SUSTAINABLE DEVELOPMENT IN SOUTH

SUSTAINABLE DEVELOPMENT IN SOUTH ASIA

V.C. PANDEY

Publications

KALPAZ PUBLICATIONS

DELHI–110052

SUSTAINABLE DEVELOPMENT IN SOUTH ASIA

(Sociology)

Rs. 825

ISBN: 81-7835-206-0

Published in 2003 in India by
Kalpaz Publications
C–30, Satyawati Nagar
Delhi–110052
E-mail: kalpaz@hotmail.com

Laser Typesetting at: Varsha Graphics, Delhi
Printed at: Mehra Offset Press, Delhi

Contents

Preface *vii*

1. **Environmental Perspectives: Towards Sustainability** **1**
Infrastructure Conservation; Challenges of Forest Management; Land Water and Food Production Management; Conservation of Energy Resources; Policy Issues.

2. **Sustainable Development in South Asia**
India; Biodiversity; Wastes and Hazardous Materials; Toxic Chemicals; Desertification and Draught; Strategies for Pollution Control; Indian Forestry Policy; Central Pollution Control Board; Environmental Impact Assessment; Ozone Cell; Environmental Education; Pakistan; Bangladesh; Nepal; Sri Lanka.

3. **Towards Ecosystem Balance** **150**
Planning and Management of Land Resources; Fragile Ecosystems; Mountain Ecosystem; Sustainable Agriculture Development; Land Degradation; Plant Nutrient Depletion; Fresh Water Resources; Sustainability of Food Production; Substantial Use of Chemicals; Radioactive Wastes; **Appendix:** Protection of the Atmosphere: Report of the UN Secretary-General—Introduction, I. Global Atmospheric Trends, II. Regional Air Pollution, III. Urban Air Pollution, IV. Issues for Further Consideration.

4. **Conserving Water Resources** **223**
Issues of Water Scarcity; Quality Issues; Trends in Freshwater Supply; Irrigation Management.

5. Sustainable Development: Role of Economy **269**
Subsidies for Sustainable Development.

Bibliography 313

Index 315

Preface

Sustainable development is one of the most urgent challenges now facing humankind. Today, land degradation and water scarcity threaten food security and livelihoods. Increasingly, air and water pollution are having a negative impact on human health and the productivity of natural resources. The 1.2 billion people who live on less than $1 a day are also the most vulnerable to environmental degradation. They depend on natural resources for sustenance, and they suffer disproportionately from poor environmental conditions.

The high level of public concern about environmental issues provides a political foundation for generating additional financing for the environment and sustainable development. Governments, international finance institutions, and the private sector all have critical and mutually reinforcing roles to play. Financing packages must be designed to involve more than one component of this "triangle" and to foster close coordination and innovative partnerships. Governments must continue to exert leadership, there is much to be gained from forging partnerships to promote sustainable development among the public and private sectors, local and national governments, national and international agencies, NGOs, and civil society. It demonstrated that economic development must not only be economically and financially viable, but also socially acceptable and environmentally sound.

The sustainable development programmes should establish the necessary mechanisms to promote local regional and international action plans and programmes for the environmental advancement. People's participation is a means and an end in sustainable development, whereby people become increasingly self-reliant economic agents in the decision making process.

This book elaborately describes the major issues of sustainable development in South Asian countries. It includes the basic concepts, paradigms, policies, management and latest details about the subject in this region. It will be a highly valuable reference tool for policy makers, researchers, scholars, environmentalists, and so on.

Editor

1

Environmental Perspectives: Towards Sustainability

As a result of the rise in global trade, the problem of non-native species invasions has increased drama-tically. Between 1965 and 1998, imports of agricultural products and industrial raw materials increased ninefold. In the process, many non-native species were unintentionally introduced as contaminants in the movement of goods. Non-native invasive species in forests can create unstable ecosystems, increase the negative impacts of fire, impede or stop vital species interactions, promote the extinction of species that are symbiotic with native forest species, and alter key ecosystem functions.

Studies show that the greater frequency of extreme climatic events affects forests significantly. High-intensity windstorms and floods become 'gap-forming' processes that favour introduced species, which tend to be reproduced more rapidly than native species. Riparian forests destroyed by floods are being continually replaced with non-native plant species. Climate change also modifies local climatic regimes, leading to species and ecosystem extinction where conditions become unfavorable for locally occurring native species. Protected areas and integrated approaches. There is clear and unequivocal agreement that protected areas remain critical centers for biodiversity conservation. Protected areas constitute important storehouses of genetic, species, habitat, and ecosystem diversity and are supported by a wide range of stakeholders. However, there is also a strong emerging consensus that for pragmatic, scientific, and technical reasons-conservation efforts must extend beyond protected areas.

There are limits to a country's set-aside areas. Even the most ambitious supporters of biodiversity protection recognize that most countries will resist designating more than about 10 percent of their land as protected areas, so there is clearly a need to balance conservation with sustainable use and sustainable development options to satisfy economic and social needs. From a scientific standpoint, the scope for biodiversity conservation would be enhanced through the adoption of a landscape approach that involves a mosaic of land uses, including protected and production landscapes. There is also evidence that many species may only be conserved within a matrix of land uses, and that such spatial arrangements are necessary for long-term solutions.

Building on its experience and responding to new guidance from the Convention on Biological Diversity (CBD), GEF is embarking on strategic changes in the way it targets biodiversity conservation, including forests. In particular, GEF has adopted a program on Integrated Ecosystem Management that deals with forest conservation issues in a broader socioeconomic and political context. Recent support provided by GEF to China and Tanzania has sought to mainstream biodiversity considerations into forest-sector reforms.Another important strategy that has emerged from this integrated approach is the use of "corridors" to connect protected areas into a much larger landscape. A mosaic of land use corridors enables wildlife to move across wider ranges, promotes genetic exchange, and helps preserve and increase existing populations.

Domestic demand for forest products is growing in relation to export demand, especially in developing countries; in fact, almost 90 percent of all commercial roundwood is traded domestically. For a variety of reasons, including the higher costs of natural forest management, forest plantations are gaining a competitive advantage over natural forests. In 2002, plantations occupied only 5 percent of the global forest cover but supplied 35 percent of global roundwood; this trend is expected to continue. The expansion of plantations affects natural forest conservation in two ways.

— Plantations decrease the pressure on natural forests for wood by generating alternative supplies. Yet their much higher productivity per hectare supplies the wood market with cheaper wood, indirectly diminishing the value of natural forests as wood producers and reducing the competitiveness of natural forests relative to alternative land uses.

— The collapse of production from natural forests would be unwelcome, particularly for the indigenous and other communities that have only recently begun to regain the authority to use their forest assets. Balancing the tradeoffs between plantation and natural forest supply, and strengthening the role of communities and smallholders in both of these activities will be increasingly important. The key issue is how to generate returns and revenue from natural forests.

The increased globalization of the forest sector poses uncertainties for developing countries, but it provides opportunities as well. Investor and consumer demands for socially and environmentally responsible forestry are beginning to drive improved management. For example, socially responsible investment funds, with more than $1.4 trillion in assets under management, are developing positive indicators for sustainable forestry investments, using certification as a bench-mark to verify sound practices in the global market. This demand for sound forestry is also giving rise to a new generation of forest companies such as Global Forest Products in South Africa and Renewable Resources LLC in the Brazilian Amazon. These companies use business models that combine profitability with sound social and environmental management. With more communities and indigenous groups involved in forest ownership, many companies are forming partnerships with indigenous and other community suppliers.

On the social and political front, significant new developments include increased community control of forests and greater attention to governance, international standards, and transparency mechanisms such as certification. As part of the global trend toward decentralization and the recognition of indigenous and community rights, many developing nations are transferring either legal or administrative control over forests to indigenous and community groups. In the most forest-rich developing countries, nearly one-fourth of the forest estate is now legally owned or officially administered by indigenous and rural communities.

Communities legally own or administer at least 380 million hectares of forest. The percentage of forest under community control has doubled in the last 10 years, and could double again by 2020. This change is supported by parallel trends in many countries to reform land tenure and enhance the security of private property rights. This transition represents great progress in rationalizing and securing forest ownership and establishing more conducive conditions for sustainable forest management, as well as a historic opportunity to dramatically improve the livelihoods of millions of forest inhabitants.

When efforts to halt deforestation in tropical forests made little progress in the late 1980s and early 1990s, some environmental groups began thinking about ways to encourage markets to give preference to timber from sustainably managed tropical forests. The result was forest certification, a procedure that uses predetermined standards to assure the quality of forest management operations. Certification may include an agreement on the right or license to use a special label on traded forest products, coupled with independent verification of compliance to these standards. Since the early 1990s, some important strides have been made in forest certification:

— The area certified by accredited certifiers of the Forest Stewardship Council has reached 22 million hectares, up from 10 million in 1998. Sweden and Poland account for 61 per cent of the total.

— In Europe, 21.9 million hectares of Finland's forests have been certified under the Finnish Forest Certification System; another 6.9 million hectares have been certified in Norway and Sweden under national certification schemes. And in Canada, about

44 million hectares of forestland have been certified according to the ISO 14001 standard of the International Organization for Standardization.

— The Pan-European Forest Certification Framework provides a mechanism for mutual recognition among different European national systems.

— The Indonesia Ecolabelling Institute (LEI) has developed criteria and indicators for the auditing of forest management on logging concessions, as well as ecolabelling of products from these concessions. LEI issued its first certificate of good forest management in April 2001 for 91,000 hectares of forest managed by a company operating in central Sumatra.

— Malaysia has formed a National Timber Certification Council.

— B&Q, a leading home improvement chain in the United Kingdom, has agreed to accept Finnish timber certified under the Finnish Forest Certification System. In the United States, several retail chains and major homebuilders have announced that they will favor certified wood products in the future. Buyers' groups have expanded, with notable commitments recently from some large retailers in Brazil.

Forest certification has pioneered the way for other certification schemes in the marine, tourism, and aquarium fish trades. Even with these encouraging developments, however, the future effectiveness of forest certification is widely debated. The area of certified forests is growing rapidly but still represents only about 2 percent of the world's total forest area, and most certified forests are located in a limited number of temperate countries rather than in tropical ones. In general, countries with large areas of tropical forest export only a low percentage of their products to the most environmentally sensitive markets in Europe. And certification does not seem to be a driver for the development of national land-use strategies that include biodiversity conservation and other sustainability factors.

Finally, certification relies on a long and detailed set of criteria and indicators that may deter implementation by logging and forest management teams. In developing countries, certification's greatest contribution to date has been to stimulate new debate on forest practice and the development of new standards in an inclusive, participatory manner. Certification is increasingly used by investors and insurers to indicate reduced risk and uncertainty in forest operations. Certification's greatest potential will most likely be in the area of forest services. Independent certification is an essential element of the institutional framework required by markets for forest services. Building this framework will be a major challenge in the coming decades. New global conventions.

The parties to the CBD have progressively strengthened the role of forests in maintaining biological diversity. A work program adopted in 1996 provides a strong basis for delivering the objectives of the convention within a broader socioeconomic context. Emphasis is on research, cooperation, and development of technologies necessary for the conservation and sustainable use of forest biological diversity. CBD also has influenced the global dialogue on forests through its recognition of the traditional forest-related knowledge of indigenous peoples. Another influential link with forests is made through the GEF, which provides funding for CBD for that support forest biological diversity. GEF's forest program accounts for almost 40 percent of its entire biodiversity portfolio, with funding of $540 million and cofinancing of $1.1 billion. Even these estimates are conservative, because forest ecosystems are included in other GEF operational programs. Protection and expansion of forests also are important elements in the UNCCD, since forests help mitigate the effects of drought and prevent desertification. Sustainable forest management is an important part of the corrective actions under UNCCD to reduce land degradation.

Other important conventions relating to forests include the Ramsar Convention on Wetlands of International Importance, the Convention for the Protection of the World Cultural and Natural Heritage, the Convention on International Trade in Endangered Species of Wild Fauna and Flora, the Convention Concerning Indigenous and Tribal Peoples in Independent Countries, the International Tropical Timber Agreement, and the Agreement Establishing the World Trade Organization. The GEF has provided substantial funding in support of some of these priorities. While the continuing lack of consensus about the elements of a global forest convention appear to preclude any consolidation of agreements into a single treaty in the near future, the scope for existing conventions to address the issue of sound forest management, including biodiversity conservation, must be a priority.

Infrastructure Conservation

Better governance in developing countries could improve incentives for conservation-oriented private-sector participation, encourage more effective models of community forest management, and generate international support and additional financial resources for public forest management. The challenge for developing countries is to create or strengthen their 'conservation infrastructure' so they have the tools and capacity needed to capitalize on and benefit from opportunities in the forest and other related sectors. Targeting policies, institutional frameworks, and human capacity is critical. Another important challenge is to develop a new generation of institutions with the capacity to deal with the complexity and unpredictability of forest systems; manage across jurisdictions, from the sub-regional to the national level; deal with forest problems in an integrative, holistic way; and create markets to enable payments for ecosystem services.

Greater integration of resource management should be sought at decentralised levels of governance. Stronger institutions are needed to address resource management issues that cross national borders, and to operate at the subnational level in situations such as large catchments. At the local level, governments should continue to support a shift in forest ownership to communities and smallholders, and pragmatic capacity building. Clear tenure rights enable local people both to protect forests from outside encroachment and to enter into business contracts. In Indonesia and the Philippines, some local groups have successfully negotiated new rights by demonstrating effective sustainable forest management. Key steps in supporting this transition include:

— *Identifying and clarifying property rights:* In most countries, additional laws are needed to strengthen property rights for forest ecosystem services; this will facilitate the development of markets for environmental services.

— *Building and enhancing local capacity:* Training and capacity building at the community level will empower local people to organize themselves to generate sustained income from forests-through ecotourism, timber certification, carbon sequestration, and other payment schemes.

— *Developing and sharing transition strategies, lessons, and best practices:* Governments and policymakers will benefit from information about successes and failures in reforming tenure systems. Equally important is the need to expand knowledge-sharing among field practitioners by arranging exchange visits to innovative, and by encouraging replication and scaling-up by communities.

— *Increasing investments:* Industrial countries as well as multilateral and bilateral organizations need to increase financial assistance for tenure reform to include assessing community claims, mapping tenure, delimiting property and devising regulations.

At the international level, financial and technical assistance agencies should increase support for forest management and conservation reforms in developing countries by:

— *Assessing the performance of public timber concessions and adopting necessary reforms:* Following the example of Cambodia, governments could review the extent to which companies holding concessions are conforming with legally agreed-upon obligations and could cancel or reissue those in default.

— *Controlling illegal logging and corruption:* A number of countries are improving the monitoring of logging activities. Reducing financially competitive illegal and unsustainable activities would help make forest conservation and sustainable management financially attractive.

— *Developing and strengthening independent certification standards and national auditing capacity:* Certification can effectively support governance, yet national-level capacity is often limited, thereby increasing the costs of adoption. Adopting systematic independent audits of government performance in public forest management. Several countries, notably Malaysia, have adopted a process of independent audits. These assessments help governments check their own performance and provide assurance to citizens and buyers.

— *Setting conservation goals:* Governments could heighten the visibility of forest conservation by creating conservation goals.

Policy reforms can encourage investment, help make forests more competitive with alternate land uses, and strengthen the role of forestry in poverty reduction. Reducing the regulatory burden on local forest producers can help them use their own forests or public stands to enter markets. In many cases, regulations can be replaced by technical assistance programmes that promote and monitor best practices, or by certification. But the requirements of forest management plans and certification programs need to be simplified if small-scale producers are to comply and benefit from them.

It is also important to level the playing field for small-scale producers. In Bolivia, forest policy reforms have included formal recognition of indigenous groups' forest rights and have exempted small-scale forest producers from some requirements. Reforms included lower concession fees, a simplified process for accessing municipal forests, and assistance with marketing and forest certification. In addition, the active involvement of local producers in forest policy negotiations will lead to more practical, realistic, and lower-cost laws, market regulations, and development plans.

Promoting community forest enterprises and joint ventures is important. There are many examples of sound community management where forest harvest levels appear sustainable, and where benefits are distributed to community members. In Mexico, for example, community-owned forests contribute substantially to community livelihoods and domestic wood supply. There are important new opportunities for smallholders and communities in managing forests, especially given the reduced supply of tropical hard-woods and the increased environmental conscience of investors and forest product companies. Capturing these opportunities will require a number of steps, including:

— *Characterizing and establishing markets for low-income producers:* Preliminary studies indicate there is high potential for low-income producers, but more research is needed to better characterize the potential in each market segment, identify where the potential is strongest, and describe the steps required to enable community participation.

— *Improving market position:* Long-term growth in timber and nontimber forest products requires building supply networks that link producers to domestic markets with increased production efficiency. To raise incomes significantly, producers need to establish a competitive position. This may mean improving production and marketing technology, product quality, and reliability of supply.

— *Strengthening producer organizations:* Where market institutions are underdeveloped, producer organizations can fill the gaps by, for example, setting up transport services, scaling up supply, or leveraging credit. Producer organizations also need to develop the skills to make capital investments and establish and maintain quality controls.

— *Promoting strategic business partnerships:* Partnerships can benefit both private industry and local producers. Industrial firms gain access to wood fiber and nonwood products at a competitive cost, while local producers can obtain high-quality planting materials, technical assistance, quality control, and investment resources for expansion, marketing, and business expertise.

— *Promoting essential business services:* Some private firms, such as A2R in Brazil, and some public making concerted efforts to build private-sector capacity in forest settings, including management services; organizational support; technical assistance for production, conservation, and processing; market information and marketing assistance; insurance; and financing. Several steps could help promote the development of markets and market-based mechanisms to finance forest ecosystem services.

  — There is a great need for more information about the biophysical relationships between forest management activities and the flow of services, and on how to ensure that the poor participate fully in and benefit from such markets.

  — All markets require enabling institutions in areas such as common assessment methodologies, property rights, certification systems, and contracts. In the carbon market, particular challenges include devising approaches to deal with leakage, permanence, and accessibility issues.

— The existing stock of knowledge comes from innovators who have forged ahead despite uncertainty. Encouraging such efforts will provide greater experience and certainty about how to develop market-based mechanisms successfully.

International market-based payment mechanisms could provide an opportunity for industrial countries to invest in developing-country forests. Innovative funds, such as the World Bank's Prototype Carbon Fund, have helped build experience and capacity in the international markets area. The new Prototype Sequestration Fund will similarly set precedents in the forest carbon markets.

Challnges of Forest Management

Forests provide a host of valuable ecological services. Although these have quantifiable economic value, they are generally provided at no cost. For example:

— Forests contain about two-thirds of known terrestrial species, have the highest species diversity of any ecosystem, and the highest number of threatened species. Most forest plant species, including timber trees and other forest products such as sago palms and rattans, depend on animal pollination for reproduction. Without a wide variety of forest habitats, animal pollination could be disrupted. Many plants, especially in tropical forests, also require animals for successful seed dispersal.

— Forest vegetation and soils hold almost 40 percent of all carbon stored in terrestrial ecosystems. And release of carbon as a result of deforestation contributes to global climate change. For example, a closed primary forest contains some 280 tons of carbon per hectare; if converted to pasture or permanent agriculture, it would release more than 200 tons of carbon into the atmosphere.

— By filtering freshwater and reducing soil erosion and sedimentation, forests play an important role in maintaining clean water supplies and reducing the severity of flooding. For example, erosion rates in slash-and-burn crop fields are 10 times higher than in natural forests. Road construction associated with logging, though only a small percentage of the logged area, can contribute as much as 80 percent of the sediment that enters streams.

— By providing shade and surface cooling, forests help moderate local temperature extremes. An estimated 99 percent of potential crop pests are controlled by natural enemies, many of which require forest habitats. If this natural pest control had to be replaced with chemical pesticides, the annual cost to U.S. agriculture alone is estimated at $54 billion.

Experience to date suggests that watershed protection can be an inexpensive way to save water and avoid the costs of filtration. In the United States, many cities have found that every $1 invested in watershed protection can save up to $200 in costs for new filtration and water treatment facilities. In South Africa, the Working for Water Program clears non-native tree species and increases stream-flow at a fraction of the cost of new diversion or reservoir programmes.

Forests also play an important economic role. Production of industrial roundwood is, of course, a vital part of the global economy. And in many developing nations, forests are an important source of livelihoods and resources, both for fuelwood and for other nonwood forest products. Many people rely on fuelwood from forests, road-sides, community woodlots, and wood industry residues as a source of energy for heating and cooking. For developing countries as a whole, fuel-wood provides about 35 percent of primary energy consumption. It is particularly significant in poorer countries, and for the poor within those countries. Nonwood forest products are an important source of low-cost building materials, fuel, food supplements, and traditional medicines. In rural Madhya Pradesh, India, for example, a study found that these products provided 40-63 percent of total annual income. In Zimbabwe, extraction from wild-lands for domestic uses accounts for about one-third of average household incomes.

Traditionally, landowners receive no compensation for the environmental services their land generates. Recognition of this problem has led to the development of innovative payment systems. In some cases, private entities have developed their own mechanisms to pay for watershed protection with little or no government involvement. In Colombia, for example, large agricultural producers in the Cauca Valley assess their own fees through water users' associations to finance watershed management practices in upland areas that will improve base flows and reduce sedimentation in irrigation canals. A regional public development agency carries out watershed management activities and provides technical assistance. A common example of new compensation systems involves public schemes, in which payments are made to private landowners and private or public resource managers. For these compensation systems to be successful, a World Bank study found that payments need to be ongoing and carefully targeted, and that care needs to be taken to avoid inappropriate incentives.

The Food and Agriculture Organization (FAO) currently estimates that about 15.2 million hectares of forest are lost every year in the tropics, largely as a result of rapid, planned, or large-scale conversion to other land uses, mainly agriculture. Even as deforestation continues in tropical zones, a host of new ideas and initiatives provide hope that the world is moving toward protecting and sustainably managing the global forest estate. These developments are particularly important:

— Increasing devolution of the rights and management of forests to indigenous and other local communities

— Increasing influence of global markets on forest management, including the growing capacity of forest plantations to help meet the world's wood demands

— Emerging demand for the environmental services that forests provide, from water purification to ecotourism

— Shifting from an excessive focus on establishing new protected areas to strategies that emphasize integrated landscape and mosaic approaches

— Widening recognition of the role of forests as carbon sinks and as a common biome for addressing synergies between the Convention on Biological Diversity (CBD), the U.N. Convention to Combat Desertification (UNCCD), and the UN Framework Convention on Climate Change (UNFCCC), among others

— Growing acceptance of governance, transparency, and accountability, including the growing role of independent certification, as indicators of good resource management

— Increasing awareness of emerging threats, including the risks posed by climate change and non-native invasive species.

In most developing countries the conservation of natural forests is a relatively small part of the much bigger picture of poverty, slow economic growth, and weak institutions. Improved conservation and management of forests depends on balanced economic development in poor countries that includes improved governance, more effective market mechanisms, secure tenure and access rights, strengthened institutional capacity, and poverty alleviation strategies that recognize the importance of forests.

Long-term challenge is to incorporate the value of forest services, and most important, the contributions of forests to the livelihoods of the poor into conventional economics. Several payment mechanisms for environmental services have been tested, but payments have not yet become a major factor in achieving forest conservation. As a climate change mitigation measure, payments for the carbon storage value of forests could be a potentially significant new development in the coming decades.

FAO estimates that there are about 3.87 billion hectares of forest. About 47 percent of the world's forests are in the tropics, 9 percent in the subtropics, 11 percent in the temperate zone, and 33 percent in the boreal zone. Worldwide, an estimated 16.1 million hectares of natural forest were lost annually during the 1990s, including 14.6 million hectares through deforestation and 1.5 million hectares through conversion to forest plantations. Of the 15.2 million hectares lost in the tropics each year, 14.2 million hectares were converted to other land uses, and one million hectares were converted to forest plantations. Against the gross annual loss of 16.1 million hectares of natural forests worldwide, there was a gain of 3.6 million hectares as a result of natural forest expansion, leaving a balance of -12.5 million hectares as the annual net change of natural forest.

The underlying causes of forest loss vary among regions. In Africa, the expansion of subsistence agriculture is the principal cause; in Latin America, the main causes are large-scale cattle ranching, clearance for government-sponsored settlements, and hydroelectric reservoirs; and in Asia, subsistence agriculture and economic development schemes account for the loss. The condition of global forests is not well documented and varies considerably from place to place. According to FAO, the principal direct causes of forest degradation include insect pests and diseases; fire; overharvesting of industrial wood, fuelwood, and other forest products; mismanagement of production forests, including poor harvesting practices; overgrazing; air pollution; and extreme climatic events such as storms. Habitat degradation caused by these factors and the overharvesting of wildlife are major contributors to the local depletion of forest-based wildlife populations. Underlying causes include poverty, population growth, markets and trade in forest products, and macroeconomic policies. About 479 million hectares (12.4 percent of the world's forest area) are in protected areas, according to FAO. It estimates that about 20 percent of all forests in North and South America are protected. By region, FAO found that:

— The bulk of tropical forests in the African Great Lakes region are unprotected.

— In Asia, most closed forests in Papua New Guinea and Indonesia are unprotected and threatened by logging, agricultural clearing, or mining.

— Europe's last few large blocks of forest area in Sweden and Finland are well protected.

— Russia's boreal forests are still largely intact, but the percentage of protected area is very low.

These estimates are based on a new global map of protected forest areas developed for FAO in collaboration with the UN Environment Programme's World Conservation Monitoring Centre (UNEP-WCMC). In addition, industrial countries reported on protected forest areas in response to questionnaires prepared by the UN. Economic Commission for Europe and FAO. Protected areas are classified according to the categories established by the IUCN. The raw data in the UNEP-WCMC database includes all land under protected management status, not just forestland. The UNEP-WCMC global protected areas map was overlaid with a global forest cover map to develop an updated global protected forests map. FAO says that there are continuing difficulties in obtaining a consistent approach for comparing forest areas that countries report as protected, so these global statistics may not be representative of the actual protection afforded to forests in different countries.

Land, Water and Food Production Management

Since the 1992 Rio Earth Summit, a great deal has changed in the forest sector, providing opportunities for expanded conservation and sustainable use of forests and biodiversity in support of poverty alleviation. For example:

— In the environmental area, important developments include increased recognition of major environmental threats such as invasive species and climate change, and the growing interest in wider approaches to forest and biodiversity protection.

— In the economic area, key trends include market changes such as the increased role of forest plantations, the greater influence of global markets on forest management, and the emerging interest in systems of payment for ecological services.

— In the social and political areas, major changes include a dramatic increase in indigenous and other community forest ownership and management, greater attention to governance, and the growing role of independent certification.

Land and water management institutions tend to be centralized, technically oriented agencies that support one or two specific aspects of management, such as water supply utilities or irrigation agencies. Although it often leads to short-term economic gains, the single-sector approach to land and water management can result in longterm environmental degradation because it fails to account for the complex linkages among various components of the ecosystem. It typically seeks to maximize the benefits of one sector, such as irrigated agriculture, without considering effects on other sectors. In addition, this approach tends to rely heavily on technical and engineering solutions, making little or no attempt to address related policy and institutional issues.

Development activities in the Senegal River valley highlight many of the unintended environmental and social impacts of the single-sector approach. Two dams were constructed on the Senegal River in the 1970s to support intensive rice production, electricity generation, and year-round navigation. Around 50 percent of the irrigation fields have been lost to soil salinization, dams and dikes have reduced traditional grazing lands from 80,000 to 4,000 hectares, water pollution from pesticides and other agrochemicals is significant, and fish production in the river and estuary has dropped by 90 percent.

A critical need in the next few decades is to improve the efficiency of water use, especially for agriculture. World Water Vision lists a range of technical and management options to improve productivity, including:

— Developing new crop varieties with higher yields per unit of water-for example, crops with comparable yields but shorter growth periods

— Switching to crops that consume less water or use water more efficiently

— Improving soil management, fertilization, and pest and weed control

— Improving the reliability of water supplies at critical crop growth periods; this would encourage farmers to invest more in other inputs and lead to higher output per unit of water

— Promoting deficit irrigation, which can increase productivity per unit of water by providing less-than-full irrigation requirements; and supplemental irrigation, which uses limited irrigation at critical periods to supplement rainfall. In the Syrian Arab Republic, for example, researchers have demonstrated that reducing full irrigation by 50 percent results in a yield loss of only 10 percent.

A broad range of irrigation technologies now available can increase water productivity. For example, drip irrigation, which uses a network of perforated plastic tubes that deliver water directly to the roots of plants, can cut water use by 30-70 percent and increase crop yields by 20-90 percent. Another efficient sprinkler system known as low-energy precision application has drop tubes extending vertically from the sprinkler arm. These tubes deliver water much closer to the plants, reducing evaporation losses. Used in combination with time-controlled surge valves, which distribute water more uniformly down furrows, these systems can produce water savings of 25-37 percent compared with conventional furrow irrigation. There are also a variety of management techniques that can improve irrigation efficiency. These include improving irrigation timing, improving canal operations for more efficient deliveries, applying water only at crucial periods, using water-conserving tillage and field preparation methods, improving canal maintenance, and recycling drainage and tail water. In addition, there are a wide array of small-scale irrigation strategies for areas with scarce water supplies. For example, check dams built across gullies can trap large amounts of runoff, which can be channeled to fields or stored for later use.

Reducing water subsidies will help promote more efficient water use. The World Water Vision recommends that consumers be charged the full cost of providing water services, including the cost of obtaining the water and of collecting, treating, and disposing of wastewater. Full cost pricing will make water suppliers accountable to users, reduce water withdrawals from ecosystems, and provide the revenue needed to cover operation and maintenance costs. Such policies must be accompanied by targeted, transparent subsidies to low-income communities and individuals. A wide variety of strategies are available to rebuild and conserve soil resources. In less-favoured areas in the East African highlands, for example, inexpensive ways to improve nutrient management include improved fallows, biomass transfer, crop residue management, manure management, and composting. In steeply sloping areas prone to erosion, solutions include bench-terracing, natural vegetative strips, stone walls, and perennial tree crop systems. In the Southeast Asian uplands, contour hedgerows are effective in controlling soil erosion. Agroforestry, which combines annual and perennial plants, can help maintain soil fertility because perennial crops help recycle nutrients and reduce erosion. Conservation agriculture is gaining acceptance around the world. Recent studies estimate that conservation agriculture is practiced on about 58 million hectares of farmland, mainly in North and South America, but also in Southern Africa and South Asia. Under this approach, farmers leave crop residues in the ground as soil cover. Rather than tilling the soil at the start of the next cropping season, they use special equipment to drill the seeds directly into the soil.

The surface cover reduces mineralization, erosion, and water loss. In addition, it inhibits the germination of weeds, protects soil microorganisms, and helps build up organic matter. Conservation agriculture does not preclude the use of chemical inputs. Herbicides are an important component, particularly in the transition phase until a new balance in the weed population is achieved. Conservation agriculture generally uses fewer chemical inputs than conventional farmers. Over the years, the use of inputs tends to decline. In the long run, disease problems do not increase if sound crop rotations are adopted. The system can be used to grow grains, pulses, sugar cane, potatoes, beets, and cassava.

Advances in information technology, such as computer simulation models that are built on digital databases and integrate satellite imagery and geographic information systems, are increasingly helping to define problems, evaluate risk, and design technologies for improved food production. The International Water Management Institute (IWMI) has integrated agricultural weather data from 56,000 weather stations around the world for the period 1961 to 1990. Available on CD-ROM and the Internet, the World Water and Climate Atlas can be used to better match crops and crop varieties to local climate conditions. A new technology called 'diffused reflectance spectrometry' helps measure soil quality in the field quickly and inexpensively. Using this technology, scientists can process between 350 and 500 soil samples a day under laboratory conditions, which gives them a new way to look at soil degradation and helps provide more timely mitigation advice. Working with the International Crops Research Institute for the Semi-Arid Tropics (ICRISAT), national research teams in Africa and Asia are field-testing an Agricultural Production Systems Simulator, which weighs tradeoffs in given scenarios for the production of various crops. In Tamil Nadu, India, for example, the system helped convince farmers to try alternative sowing dates and more efficient water management for groundnut production.

Many governments are now in the process of transferring responsibility for irrigation systems to local farmers' groups or other private organizations. Water users' associations are an effective way to improve efficiency, productivity, accountability, and responsiveness to farmers. They give users the authority to operate and maintain water systems, collect fees, hire professionals, and manage water rights. Many low-cost irrigation methods for farmers can dramatically improve productivity. For example, human-operated treadle pumps, which are operated by pedaling up and down on two long poles to lift groundwater to the surface, can irrigate about one-fifth of a hectare. One pump costs about $35, including installation of the tubewell, but farmers can usually get their investment back in less than a year. In Bangladesh, farmers have purchased more than 1.2 million treadle pumps, which are operating on about 250,000 hectares. International Development Enterprises, a nonprofit organization that is marketing the pumps, estimates that the total market could be 10 million pumps, including 6 million in India and 3 million in Bangladesh. In Kenya, the Asian treadle pump has been reconfigured into a lighter, portable device called a pedal pump. Approtech, a local NGO, is selling the pump for about $70 in Kenyan towns and villages. Many initiatives that promote sustainable use of land and water resources for food production are taking place at the river basin or ecosystem level. A critical goal is to meet the needs of both upstream and downstream users.

In Cameroon, for example, a dam constructed in 1978 for rice irrigation greatly restricted the seasonal flooding of the downstream floodplain along the Logone River. A decade later, IUCN began a programme to rehabilitate the floodplain, including the 171,000-hectare Waza Park. Pilot water releases through newly constructed openings in the main river levee have restored about 60 per cent of the affected floodplain. The World Bank financed an environmental flow assessment that studied the complete river ecosystem. Based on the findings of the assessment, the design of the projects Mohale Dam was changed to a multiple outlet structure. This will allow releases of varying quantity and quality, including occasional flood flows, to meet the requirements of downstream ecosystems. Mexico's 1992 National Water Law authorizes the creation of river basin councils to provide a forum for identifying and evaluating problems and needs; developing consensus between the various government entities, water users, and other interested parties; recommending actions and obtaining commitments to implement them; and ensuring continuing commitment and compliance with agreed-upon initiatives. The councils are responsible for making the planning process dynamic, participatory, and results-oriented. There are several encouraging examples of effective local responses to drought conditions in developing countries.

In Burkina Faso, the Mossi plateau receives only about 700 millimeters of rainfall per year, which varies in extent, duration, and intensity. Since 1976, rainfall levels have been falling, leading to migration, food shortages, and land degradation. At the village level, self-help groups known collectively as the Naam Movement developed a number of strategies to manage water shortages. As one response, they built diguettes, or stone lines constructed along contours that were designed to temporarily restrict water movement across fields, increase infiltration time, and catch organic debris. The lines, which are often reinforced with vetiver grass, are effective at increasing agricultural production, reducing soil erosion, reclaiming degraded fields, and replenishing aquifers. They were built throughout the Mossi plateau and significantly increased food and water security.

Many other traditional water harvesting technologies were also spread through Naam groups, including zai, which are small pits dug in the field with a little compost to trap water; demilunes, or half-moons, which were constructed out of earth on the downside of a contour and used to trap water; and erosion bunds, which were dug on contours with a depth of about half a meter to increase water availability for crops.

Successfully promoting environmentally sound food production requires action in five key areas: mainstreaming integrated approaches to land and water management; strengthening the enabling environment; adopting good management practices and environmentally sound technologies; expanding and accelerating capacity development; and strengthening partnerships. Integrated land and water management approaches provide a comprehensive framework for countries to manage land and water resources in a way that recognizes political and social factors as well as the need to protect the integrity and function of ecological systems. Resource owners, managers, upstream and downstream users, and other stakeholders should participate in resource allocation and management decisions, taking into account ecological, economic, and social factors. Such an approach minimizes conflicts over resource allocation and management. It also facilitates the integration of technical and engineering solutions with needed policy and institutional reforms. Traditional or indigenous systems of natural resources management are based on the same principles of integration. Several countries have established river basin management programmes in an attempt to use integrated approaches. For example, the Murray-Darling Basin (MDB) Initiative in Australia, which was started in 1987, has:

— Introduced improved land management techniques to minimize the amount of irrigation water being added to the water table. New crops and more efficient irrigation technology will help support more sustainable land use.

— Constructed engineering works to intercept highly saline groundwater and pump it to suitable disposal sites before it flows into the main river system.

— Adopted new operating rules to reduce evaporation losses from reservoirs.

Throughout Australia, farmers and other rural industries are working with government and other rural communities to solve rural problems. More than 2,000 voluntary landcare community groups are currently working to develop more sustainable systems of land and water use within catchments.

Conservation of Energy Resources

Energy is vital for economic growth and development. It can improve the quality of people's lives and their productivity and can extend the working day and provide additional time for activities such as education and health care. And in developing nations, modern forms of energy can liberate millions of women and children from the burden of gathering water and fuelwood. In the developing world, energy availability is limited. Some 2 billion people who do not have access to electricity must rely on traditional fuels such as dung and fuelwood. To reduce poverty and meet growing demand, developing countries must generate more energy. Energy-especially from fossil fuels-has significant environmental implications. Local air pollution causes perhaps 4 million premature deaths per year, mostly of young children exposed to dirty cooking fuels.

The economic costs of air pollution are substantial, perhaps $350 billion per year, or 6 percent of the gross national product of developing countries. Emissions of sulfur dioxide and nitrogen oxide also have been found to damage crops, forests, rivers, and lakes. In terms of climate change, the risks posed by the current approach to energy are at best difficult and at worst potentially catastrophic. Fossil fuels (coal, oil, and natural gas) now account for about 80 percent of world consumption of primary energy. The combustion of fossil fuels adds carbon dioxide (CO_2) to the atmosphere.

CO_2, in combination with other greenhouse gases such as methane and nitrous oxide, traps heat in the upper atmosphere. Though the process is complex and not completely understood, there is consensus among scientists that emissions of greenhouse gases have altered the global climate, and that a further expansion in these emissions could have devastating environmental effects.

Energy production and consumption trends are sensitive to policies and incentives and therefore can change, particularly as new knowledge about the environmental consequences of an approach dominated by fossil fuels becomes available and is widely disseminated and understood. Since the mid-1980s, many policymakers, government officials, and business leaders-including those from oil companies- have changed their thinking about sustainable energy development. Actions have centered on three main areas:

— improvements in efficiency to obtain more energy services with less primary energy use,

— the spread of renewable energy sources, and

— efforts to provide more than 400 million rural households with access to modern energy services.

Private investors, governments, and multilateral assistance agencies are shifting their attention and investment shares to renewable energy. At the 2000 G-8 Summit in Okinawa, Japan, assembled ministers for the first time publicly recognized the importance of renewable energy, saying, "We call on all stakeholders to identify the barriers and solutions to elevating the level of renewable energy supply and distribution in developing countries." Shell and British Petroleum have each committed $500 million for renewable energy investments.

In addition, some countries, including China and India, are proposing domestic targets for renewable energy that range from 5 to 15 percent of new electricity supply within 10 to 20 years. A transition to renewable energy is inevitable- not because fossil fuel supplies will run out, but because the costs and risks of using these supplies will continue to increase relative to renewable energy. Costs will increase as the environmental effects of fossil fuel use are incorporated into the costs of energy and as the cheapest reserves are depleted.

Renewable energy helps alleviate fuel price risks. As the costs of using it continue to fall, renewable energy is expected to overtake fossil fuels as the lowest cost, least-risk investment over the next several decades. Development agencies, many governments, and environmentalists would like to accelerate the process so that it occurs within the next few decades, because this switch will have enormous economic, social, and environmental benefits. In 1998, they accounted for nearly 80 percent of primary energy consumption, followed by renewables and nuclear energy. Oil accounted for about 35 percent of the total, followed by coal and natural gas. Wood, dung, and other biomass fuels are the dominant fuel sources for poor people; as incomes rise, people move up the "energy ladder" to charcoal, coal, and kerosene, and ultimately to electricity and liquefied petroleum gas (LPG). The poor pay more for-or spend more time getting- energy services.

In many cases, studies have found that poor households could significantly reduce their daily costs if they could move up the energy ladder to LPG or electricity. In turn, the gains in purchasing power would be applied to basic needs for food, shelter, clothing, health, education, and additional fuel. Access to modern energy sources could, therefore, have a substantial and positive impact by reducing poverty and increasing rural jobs. From 1970 to 1998, global use of primary energy expanded by about 2 percent each year, according to the World Energy Assessment. But during the latter part of that period, in the 1990s, annual growth slowed to about 1 percent, largely because of the economic collapse of transitional economies in Eastern Europe and the former Soviet Union and the 1997-98 financial crisis in Asia.

Energy use in developing countries has increased three to four times faster than in western industrial countries. As a result, developing countries' share of energy use rose from 13 percent in 1970 to almost 30 percent in 1998. Still, the gap in per capita electricity use between industrial and developing countries stayed about the same. In the least-developed countries, annual per capita electricity use is estimated at 83 kilowatt-hours-only about 1 percent of the 8,053 kilowatt-hours consumed per capita in OECD nations.

Today, world energy use will grow at an annual rate of about 2.6 percent in developing countries, according to the World Energy Assessment. By 2015, the World Bank estimates that developing countries will have matched the total consumption of industrial countries; by 2050, they will have doubled it. Even at that point, however, energy consumption per capita in developing countries will still be only one-fourth that in industrial nations. Fossil fuels will still account for almost two-thirds of primary energy production by 2030.

In about half of the world's households, people use biomass and coal for cooking and heating. These fuels emit large amounts of pollutants, which in many cases are not vented from the home and create substantial indoor air pollution. The principal health effects include chronic respiratory diseases such as bronchitis and asthma. In India, studies have found that household use of solid fuel causes about 500,000 premature deaths each year among women and children under the age of 5. This is 5-6 percent of the national burden of ill health, and 6-9 percent of the burden for these two population groups.

The global impact is thought to be about four times larger, or about 2 million premature deaths a year among women and young children. In communities and urban areas, fuel combustion emits large amounts of fine particles that lodge deep in the lungs and have significant health effects. Atmospheric particle concentrations and other pollutants are thought to cause 170,000-290,000 premature deaths annually in cities in China and 90,000-200,000 deaths in India's urban areas.

The causes of urban pollution in developing countries are varied, but include power plants and large industries with limited pollution controls; large numbers of small boilers, engines, and open fires; two- and three-wheel vehicles with highly polluting two-stroke engines; and emissions from cars and trucks powered by diesel fuel.

These pollutants can be transformed into acids in the atmosphere. Studies have found that acid deposition can harm aquatic life in lakes and rivers. At high elevations, acid deposition can increase the susceptibility of forests to natural stresses and cause a loss of nutrients in the soil. Acid deposition also can be harmful to humans; for example, many respiratory diseases are likely caused or aggravated by sulfur particulates and nitrogen oxides in acid fog.

At the global level, fossil fuel combustion plays a major role in the buildup of carbon dioxide. Increases in the atmospheric concentration of CO_2 closely parallel the rise in global fossil fuel burning over the past 150 years. Since the pre-industrial period, CO_2 concentrations are estimated to have risen about 29 percent, causing an increase in near-surface air temperatures of 0.3-0.6 degrees Celsius since the late nineteenth century.

The Intergovernmental Panel on Climate Change (IPCC) estimates that as CO2 concentrations continue to increase, global average surface temperatures will be 1.0-3.5 degrees Celsius higher in 2 100 than in 1990. At mid-latitudes, the increase is likely to be 1.3-2.0 times higher than the global average; in higher latitudes, the increase could be three times the global average. The likely effects of global warming include disruptions in the productivity of farms, forests, and fisheries; changes in the geographic distribution of human disease; increased frequency and intensity storms and floods; and rising sea levels.

The cost in developing countries is estimated at 5-9 percent of gross domestic product (GDP)-considerably worse than in industrial nations. The cumulative rise in carbon emissions varies considerably, depending on the future fuel mix. In a coal-intensive scenario, carbon concentrations in the atmosphere could rise from the current 370 parts per million by volume (ppmv) to about 730 ppmv 2100, about twice current levels. Under more sustainable scenarios, concentrations are projected to rise to the 450-600 ppmv range. In nearly all scenarios, concentrations continue to rise throughout the twenty-first century.

Virtually all future energy-use scenarios show that sustainable futures are not possible if development continues along a business-as-usual path. These scenarios require at least moderate policy and behavioural changes that are consistently applied over several decades. In time, such changes could result in a substantially changed energy future.

The 1992 Rio Earth Summit had a variety of direct and indirect impacts on sustainable energy development. Two immediate outcomes included the UNFCC and the establishment of the GEF. The climate convention and the subsequent Kyoto Protocol have already led to some adjustments in energy consumption and greenhouse gas emissions among a few of the signatory countries. GEF was initiated in 1991 as a pilot program to earmark multilateral funds for developing-country-based projects with global environmental benefits. Following the Rio Earth Summit, GEF was designated as the financial mechanism for both the CBD and the climate change treaty. In the energy area, GEF has since 1991 provided more than $1.2 billion in grants for projects with a total value of more than $6 billion. The Rio Summit also helped strengthen and legitimize the role of NGOs. Further, it increased the political importance of science, technology, and the environment in developing countries, which in some cases resulted in the creation of cabinet-level environment departments.

Especially in rural areas, there have been significant improvements in access to commercial energy over the past decade, including access to LPG, modern biogas, and village-scale electricity grids. Use of renewable energy, including solar, wind, and small hydropower, also has increased dramatically. For example, solar home systems using photovoltaic (PV) technology, which was virtually unknown in 1992, now provide lighting, television, and radio to more than 1 million rural households. Thousands of rural communities now receive drinking water from solar PV-powered purifiers and pumps.

Small hydropower and biomass generation capacity worldwide increased 20-30 percent over the past decade, to 25,000 megawatts and 16,000 megawatts, respectively. More than 50 million households are served by small-hydro village-scale mini-grids, mostly in China. Wind power generation capacity has increased from virtually zero to over 1,700 megawatts, mostly in India. In addition, the number of households served by solar hot water heaters has tripled, to roughly 10 million households, mostly in China. Programs for improved biomass cooking stoves in China, India, and several African countries have benefited some 220 million households through reduced fuel costs or fuelwood collection burdens.

With the encouragement of the World Business Council for Sustainable Development and other business councils in industrial and developing countries, a large number of leading industries have become increasingly engaged in renewable energy and energy efficiency investments. It is estimated that between $500 million and $1.5 billion of renewable energy projects in developing countries are being financed each year, a market that is growing 5-10 percent annually.

During the past decade, commercial markets for renewable energy have expanded, shifting investment patterns away from traditional government and international donor sources to greater reliance on private firms and banks. These changing investment patterns have made it more important to think about markets for renewable energy, along with the policy and social conditions that underlie markets, rather than simply about the technologies themselves and their economic characteristics.

Changing investment patterns also elicit increased decisionmaking and participation from a wider variety of stakeholders-not just traditional donor agencies and governments, but also manufacturers, rural entrepreneurs, individual households, local technicians, NGOs, community groups, utility companies, and commercial banks.

With exceptional wind resources, the facility was expected to provide an unprecedented capacity factor of 46 percent when it began operation in late 2000. Ownership of the wind farm will be ceded to the Moroccan national electric utility, Office National de l'Electricité (ONE), at the start of operations. The power purchase agreement with the consortium extends 19 years and provides full cost recovery.

In 2000, ONE solicited bids for two additional wind farms totalling 200 megawatts. In the Dominican

Republic, the U.S. firm Soluz is developing a subsidiary, Soluz Dominicana, as a successful fee-for-service business. The company targets up to 50 percent of the population in the rural communities it serves and charges $10-$20 a month for electricity service from solar home systems. By continuously improving this business model, Soluz expects to expand Soluz Dominicana to include 5,000 fee-for-service customers. At this scale, revenues should cover the direct costs of operations. Soluz has begun replicating the fee-for-service concept in Central America by establishing Soluz Honduras. In Cebu in the Philippines, the WorldWater Corporation will supply water to about 100,000 people through a program that combines solar-powered water pumping technology, full cost recovery through pay-for-service methods, and community education about the benefits of the technology. Under the full program, a total of 110 barangays (villages) in 26 municipalities will be provided with solar-powered water pumping and distribution systems.

Many developing countries are either beginning to consider or already have power sector reforms in place, driven primarily by free-market, privatization, and institutional efficiency agendas. Globally, six key trends in power sector reform are most relevant to sustainable energy in developing countries: competitive wholesale power markets and removal of price regulation on generation self-generation by end-users smaller-scale generation facilities and technologies privatization or commercialization of utilities unbundling of generation, transmission, and distribution competitive retail power markets.

Since 1980, energy conservation and increased energy efficiency have been pushing downward the energy required to produce a unit of GDP. Among developing countries, China is a prominent example of declining energy intensity in the economy. While the economy grew on average 12 percent per year from 1980 to 1995, primary energy consumption only grew on average about 4 percent annually-an unprecedented situation for a developing country.

Chinese energy consumption in 1995 would have been 2.2 times greater had the economy used energy at the same intensity as it did in 1977. This has been attributed to policies directed at energy efficiency, particularly reductions in industrial intensities. It is also the result of a concerted drive away from central planning and toward a market economy, which has raised energy prices (often within a two-tier system of coexisting state prices and market prices) and forced enterprises to consider profitability and cost minimization.

In developing countries, many promising approaches to promote energy efficiency and renewable energy have been tried over the past decade. Energy-efficiency labels for consumer appliances are a prominent part of efficiency strategies in Brazil, China, the Philippines, and Thailand. In China, for instance, new refrigerator standards were enacted during development of a GEF project to promote the market for high-efficiency units, and they have contributed to developing the market for more energy-efficient products.

In Thailand, the national electric utility (EGAT) has actively promoted both refrigerator and air conditioner labelling. In 1994, EGAT negotiated a voluntary refrigerator libelling scheme with manufacturers. In 1998, the libelling scheme was made mandatory, and in 1999

EGAT reached an agreement to increase energy efficiency requirements for each label by 20 percent.

EGAT was unable to negotiate a labelling agreement with the air conditioner industry, which is diverse and fragmented. Instead, it began offering both interest-free consumer loans to cover the incremental cost of high-efficiency units and rebates to shop owners who sell high-efficiency units.

Voluntary agreements with the private sector have proven to be one of the most cost-effective approaches to promoting energy efficiency. However, such initiatives are generally limited to situations where the gains from switching to more efficient technologies are large to neutral and the switching costs are not inordinately high. In Thailand, for example, the World Bank and Global Environment Facility (GEF) supported a comprehensive 5-year demand-side management program with EGAT. As part of this program, EGAT reached a voluntary agreement with all five Thai light manufacturers and one importer to switch from lower-efficiency to higher-efficiency fluorescent tubes.

EGAT supported the manufacturers with an $8 million consumer information program, which explained that thin tubes give you more light for your money. In one year, the more efficient tubes increased their market share from 40 to 100 percent, so that all new tubes sold currently are higher-efficiency models.

In China, a GEF/UNDP project to transform the market for energy-efficient refrigerators has just begun, but it has already influenced the market for energy-efficient refrigerators. New refrigerator standards, enacted with support from the project preparation budget, also contributed to the future market. In Poland, a GEF/IFC project has had a significant impact on the market for compact fluorescent lamps (CFLs). Lower CFL prices through a manufacturer subsidy, combined with a mass media campaign, resulted in sales of over 1.2 million CFLs from 1995 to 1997.

The percentage of Polish households using CFLs increased from 10 to 30 percent. In Mexico, the national utility CFE sold 2.5 million CFLs in 2.5 years through promotional campaigns and sales through utility billing offices. Sales were higher than the 1.7 million initially targeted, and the utility has launched other CFL programs since the first program ended. The Brazilian ethanol fuel program is a model for renewable energy development worldwide. Under the ProAlcool program, production of ethanol was stimulated through a combination of policies, including low-interest loans for the construction of ethanol distilleries, guaranteed purchase of ethanol by the state-owned oil company at a price considered adequate to provide a reasonable profit to ethanol producers, pricing of ethanol to be competitive with a gasoline-ethanol blend, and sales tax incentives during the 1980s to stimulate the purchase of ethanol vehicles.

In the late 1970s, ethanol producers received heavily subsidized loans to finance their capital investments, and the government reached an agreement with automobile makers that led to large-scale manufacturing by 1980 of vehicles that ran on ethanol. Between 1979 and 1983, total production of ethanol more than doubled. By 1998, ethanol provided about one-third of the fuel consumed by cars and light trucks in Brazil. During 1976-96, ethanol production saved Brazil about $33 billion in oil imports. It now supports about 700,000 jobs in rural areas at a low investment cost per worker. From an environmental perspective, the use of ethanol has had many benefits. It reduced lead, sulfur, hydrocarbon, and carbon monoxide emissions in Brazil, while nitrogen oxide emissions remained about the same.

Ethanol fuel played a significant role in reducing urban air pollution in Brazil's large cities. In addition, the nation avoided about 13 million metric tons of carbon emissions due to ethanol substitution for gasoline in 1996-97, which is equivalent to nearly 30 percent of its actual carbon emissions from burning fossil fuels. On the downside, however, burning sugarcane leaves and tops in the field produces air pollution, and disposal of stillage from ethanol production can pollute rivers and groundwater. Considerable attention is now being devoted to expanding uses for sugarcane and ethanol residues, including cogeneration of electricity from bagasse and leaves and production of animal feed.

China's latest five-year plan calls for a fivefold increase in wind power, to 1,500 megawatts by 2005. The plan also proposes to require that 5 percent of all new power generation come from renewables, which could mean an additional 20,000 megawatts by 2010. Such policies must overcome political and institutional hurdles, must fit into utility-sector restructuring, and must resolve how the extra costs of renewables will be allocated among utility consumers or society-at-large.

Dealers typically sell systems for cash to the wealthiest rural households. In a few cases, dealers or third-party financiers extend consumer credit that improves afford-ability and thus allows less-wealthy rural households to purchase systems. In Sri Lanka, several rural entrepreneurs have sold more than 5,000 solar home systems through a unique microfinance model. In this case, dealers market, sell, service, and warranty their products to rural consumers through their own local sales/service offices.

Consumers obtain loans from Sarvodaya, a national microfinance institution with many local branches and strong ties to the communities in which it operates. A customer signs a credit agreement with Sarvodaya, which pays the supplier and is responsible for repayment and collections. Productive uses of electricity can increase incomes and provide significant social and development benefits. In turn, as incomes rise, rural populations are able to afford even more energy services.

Brazil has recently adopted several policies to promote the use of grid-connected renewable energy. Utilities are allowed to purchase renewable power at higher prices than conventional electricity, with the cost difference spread among the whole customer base. Independent power producers may supply electricity on a competitive basis to any third party, and receive open access to the transmission and distribution system based on wheeling fees. Small hydro producers receive 50-percent discounts on transmission wheeling fees. In India, GEF support for wind power coincided with the explosive market growth of the mid-1990s, which was fuelled by favourable investment tax policies, availability of commercial financing, and a supportive regulatory framework.

Transparent power purchase tariffs, transmission wheeling, third-party sales, guarantees for local utility power-purchase contracts, and power "banking" contributed to development of the market. By 2000, almost 1,200 megawatts of wind capacity had been installed in India, virtually all of it by the private sector.

In addition, dozens of domestic wind turbine manufacturers had emerged, many of them joint ventures with foreign partners. Exports of turbines began, and high-technology turbine designs with variable-speed operation were being produced. Over the next few decades, it is essential to reduce the consumption of fossil fuels through energy efficiency measures and to expand the use of renewable energy sources.

New financing mechanisms and institutions that can effectively channel small amounts of credit Transfer of technical know-how through alliances and joint ventures. Governments, NGOs, and the private sector could create strategic alliances to promote specific clean energy and development goals. Networks of institutions also could play a greatly expanded role in information sharing, training, knowledge transfer, and monitoring progress on agreed-upon targets.

In January 2002, experts from around the world participated in a GEF Roundtable on Sustainable Energy, chaired by Professor José Goldemberg, one of the world's leading authorities on energy and development. The meeting offered a vision and set of actions to promote clean energy for sustainable development. Participants included representatives of industrial- and developing-country governments, private businesses, NGOs, and multilateral agencies. The GEF Roundtable advanced 10 key priorities for incorporating clean energy into sustainable development in the coming years. Important reductions in technology costs will arise from expanded markets in industrial countries. Clean energy targets adopted in industrial countries mean expanded markets and reduced costs for energy efficiency and renewables, both of which benefit developing countries. Governments should adopt targets according to their respective conditions. Tax and subsidy policies should treat fossil fuels and renewable energy sources equally. Capital is available for clean energy if new mechanisms can channel funds to those who need it, and can divide large pools of credit into smaller increments with low transaction costs.

Renewable energy certificates are another policy for encouraging competitive investment and access. Modern cooking fuels, such as biogas and LPG, should be rapidly integrated into development programs, because of their health and economic benefits. Linkages to agriculture and forestry and sustainable biomass harvesting are important. The special situation of women, who spend much time gathering fuelwood and who receive the greatest exposure to indoor air pollutants, should not be neglected. Integration of renewable energy into agriculture, education and health care, and rural industries is often the least-cost option for addressing these productive and social needs without relying on purchases of nonrenewable fuels.

Renewable energy needs to be on the agendas of donors and officials working in these sectors. Despite significant progress in improving energy efficiency, significant reductions in energy intensity-that is, reductions in energy use in providing goods and services-remain possible, especially in transport, buildings, and industry. Opportunities for such reductions exist even in countries with low per-capita energy use. Rural entrepreneurs are key drivers of new clean-energy technologies, particularly for household lighting and productive uses in small industry, agriculture, and water supply. But few clean-energy enterprises exist, and the challenges of rural-enterprise development and financing are large.

Policy Issues

The management and conservation approaches must be supported by appropriate policies, regulations, and institutional arrangements, for best results. Countries should give priority to strengthening these arrangements in ways that facilitate wider adoption of integrated and cross-sectoral approaches to land and water management. Subsidies and pricing of inputs such as land, water, seeds, and agrochemicals are major policy issues. There is ample evidence that underpricing of natural resources and subsidies for agricultural inputs can lead to overexploitation of those resources and degradation of the environment. Full-cost pricing of water is desirable in the long run, but there are many alternatives that could be politically easier to initiate now. Under a tiered pricing scheme, for example, farmers would be charged the customary rate for perhaps 80 percent of their water use, a much higher rate for the next 10 percent, and the full marginal cost for the last 10 percent. Another major policy issue is the security of land tenure and water rights.

Resource users are less willing to make investments to protect the environment when they have no ownership or when access is restricted. In the absence of such security, they focus on maximizing short-term benefits, often to the detriment of the environment. Policies on subsidies, pricing, tenure security, and other key issues should promote equitable and reliable resource access, efficient resource use, and environmental protection. An important priority is to facilitate the development and wider adoption of good management practices and technologies, such as low or zero tillage and farming systems that use drought-resist-ant or low-water-consuming crop varieties as well as more water-efficient irrigation systems. The development and adoption of better management practices and technologies could be facilitated by collaboration among public and private international agricultural research centers, national research centers, policymakers, NGOs, and local resource users. It is noteworthy, for example, that in Bangladesh the treadle pump mentioned earlier has spread entirely through activities of the private sector, with no government subsidies. A significant support system in Bangladesh-70 manufacturers, 830 dealers, and 2,500 installers-has also helped create jobs and raise incomes.

The 16 centers supported by CGIAR are playing a valuable role in facilitating the adoption of more sustainable practices. For example, the International Institute of Tropical Agriculture (IITA) is using integrated pest management strategies in Sub-Saharan Africa. In dry savannah and Sahel sites, striga (a parasitic weed), stemborers, and poor soil fertility are badly damaging cereal-based cropping systems. In Kenya, farmers are fighting striga and stemborers by combining a striga-tolerant maize variety developed by the Kenya Agricultural Research Institute with the fodder legume desmodium in an intercropping and habitat management system that includes the use of Napier grass. More than 100 farmers in experienced a 20-percent increase in maize yields, and have a new market opportunity for the sale of desmodium and Napier grass. The best information on the enabling environment and on resource management practices and technologies will not result in wider adoption of integrated land and water management approaches-unless there are people with the skills needed to plan and implement such programs.

Governments need to expand and accelerate capacity development activities through in country formal and informal educational programs, advanced training, and staff exchanges among developing countries and between developed and developing nations. Capacity development programs should be tailored to the needs of specific stakeholder groups involved in a particular resource management issue, and should draw on the expertise and experience of local and international organizations. These programmes can help raise environmental awareness, improve technical skills, and provide facilities and equipment to support integrated natural resource management activities. There are four priority groups for capacity development: national and local economic and development planners; resource owners such as government entities, local communities, individuals, and private firms; resource managers such as government and private-sector employees and local communities; and resource users such as government agencies, local communities, and the private sector.One of the positive lessons from the Green Revolution is that partnerships involving a broad range of government and nongovernmental stakeholders, including government and private research institutions, bilateral and multilateral development agencies, and foundations, can play a major role in addressing the issue of food insecurity. Countries need to strengthen existing partnerships or create new ones to provide an effective mechanism to achieve food and environmental security through integrated land and water management.

Partnership arrangements can help mobilize funds from a variety of sources, including local and national budgets, bilateral development cooperation agreements, and country assistance programs of multilateral agencies and foundations. Improved coordination would help to avoid duplication of effort as well as piecemeal approaches to addressing food and environmental security issues. Partnerships can provide legitimacy and technical resources to a program, which in turn can improve opportunities to leverage in opportunities to leverage in country policies and institutional reforms in support of integrated land and water management. Partnerships can also help to strengthen information exchanges.

2

Sustainable Development in South Asia

Sustainable development is one of the most urgent challenges now facing humankind. Today, land degradation and water scarcity threaten food security and livelihoods, particularly in Africa. And, increasingly, air and water pollution are having a negative impact on human health and the productivity of natural resources. The 1.2 billion people who live on less than $1 a day are also the most vulnerable to environmental degradation. They depend on natural resources for sustenance, and they suffer disproportionately from poor environmental conditions.

The high level of public concern about environmental issues provides a political foundation for generating additional financing for the environment and sustainable development. Governments, international finance institutions, and the private sector all have critical and mutually reinforcing roles to play. Financing packages must be designed to involve more than one component of this "triangle" and to foster close coordination and innovative partnerships. Governments must continue to exert leadership, there is much to be gained from forging partnerships to promote sustainable development among the public and private sectors, local and national governments, national and international agencies, NGOs, and civil society. It demonstrated that economic development must not only be economically and financially viable, but also socially acceptable and environmentally sound. This chapter elaborately describes the major issues of sustainable development in South Asian Countries.

India

According to environmental studies, the current Indian gross Carbon dioxide emissions on a per capita basis is merely 1/6th of the world average. Fresh land availability is sparse as already 4% of the geographic area is under nature reserves / forest land. The Department of Space in India has mapped the entire country on a 1:1million scale to identify various land use categories. The study has shown that wasteland area is around 53.3 mn hectares. The remote sensing forestry data can be used for GHG sink development and impact assessment of land use change. The consumption of CFC has been reduced to 60% of the base-level consumption. Use of halon has been reduced to 20% of the consumption of the base-year. Some studies suggest that as the greenhouse effect gains strength, the cyclones will become more frequent and more destructive making island archipelagos such as Lakshadweep highly vulnerable. The danger of frequent storms which generally originate in the Bay of Bengal is, however, higher in the Andamans and Nicobar than Lakshadsweep. Also, as sea level rises, the fresh water aquifers of the islands will be subjected to saline intrusion.

The metros and other big cities of the country are the worst affected chiefly because of lopsided urban planning and incorrect location of industrial units. India's efforts at protecting the ozone layer are guided by the need to integrate environmental protection with development while formulating policy and implementing programmes. The objectives of the ozone depleting substances (ODS) phase-out need to be achieved with minimum economic dislocation and minimum obsolescence costs. Indigenous production of products and substitutes require encouragement, and technological choices need to be carefully made.

Biodiversity

Approximately 5.3% of the total geographical area of country has been earmarked for extensive in situ conservation of habitats and eco-systems through a protection area network of 80 National Parks and 44 Wildlife Sanctuaries. This network has played a significant role in restoring viable populations of large mammals such as the tiger, lion, rhinoceros, crocodiles, elephants, etc. Attention has been paid to ex situ conservation measures as they complement and are important to situ conservation. According to a recent survey, the Central and State Governments together run and manage 33 Botanical Gardens. In addition, universities have their own Botanical Gardens. There are 275 centres of ex situ wildlife preservation in the form of zoos, deer parks, safari parks, aquaria, etc. The Government of India has set up a Central Zoo Authority to oversee, monitor, and coordinate the management and the development of zoos in the country.

Surveys of the floral and faunal resources in the country are carried out by the Botanical Survey of India established in 1890 and the Zoological Survey of India established in 1916. The National Institute of Oceanography and several other specialized institutions and universities further strengthen the taxonomic data base. The diversity of the country's biological resources is yet to be fully surveyed. Approximately 65% of the total geographical area has been surveyed to date. Based on this, over 47,000 species of plants and 81,000 species of animals have been recorded. The vascular flora which form the conspicuous vegetation cover comprises about 15,000 species. Several thousands of them are endemic to India and they have so far not been reported from anywhere else in the world. This list is being constantly upgraded, especially in respect of lower plants and invertebrate animals. The biological diversity of the country is so rich that it may play a very important and crucial role in the future survival of mankind if it is conserved and used with the utmost care. Today, two hot spots in biological diversity have been identified in the country, namely, the Eastern Himalayan region and the Western Ghats. A comprehensive status report covering the various facets of biodiversity conservation in India is under preparation.

The collection and preservation of genetic resources is accomplished through the National Bureau of Plant Genetic Resources for Wildlife for crop plants; the National Bureau of Animal Genetic Resources for domesticated animals; and the National Bureau of Fish Genetic Resources for economically valuable fish species. These Bureaus are assigned the task of collecting germplasm and supplying these on request to Indian and foreign agencies for research purposes. Conservation and sustainable use of biological resources based on local knowledge systems and practices is ingrained in Indian ethos and way of life. Formal policies and programmes for conservation and sustainable use of biodiversity resources date back several decades. The concept of environmental protection is enshrined in the Indian Constitution in Article 48(a) and 51(g). Major central acts relevant to biodiversity are: the Wildlife (Protection) Act, 1972; the Forest (Conservation) Act, 1980; and the Environment (Protection) Act, 1986. The various central acts are supported by a number of state laws and statutes concerning forests and other natural resources.

Following the ratification of the Biodiversity Convention by India, several steps have been initiated to meet the commitments under the Convention and to bring the legislative, administrative, and policy regime regarding biological diversity in tune with the Articles of the Convention. A National Action Plan on Biological Diversity is being finalized which will consolidate the ongoing conservation and sustainable use efforts including capacity building and biosafety measures. In addition, the following activities are being undertaken: biosafety protocol; biodiversity information network; capacity building in taxonomy; consultation with the State Governments; traditional knowledge and benefit sharing; and legislation.

Policies and strategies directly relevant to biodiversity include: the National Forest Policy as amended in 1988; the National Conservation Strategy, and Policy Statement for Environment and Sustainable Development; the National Agricultural Policy; the National Land Use Policy; the National Fisheries Policy (under preparation); the National Biodiversity Policy (under preparation); the National Wildlife Action Plan;

and the Environmental Action Plan. A programme called eco-development for in situ conservation of biological diversity involving local communities has been initiated in recent years through World Bank assistance. The concept of eco-development integrates the ecological and economic parameters for the sustained conservation of ecosystems by involving local communities with the maintenance of earmarked regions surrounding protected areas. To conserve representative ecosystems, a Biosphere Reserve Programme is being implemented.

Eight biodiversity rich areas of the country have been designated as Biosphere Reserves applying the United Nations Educational, Scientific and Cultural Organization's Man and the Biosphere criteria. India is one of the 12 mega biodiversity centres in the world, representing two of the major realms and three of the basic biomes of the world. The country is divided into 10 biogeographic regions: Trans-Himalayan, Himalayan, Indian Desert, Semi-Arid, Western Ghats, Deccan Peninsula, Gangetic Plains, North-East India, Islands, and Coasts. Programmes have also been launched for scientific management and wise use of fragile ecosystems. Specific programmes for management and conservation of wetlands, mangroves, and coral reef systems are being implemented. National and state level committees oversee and guide these programmes to ensure strong policy and strategic support.

The Convention on Biological Diversity was signed and ratified by India in February, 1994. The Convention on International Trade in Endangered Species of Wild Fauna and Flora was signed in 1976. India believes that National action regarding conservation and sustainable use of biodiversity and equitable sharing of benefits arising from the use of genetic resources demands appropriate actions on the part of international community. Some key issues in this regard are as follows: Development of a suitable enabling environment by the other parties, particularly the developed countries, to ensure benefits to countries of origin. These benefits should not only include measures like royalty payment or monetary compensation, but also location of research and technologies in the countries of origin in accordance with the provisions of the Convention.

Development of a credible internationally regime for recognizing the intellectual and physical property rights of local communities. Development of such a regime may take time, pending which all patent applications should be required to disclose:

a) the source and origin of the genetic material used;

b) knowledge and practices about the use of the genetic resources by the local communities and identification of such communities; and

c) a declaration that laws, practices, and guidelines for the use of such material and knowledge systems in the country of origin have been followed.

Capacities of biodiversity rich countries should be built to enable them to bio-prospect and develop products from genetic resources. Introduction of transgenics, alien species should be only permitted with appropriate safeguards.

Biosphere Reserves

Biosphere reserves are multi-purpose protected areas to preserve the genetic diversity in representative eco-systems. The major objectives of biosphere reserves are: (i) to conserve diversity and integrity of plants, animals and micro-organisms; (ii) to promote research on ecological conservation and other environmental aspects and (iii) to provide facilities for education, awareness and training. So far eleven biosphere reserves have been set up. They are Nilgiri; Nanda Devi; Nokrek; Great Nicobar; Gulf of Mannar; Manas; Sunderbans; Similipal; Dibru Saikhowa; Dehong Deband and Pachmarhi. Comprehensive guidelines for them emphasize formulation of eco-development and demonstration projects, development of data-base, conservation plans of key species, establishment of research stations and implementation of social welfare activities.

Wetlands, Mangroves and Coral Reefs

India's wetland eco-systems distributed in different geographical regions from the cold arid zone of Ladakh in the North to the wet humid climate of Imphal in the East, the warm arid zone of Rajasthan in the West to the tropical monsoon Central India and the wet and humid zone of Southern Peninsula. Most of the wetlands in India are directly or indirectly linked with major river systems such as Ganga, Brahmaputra, Narmada, Tapti, Godavari, Krishna, and Cauveri.

Forests

Analysis of State changes in forest cover for 1991-1993 reveals that the country can be broadly classified into two regions, namely the Northeast region and the rest of the country due to the peculiar situation of shifting cultivation. While there has been a decrease of 635 km2 of forest cover in the north-eastern region, there has been an overall increase of 1560 km2 in the rest of the country, giving a gross increase of 925 km2 in the forest cover. However, in terms of qualitative forest cover loss, the dense forest in almost all the major states has gone down. On the whole, the country has achieved a partial success in the protection of forests. The wildlife scenario in India is not very encouraging. According to the All India Tiger Census of 1993, the tiger population has declined. There has been a loss of 553 tigers between 1989 and 1993. In spite of the stringent and tough provisions of the Wildlife Act, wildlife poaching still continues. There has been a change in the demand pattern from tiger skins to their bones. Full analysis of this change is required so as to prevent poaching at the initial stages. Wildlife conservation has assumed new dimensions under the Eco-Development Scheme in and around National parks and sanctuaries.

Forest based livestock farming and forest are highly interdependent. Livestock development in the country has taken in two different areas in two different pretexts. The first pretext, which relates with dairy and poultry, is on an industrial base, involving more of person's management rather than persons of husbandry. However, in the second, which relates with the poor class of people/ rural poor, is resource based and depends upon forest, grassland and pastures. Therefore, forest based livestock farming needs more attention in order to result in both improvement of the economic condition of the farmers and conservation of the forests. Major forest areas in India and other developing countries are owned and managed by government, and local people have rights and concessions over the usufructs. The main problem area of most developing countries including India is of financial resources or funding. Financial resources have been identified only as a supporting function under the Principle function of policy implementation. This needs reconsideration. It is suggested that one of the IAMs must be assigned this exclusive function. It should perhaps be mandatory for this IAM to ensure that funding is based on the National Forest Action Plan prepared by the country and not on other parameters.The Government has taken initiatives to identify the criteria and indicators for sustainable forest management. All the State Governments and various concerned Ministries of the Government of India, including Ministry of Rural Development, Department of Land Resources and the Planning Commission are being requested to see the National Forestry Action Programmes for drawing out linkages with the land management strategies. India's policies and programmes in forestry, particularly over the last fifteen years, have been largely in consonance with the Forest Principles adopted during the United Nations Conference on Environment and Development (UNCED). The Forest (Conservation) Act of 1980 initiated a process by which India's forests were treated as an environmental and social resource rather than as a revenue or commercial resource. The strictest controls have been placed on the diversion of forestland to other uses. In the rare cases when this is permitted for developmental purposes, compensatory afforestation is a prior requirement.

Biodiversity conservation has been made an integral part of forest conservation. Various conservation measures have been taken to strengthen legislation and eco-development efforts. The Wildlife (Protection) Act, 1972 and its amendments to 1991 provide the legal framework for conservation of wildlife in the country. The amendment of 1991 is significant as it provides protection not only to wild animals and birds, but also to plant species. Thus, it addresses forest ecology in its totality. Realising the role of forests in controlling soil erosion, moderation of floods, recharging of ground aquifers, as habitat for wildlife, conservation of bio-diversity and gene pool, etc., several programmes have been launched from as early as the Second Five Year Plan. The Indian Forests Act 1927 is the main act, which regulates the management of forest by the States. A two-pronged strategy to increase forest cover has been adopted which essentially comprises of: 1) To improve canopy cover in the forest land; and 2) To undertake afforestation in non-forest and degraded lands preferably contiguous to forest blocks.

A National Afforestation and Eco-Development Board (NAEB) has been created for promoting afforestation, tree planting, ecological restoration, and eco-development. The NAEB pays special attention to the regeneration of degraded forests. The NAEB serves as a vital interface between external agencies and the State Governments. Compensation for forest owners providing non-market environmental benefits to society is not a relevant issue in the context of India, as more than 95% forests are owned and managed by the Government. Most of the forest in the country recognizes the customer rights and concessions of the local people over it. The issue of forest certification is being examined by the Government, and no final view has been taken on the issue. India's National Forest Policy of 1988 formulated four years before the Earth Summit embodies the direction emphasized in the Rio Principles. The Government's commitment to the management of forests through the participatory process is reflected in the active involvement of tribal and village communities and voluntary agencies. This strengthens the activities of State Forest Departments in forest protection and regeneration initiatives. Various problems and conflicts arising out of the tribal forest interface are resolved through administrative measures including the creation of village-based Forest Protection Committees, an experiment, which has met with remarkable success in some parts of the country. Tree planting is the main focus, particularly through the Area Orientated Fuel wood and Fodder Scheme, and the Integrated Afforestation and Eco-Development Programme. Efforts are being made to ensure that weaker sections of society and women emerge as the major beneficiaries of the activities of NAEB. Up to 1994-95, about 237,781 ha of degraded forests has been planted under the Area Oriented Fuel wood and Fodder Project. The monitoring and evaluation of the plantations is required to assess the survival of the seedlings.

Participatory Forest Management as an effective means of regenerating degraded forests has been increasingly gaining ground in India. In 1990, the Government issued guidelines to State Governments highlighting the need and the procedure for the involvement of village communities and voluntary agencies in the protection and development of degraded forests. In response to these guidelines, 22 out of 25 States have issued orders for creating resolutions enabling mechanisms for public participation in the management of degraded forests. The participatory forest management approach promotes active participation and involvement of the people in forest conservation and development, including the development of micro-level plans and their implementation. At present, approximately 10 million ha of forest area is being maintained through more than 36,000 Village Forest Protection Committees. Although many States have accepted the initiative in principle, effective implementation of the new approach at the field level has taken root only in a few States. One of the important elements of the Participatory Forest Management System relates to the use of indigenous capacity and local knowledge regarding various aspects of conservation, development, and use of forests. The rural people, particularly women, have an intimate knowledge about various species, growth characteristics, utility, and medicinal value. They are also well informed about the species to be planted in a given locality to satisfy the specific requirements of fuel, fodder, timber, and other non-wood forest products. In participatory forest management, planning and implementation of most of the activities related to regeneration and protection are completed with the active involvement of rural people.

There is a symbiotic relationship between tribal people and forests. In 1991, various issues related to forest-tribal interface were examined and detailed guidelines issued by the Government of India to the State Governments in order to ameliorate the socioeconomic conditions of tribal people. These guidelines cover a number of subjects including addressing old encroachments of forest lands, disputed claims over forest land, elimination of intermediaries to stop exploitation, conversion of forest villages to revenue villages, and payment of compensation for loss of life and property due to depredation by wild animals. A review of social forestry programme launched during the 1980s resulted in a consolidation of gains and a strengthening of the weaker links. The conservation of the existing natural forests with emphasis on natural regeneration is given increasing focus. The current approach towards afforestation and forest conservation is to integrate the activities and expertise of different sectors so that various pressures responsible for forest degradation are adequately addressed. Introduction of the Eco-Development Programme has been one of the recent developments in the field of wildlife management. The objective is economic development for the people residing in and around sanctuaries and National parks, in order to reduce their dependence on forest products and improve the ecological health of the protected areas. The scheme aims to increase land and forest resource productivity so that alternative avenue of employment and income are made available in the immediate neighborhood of people.The Eco-Development Programme proposes a package of activities including developing agriculture, improving land productivity and developing minor irrigation, raising fodder and fuel plantations, providing livestock care and improvement, introducing fuel saving devices, providing medical care including family planning, and creating environmental awareness. It is increasingly thought that the eco-development concept should not be limited to protected areas. It is believed that the scope and content of such schemes should be extended to cover other villages lying in the immediate vicinity of forests. The comprehensive State Forestry Projects, which have been recently launched by a number of States, incorporate elements of eco-development as a means of ensuring sustained development of forests.

The cross-sectoral issues like rural employment, water and soil conservation, fodder production, firewood production to meet energy requirements of 80% of the rural population, etc. has been taken care of in the National Forestry Action Programme. The forestry management in the country is being practiced on the basis of sustainable management for more than a century. However efforts are being made to ensure that the management plans of the forest areas are prepared taking advantage of the important latest technology like GIS, etc. and so as to reduce the period of preparation as well as the period of management plans in the country. Accordingly a comprehensive working plan code is being prepared for the whole country.The assessment of forest cover in the first three cycles (1987,1989 and 1991) was based only on visual interpretation of satellite imagery, while the fourth cycle (1993) has been subjected to computer analysis. As a result, it has been possible to systematically interpret a part of the area more objectively. As per the latest 1997 assessment forest cover of the country is at 6,33,397 sq. kms. Thus in the comparison of forest cover figures of 1995 and 1997 assessments, there is a slight decrease of forest cover from 6,38,879 sq. kms in 1995 assessment.

India has been participating in all the IPF/IFF meetings and India agrees with the overall action relating to National Forest Programme, Forest assessment, criteria and indicators, traditional forest related causes and underline causes of deforestation. However, India has taken a view that there has to be an instrument to coordinate the efforts of various international instruments and institutions. Accordingly, India has moved for creation of a permanent forum like Global Forest Facility on the lines of the Global Environmental Facility (GEF), to further carry out the dialogue and discussions on the contentious and unresolved issues. India has also taken a view that financial resources/funding is one of the major problem areas and therefore, it is necessary to assign this exclusive function to one of the International Arrangements and Mechanisms (IAMs).In consonance with the recommendation of IPF, India has prepared the National Forest Action Programme in the year 1999 in consultation with FAO which incorporates the agreed commitments by India. India's economic and trade policies which have a bearing on forest and forest products are being progressively fine-tuned to facilitate the conservation and sustainable use of forests. This is reflected in liberal imports of forest products to relieve pressures on forests, nationalization of trade of certain forest products, incentives for wood substitution, subsidies for the use of fuel-saving devices and alternative sources of energy supply such as biogas and solar energy, and financial incentives to supply seedlings free of cost or at subsidized rates. India has actively participated in the deliberations of the Intergovernmental Panel on Forests, established by the Commission on Sustainable Development.

Mountain Ecosystems

As a major ecosystem representing the complex and interrelated ecology of our planet, mountain environments are essential to the survival of the global ecosystem. Mountains are, however, vulnerable to human and natural ecological imbalance. The Himalayas represent one of the most fragile mountain ecosystems and, furthermore, sustain a large human population. This sets them apart from Alpine or other ranges, where human habitation is not so high. Mountains and their people deserve consideration and attention, so that local knowledge can be used, and sustained and accelerated development becomes a reality in the context of the promotion and protection of the ecosystem as a whole. The Himalaya system is vast and diverse, and represents the youngest mountain system in the world. It occupies 18% of the geographical area of India and regulates climate of the entire Indian sub-continent. The existence of valuable flora, fauna, and minerals exclusive to the region is unique. The Himalayas feed the major river systems of the Indian sub-continent.

Mountains are an important sources of water, energy, minerals, forests, and agricultural products; and serve as areas of recreation. They are store houses of biological diversity, home to endangered species, and an essential part of the global ecosystem. Therefore, the development of mountains has to be viewed in a holistic manner, encompassing economic development, technological improvement, environmental protection, and human resource development. All these activities are interrelated and gains in one will produce benefits in others.

In India, a number of important priority activities have been augmented and strengthened as a follow up of Agenda 21. While a large number of existing institutions in the region have continued their efforts, the Government has established the GB Pant Institute for Himalayan Environment and Development with the specific mandate for generating and strengthening knowledge about the ecology and sustainable development of the Indian Himalayas. The Institute is also involved in integrating and collecting traditional knowledge for sustainable and integrated development of watersheds. Some of the major achievements are as follows:

— suitable models for efficient upland farming systems have been developed to apply soil, water, and nutrient conservation techniques in watersheds of the Sikkim and Garhwal Himalaya;

— integrated approaches for the management of irrigation systems were developed in selected areas of Kumaun keeping in view rural water supply and sanitation;

- sustainable natural resource management models are being developed in selected villages of the Nanda Devi Biosphere Reserve with the people's participation;
- preliminary studies on biodiversity assessment have been completed in selected Protected Areas of the Kumaun and Himachal Himalaya;
- an environmental awareness programme and biodiversity conservation for school children was continued in the district of Pithoragarh of the Kumaun Himalaya;
- resource use in the Kullu valley has been studied to evolve sustainable practices;
- conventional and in-vitro propagation protocols for selected multipurpose tree species have been developed;
- microbial interventions for improved plant species have been developed; and
- several on-site training programmes on nursery technology, conservation practices, and protected cultivation have been organized in remote villages with the participation of farmers and NGOs.

Ocean and Costal areas

Fisheries: Fisheries play an important role in the Indian economy and supports about 6.0 million full time or occasional fishermen. It continues to be a thrust area of India's development programmes due to its vital contributions to employment generation, food security and foreign exchange earnings. Fish production in India reached a level of about 5.40 million tonnes in 1998 and the country is now sixth largest producer of fish in the world. Out of this, 2.90 million tonnes is from the marine sector. The earnings from export of fish and fishery products crossed US$1.30 billion in 1998. While fish production form 0-50 m. zone has been harvested to maximum sustainable yield levels, the zone beyond 50-200 m and 200-500 m has been harvested up to about 50% levels.The oceanic resources are harvested up to 10% of the potential. In the Indian Ocean context, the over-exploitation and destruction of eco-system and habitat is not alarming as in some other parts of the World. The recent review of the state of World fishery resources by FAO has revealed that while the Atlantic Ocean and in different parts of the Pacific Ocean the fishery resources are largely over-exploited, in the Indian Ocean fish production is on the increase with relative stability and healthy state of fish stocks. Various measures are being undertaken to optimise and rationalise the fishing fleet as well as the fishing effort by area-wise deployment of different categories of fishing vessels, regulation of fishing, gear and mesh size, uniform closed fishing season, development of deep sea fishing including diversified fishing, replenishment of fish stocks by undertaking projects on sea ranching, setting up of artificial reef, etc.

Enhancement of Marine Living Resources: The seas around India, including Island Groups, are endowed with a variety of finfish and shellfish resources. The over-exploitation of these commercially important resources has resulted in significant depletion of their population. The objectives of the work contemplated in the present technology development programme are steps towards conservation of these resources through breeding and sea ranching.

Oil Spills and Shipping: The western part of the Indian Exclusive Economic Zone, i.e., the Arabian Sea adjoining the peninsular India, forms the main international route for oil tankers originating from the Gulf. It has been estimated that some 450 mt. of crude oil is transported annually along this route, involving approximately 2500 laden tankers. Considering the large volume of oil transported and increased ocean traffic, the probability of tanker accidents is high. The last major accident in the area occurred in January 1993 when a few thousand tonnes of oil spilled into the Andaman Sea. Any accidental spillage of oil along the tanker route will cause severe and in some cases irreparable damage to the marine ecosystem. In addition to offshore oil exploration and production activities, transfer operations of oil at single buoy mooring stations, as well as lightening and bunkering operations in major ports, cause spillage of oil.

Disposal of Domestic and Industrial Waste: It has been estimated that a large quantum of domestic sewage reaches the coastal environment each day. These wastes contain degradable organic matter, which utilizes enormous amounts of oxygen from seawater for its oxidation. The resultant fall in oxygen in seawater leads to a decrease in the population of marine flora and fauna. Domestic wastes in certain coastal areas are discharged without treatment due to lack of such facilities in most cities and towns.

Under the Integrated Coastal and Marine Area Management Programme of the Department waste assimilation capacity and preparation of model Integrated Coastal and Marine Area Management plans, etc., have been envisaged. With a view to control marine pollution from land based activities information relating to assimilation capacity of coastal waters, particularly with reference to the thermal waste discharges including fly ash, aquaculture waste and sewage and other industrial wastes. Studies have been initiated on discharge and assimilation of fly ash and other pollutants from industries located along Ennore Creek, North off Chennai. Application of modern tools like computer based modelling for prediction of the impact of the various integrated activities occurring in the coastal areas is also incorporated in the Integrated Coastal and Marine Area Management Programme.

Constant monitoring of the health of the seas and taking up remedial measures for preventing and controlling pollution from land based activities is another activity, for ensuring sustainable development of the seas around India. The various measures taken up by the Government for regulating the activities along the coastal zone, fishing and fisheries, etc., have a definite role to play in sustainable development and utilisation of the ocean and its resources.

The Ministry of Environment and Forests, New Delhi and Department of Ocean Development are responsible for decision-making in the area of oceans and seas. The management of resources in high seas is with Department of Ocean Development, while management of resources in the Coastal Water lies with Ministry of Environment and Forests. In India, the UN Convention on the Law of the Sea was signed in 1995 and ratified in June 1996. India has also ratified the International Convention for the Prevention of Pollution from Ships (MARPOL Convention 73/78) and adopted the provisions in the Merchant Shipping Act. Fisheries are regulated under the Marine Fishing Regulation Act (MFRA).

The Notification on Coastal Regulation Zone 1991 (as amended from time to time) lists certain prohibited and regulated activities related to integrated coastal zone management and sustainable development. Its provisions also prohibit and regulate developmental activities in the Coastal Regulation Zone. The effluents/discharges from various resources have to meet the standards listed in the EP (Act) 1986 before being discharged in the marine waters. To address integrated coastal zone management and sustainable development, the following legislation has been adopted:

— Environment Protection Act (EPA), 1986, under which

— Coastal Regulation Zone 1991 has been notified.

— Forest Conservation Act, 1980.

— Standards for discharging effluents are listed in the Environmental Protection Act 1986.

In the area of fisheries development, the following are the legislation/rules/acts in force in the country:

The Maritime Zones of India (Regulation of fishing by Foreign Vessels) Act, 1981 provides fishing regulations for foreign fishing vessels for operation in Indian waters. The Coast Guard and the State/UT Police has been authorised under the Act to apprehend and prosecute unauthorized foreign fishing vessels/crew for fishing/poaching in Indian waters.

The Marine Fishing Regulation Acts enforced by the coastal States of India provide for regulating fishing and conservation measures in the territorial waters. These include: regulation of mesh size to avoid catching of juvenile fish, regulation of gear to avoid over-exploitation of certain species, reservation of zones for various fishing sectors to provide exclusive rights to traditional fishermen to fish unhindered in near shore areas and also for declaration of closed seasons during fish breeding period to avoid catching of young juvenile fish.

A committee was constituted by the Government of India in March, 1995 to review the Deep Sea Fishing Policy. On the basis of the recommendations of this Committee, the Deep Sea Fishing Policy of 1991 was rescinded and no new permits, extensions or renewal of the permits under the above policies has been given. The Government has also constituted a National Level Review Committee in 1996 to assess the area-wise requirements of different categories of fishing vessels below 20 m. and conservation of fishery resources, etc. A number of measures have also been taken by the government to conserve marine fishery resources and over-exploitation as per the provisions made in the Central/State Acts/ Rules. Measure have also been taken to introduce resource-specific fishing vessels for oceanic fisheries.

A national and 13 State/U.T. level coastal management Authorities have been set up to identify and prepare an Integrated Coastal Zone Management Plan for ecologically important stretches. To address the preservation and sustainable use of fragile ecosystems, State/Union Territory level Waste Zone Management Authorities have been set up, and these will prepare an Integrated Coastal Zone Management Plan for ecologically important zones. Major Groups are involved through public hearings that have been made mandatory before any project listed in EIA notification is cleared.

The Coastal Ocean Monitoring and Prediction Systems (COMAPS) is a programme being carried by the Department of Ocean Development since 1990-91 with the objective of constantly assessing the health of Indian seas on a long-term basis. The status of marine pollution in the coastal waters has been assessed and current level of pollution int he waters has also been determined. Further, it is planned to include physical oceanographic studies and incorporate the techniques for determination of waste assimilation capacity of water bodies to have predictive capabilities on pollution levels, which will enable establishing site specific regulatory measures to maintain the desired quality of the coastal waters.In 1998, the Department took up an infrastructure development and capacity building programme to facilitate adoption of the concept of Integrated Coastal and Marine Area Management (ICMAM) by coastal areas in the coming years. The programme focuses on development of expertise in ICMAM oriented activities and dissemination of knowledge gained to the coastal areas through organized training programmes. Towards accomplishing these activities, the following priority activities are being undertaken: Capacity Building and Infrastructure. With regard to the management of Marine Environment and Biodiversity as well as for their monitoring, major activities relate to the monitoring of the health of India's coastal waters and to capacity building and infrastructure development to facilitate adoption of the concept of Integrated Coastal and Marine Area Management (ICMAM).

Ocean Science & Technology Cells (OSTCs): The Department of Ocean Development has been sponsoring research projects in different disciplines in a large number of national laboratories and academic institutions with the guidance of a Research Advisory Committee. Special grants are given to selected academic institutions to build infrastructure. Research Fellowships and Research Associate ships are granted for Post-Graduate and Post-

Doctoral Research in Marine Science in Universities and national laboratories. With a view to have a coordinated approach to promote specialisation in marine science in different universities, the Department formulated a scheme for establishing Ocean Science and Technology Cells (OSTC) in consultation with the Universities engaged in research in Marine Science. These cells in the academic institutions will grow into Centres of Excellence in due course. So far 8 OSTCs have been established. To create awareness among the wide section of the society, the Department of Ocean Development organises and sponsors seminars, symposia, workshops and conference at Universities, national laboratories, scientific institutions, Government and Non-Government Organisations with national and international participation. In addition, Department brings out quarterly newsletter, technical reports and books. Data Bank and information networking exist between the coastal states and decision-making body with regard to ecologically important resources, economically important resources, etc.

With a view to synergise and generate reliable coastal and ocean data and data products, the various related projects of the Department of Ocean Development were restructured and reoriented in 1997-98 as Ocean Observation and Information Services (OOIS). This programme has four major elements viz., Ocean Observing System using Conventional and Satellite Remote Sensing Observations, Ocean Information Services, networking different ocean observations and marine data centres to serve the user demands, Satellite and Coastal Oceanographic Research utilising the advances in Satellite Remote Sensing Technology, and Ocean Dynamics & Modelling to establish predictive capacity of ocean parameters. Geographic Information

System has been introduced as a means of Decision Supporting System in the management of critical habitats like mangroves, coral reefs, areas rich in biodiversity, etc., under the Integrated Coastal and Marine Area Management programme.

The Department of Ocean Development sponsors R&D projects in academic institutions, National laboratories and societies. These projects train and orient the scientists in specific fields in the ocean sector and deploy them in the R&D activities. Some of these scientists associate themselves with the Universities and improve their academic qualifications also. The Department also provides Research Fellowship to do doctoral and post doctoral work to enhance their potentials, knowledge and expertise. The Department also sponsors short term training programmes in specified areas. The Department has plans to establish adequate infrastructure to train coastal states on the advanced tools and techniques for planning coastal zone management systems.

Oceanographic data are essential for understanding the oceanic processes and undertaking developments relating to ocean sector. The UNBED (1992) emphasizes the need for Global Ocean Observing System (GOOS) to collect long term systematic scientific oceanographic data at a national, regional and global level. The world climate research programme needs effective contributions for oceanographic observations. Thus the need of the hour is reliable oceanographic data and data products of quality which are application oriented and user driven. The application areas are Weather Climate prediction, Fisheries, Port and Harbour Development, Navigation and Shipping, Environment Pollution Monitoring, Coastal area development and R&D in oceanography.

Over the years the Fisheries Survey of India has assessed the fishing resources up to 50-70 m. depth and published the fishery atlas. It is also noted that the fishery resources in India's coastal waters up to 50-70 m. depth is almost fully exploited. Some of the species are over-exploited and are endangered. In addition, the marine pollution has led to degradation of the marine resource potential and marine biodiversity. Indian R&D institutions have carried out studies on fish biology and technologies for culture fisheries, controlled harvesting, etc. to aid sustainable resource utilisation. The Department of Ocean Development has initiated a multi-disciplinary and multi-institutional programme aimed at making an assessment of the marine living resources beyond 70 m. depth within the Indian EEZ and correlating the marine living resources potential with the oceanographic parameters in 1997-98. The major objectives of this programme are to have a realistic and reliable information on the potential of marine living resources in the Indian EEZ for sustainable development and management and to enhance the marine living resource potential of Indian seas. In addition, it is planned to develop technologies and implement pilot projects to increase the productivity of India's coastal waters selectively by sea ranching and mariculture and thereby augmenting the sea food production and improving the life of our coastal community.

Design and development of a remotely operated underwater mining system with collector module, lifting module and instrumentation and Control Systems, was initiated in 1990. In 1996, India reoriented its polymetallic nodules programme to establish the technologies in a phased manner. India is implementing a joint developmental programme on seabed mining technology with the participation of the National Institute of Ocean Technology (NIOT), Chennai and the University of Siegen, Germany, with the initial efforts to demonstrate shallow bed mining technology in Indian seas up to 500 metres depth. Successful exploration of sulphides, phosphorites, placer deposits and other seabed minerals in the Exclusive Economic Zone or India. Technology development for extractive metallurgy from polymetallic nodules, marine acoustic instrumentation, ocean energy including Ocean Thermal Energy Conservation, etc., is also given appropriate priority. For acquiring surface meteorological and upper oceanographic parameters on real-time basis 12 moored data buoys have been deployed along the Indian coastline at selected locations. These buoys are equipped with sensors for accurate measurement of a number of oceanographic parameters. The data are disseminated to the India Meteorological Department for forecast of cyclones, and to other scientific and research institutions, port authorities, National Hydrographic Office, etc., for wider utility and application. The transmission of the data between the buoys and a store station is effected through a two-way communication system of INMARSAT-C satellite. The oceanographic data are also collected through drifting buoys and are transmitted via ARGOS satellite to various user agencies.

The programme and activities of the Department of Ocean Development are fully funded by the Government of India, from the National Budget. External assistance is also available for specific programmes such as National Data Buoy Programme and the Capacity Building Component of Integrated Coastal and Marine Area Management from NORAD and World Bank, respectively. In addition to active participation at the UN on ocean matters, India actively participates in Intergovernmental Oceanographic Commission, UN Convention on the Law of the Sea, Antarctic Treaty System, Regional Seas Programme. India also has scientific and technical bilateral cooperation with other nations.

Wastes and hazardous materials

At present, solid wastes are utilized to the extent possible by the following processes: conversion of garbage into energy pellets; anaerobic digestion/biogas generation from garbage; and composting by vermiculture and other means. A pilot plant has been set up in Bombay for the conversion of garbage into energy pellets. It is proposed to set up ten more such plants for which external assistance is likely to be sought. The process of anaerobic digestion/biogas generation from garbage is being applied at medium and small scale levels at several places in India, and is being encouraged at other places. The conversion of garbage into compost by vermiculture and other processes is also being promoted. All these processes not only help in waste utilization but also in producing energy or useful products. Apart from organic wastes, several other urban wastes such as wastepaper, plastics, glass, rubber, textiles, metals, coconut shells, etc. are extensively recycled. This is encouraged by the Government. Some of the industrial wastes such as fly ash, blast furnace slag, lime sludge, phosphogypsum, red-mud, etc. are generated in large quantities and are sources of environmental pollution. Reuse and recycling of these wastes is being encouraged. Fiscal incentives in the form of excise duty exemption have been provided on the production of building materials using fly ash or phosphogypsum. An exemption of custom duty is also applied on imports of equipment and machinery for the conversion of these wastes to useful purposes.

The collection and disposal of solid wastes is another area of concern for city management in India. No city collects and disposes of its solid wastes in a safe manner and the coverage is often inadequate. An ORG study of 24 cities in 1989 revealed that, while daily solid waste generation was about 15,000 tonnes, only 11,500 tonnes was collected, leaving almost one-fourth to degenerate within the city environment. Even when the collection rate is high, say 90%, the collection frequency is not satisfactory. There is no relationship between solid waste collection and city size. Furthermore, collection does not necessarily suggest regular service and the frequency varies from twice a week in the mega cities to fortnightly collection in the intermediate towns. This relates to domestic wastes as collection of industrial and commercial wastes is more regular. The disposal of wastes is another issue of concern to city managers. The method seems to improve with the level of urbanization, from open-dumps in the small and intermediate towns to sanitary landfills in the mega cities.

The major environmental concerns in an urbanizing India relate to high levels of water pollution due to poor waste disposal, inadequate sewerage and drainage, and improper disposal of industrial effluents. The dumping of solid waste in low-lying areas contributes to land and groundwater pollution. All these developments have contributed to the deterioration of the urban environment, a critical concern that requires specific interventions to achieve sustainability of human settlements. In order to improve the management of urban solid wastes and sewage related issues, there is need for capacity building, awareness and training, improved technologies, and the creation of infrastructure facilities. The lack of adequate financial resources, especially at the municipal and local levels remains a constraint.

In India, a National Waste Management Council (NWMC) has been constituted by the Ministry of Environment and Forests to provide advice on various matters related to waste management including the incentives/disincentives required to facilitate waste utilization. Representatives of concerned Central and State Government departments, municipal corporations, industry associations, experts, NGOs, and media people meet from time to time under the Chairmanship of the Minister for Environment and Forests. There are three Centrally sponsored schemes for pollution abatement of rivers presently under implementation by the Ministry. These are the Ganga Action Plan (GAP) Phase I, Ganga Action Plan Phase II, and National River Conservation Plan. The main objective of the Ganga Action Plan is to improve the water quality of the Ganga to acceptable standards by preventing the pollution load reaching the river. The Action Plan primarily addresses itself to the interception, diversion, and treatment of 873 million litres per day of municipal sewage out of the estimated 1,340 million litres per day from 25 towns, 6 in Uttar Pradesh, 4 in Bihar, and 15 in West Bengal.

Under the GAP, emphasis has been given to the improvement of sewage treatment technologies. As a result, the programme has led to the development of some appropriate technologies like the Upflow Anaerobic Sludge Blanket (UASB), improved oxidation ponds, sewage treatment through plantation, etc. These technologies are cost effective in terms of operation and maintenance and, thus, will reduce the burden on the State Government. These developments will make the Ganga Action Plan and future programmes sustainable. The programme also emphasizes resource recovery from sewage treatment to improve its sustainability. These aspects include utilization of biogas for co-generation of power, and sale of treated sewage and sludge (a bio-fertilizer and nutrient rich treated effluents for agriculture). Pisciculture is proposed in most of the stabilization ponds constructed under GAP. The Plan serves as a model for other river systems. Thus, action plans for the rivers Yamuna, Gomti, and Damodar are being developed. For proper management of urban solid wastes, it is essential to know the quantity and nature of wastes being generated and utilized. The Ministry of Environment and Forests has initiated a scheme to survey the solid wastes generated, utilized, and disposed off in important towns of the country. A scheme to develop pilot projects, conduct surveys, and fund promotional activities in the following areas have been initiated to emphasize waste reduction, recycling, and reuse in industries, and better management of municipal solid wastes: a) survey of urban municipal wastes in important cities and the setting up of pilot plants on the utilization of municipal solid wastes; b) establishing pilot plants to utilize industrial wastes; and c) development and other promotional activities for municipal and industrial wastes.

With rapid growth of population and industrialization during the last two decades, there has been a tremendous increase in the generation of domestic, urban, and industrial wastes. Although a major part of the wastes generated are non-hazardous, substantial quantities are hazardous wastes. In spite of the several steps taken for the management of wastes generated by various sources, only a small proportion of solid wastes are properly utilized and disposed of, with the result that some wastes cause environmental degradation and health risks. The Hazardous Wastes Rules, under the authority of the Environment Act, 1986, were announced by the Ministry of Environment and Forests in July, 1989. These Rules regulate the generation, collection, storage, transport, treatment, disposal, and import of hazardous wastes. The Rules apply to 18 categories of hazardous wastes which have been identified and listed in the Schedule annexed to the Rules. One of the important stipulations under the Rules is that the importation of hazardous wastes from any other country to India is not permitted for dumping or disposal. However, importation is allowed for processing or reuse as raw material, after examination of the merits of each case by the competent authorities. Under Rule 11 of the Hazardous Wastes Rules, 1989, the exporting country or exporter is required to communicate details about the proposed transboundary movement of hazardous wastes to the Central Government. The importer is also required to provide details regarding the wastes to the relevant State Pollution Control Boards. After examining the details provided by the importer/exporter, suitable instructions are issued by the concerned authorities. The Port Authorities are also advised.

The wastes from other countries are exported in large quantities and are received in bulk shipments. Such shipments enter through India's ports and the Ports and Customs Authorities have a major role in checking and granting permission for entry of these shipments. The hazardous wastes are included in the restricted lists of imports requiring a license, which is granted subject to the recommendation under the Hazardous Wastes Rules.

Intimations are required to be given by the exporter/ importer concerning the proposed transboundary movement of the hazardous wastes. Under the Hazardous Wastes Rules, complete information on the exporter, importer, source of generation, type of waste and its constituents, method of disposal, safety data sheet, etc., is required on Form 6 of these Rules.

According to the Basel Convention, the exporter should seek prior consent in writing from the importing country's Competent Authority (Ministry of Environment and Forests) before the commencement of the shipment. A movement document should accompany the consignment. Due to indiscriminate exports, including those from non-signatories to the Basel Convention, huge quantities of hazardous wastes may reach Indian ports.

In order to arrest this phenomena, cyanide waste (waste category No. 1), and mercury and arsenic bearing wastes (waste category No. 4) under the Hazardous Wastes Rules have been prohibited for export and import from December 26, 1996.

The Basel Convention on the Control of Transboundary Movements of Hazardous Wastes and their Disposal was signed by India in 1992. The Ministry of Environment and Forests has been designated as the Competent Authority for the Convention. The Convention seeks to promote the reduction in the generation of waste and calls for international cooperation in development of cleaner technologies. Forty-seven categories of waste are included in the Convention.

The third meeting of the Conference of the Parties to the Basel Convention held in September 1995 adopted the decision to amend Article 4(a) of the Convention to ban immediately all transboundary movement of hazardous wastes from European Community (EC) and Organisation for Economic Co-operation and Development (OECD) countries to non-OECD countries for final disposal (that is for dumping). In addition, such movements of wastes destined for recycling and recovery were to be phased out by December 31, 1997. This ban would only be applicable to those wastes that are characterized as being hazardous under the Convention. The task of hazard waste classification has been entrusted to the Technical Working Group of the Basel Convention.

Developing countries have become major recipients of hazardous wastes generated in the industrially advanced countries. Due to stringent legislation and regulations, and the prohibitive costs of treatment and disposal of such wastes in the developed countries, producers of such wastes and their agents find it cheaper to ship hazardous wastes to developing countries. The Ministry of Environment and Forests has been receiving communications seeking permission to import hazardous wastes. These include metal- containing wastes (ferrous and non-ferrous), waste oil, oil sludge, etc. These are processed in accordance with the requirements of the Hazardous Wastes (Management and Handling) Rules and the Basel Convention. A Committee has been constituted for this purpose.

There is a legal framework in India for the management of radioactive wastes and an independent regulatory body with responsibilities to carrying out statutory control with regard to health, safety, and environmental protection. India is concerned with the environmentally sound management of radioactive wastes. The need for the establishment of a nuclear waste management system in the country was recognized at an early stage of India's nuclear programme. The system takes care of all radioactive waste generated from nuclear facilities as well as nuclear materials from industry, research, and medicine. Documentation and dissemination of information regarding waste generation storage and disposal is also undertaken though there is scope for increased interaction and exchange of information, especially among the developing countries.

Toxic Chemicals

Chemicals occupy an important place in India's effort to meet the social and economic goals of the community. However, many chemicals are toxic, highly reactive, explosive or flammable, or have a combination of these characteristics, and represent a potential risk to human, animal and plant life, and the environment in general. Extreme care is necessary in handling such chemicals at all stages of manufacture, processing, transportation, and use. The risk of poisoning from exposure to dangerous chemicals is acute and casualties occur each year. The adverse effects of pesticide poisoning are well known. In 1982, it was estimated that while developing countries accounted for only 50% of the use of pesticides worldwide, over 50% of pesticide poisonings occurred in these countries. A global survey undertaken in 1984-86 indicated that while most developed countries had well-established capabilities for poison control, very few developing countries had such facilities.

To reduce the risk, the long-term objective of Government is to eliminate the use of chemicals. However, the technological information on viable alternatives is generally not available. Consequently, the immediate and complete elimination of toxic chemicals seems difficult. Purification techniques and other end-of-pipe measures are capital and energy intensive and, taken alone, have not yielded the desired success in reducing the discharges of hazardous substances. Considerable research expertise exists in India on issues related to the manufacture, use, and handling of toxic and hazardous materials. However, the difficulty lies in the inadequate exchange of information and the training of persons actually involved in such processes. It is recognized that capacity building is essential in industry especially at the factory and plant levels.

In India, the Environment (Protection) Act, 1986 lays down procedures and safeguards to regulate the handling of hazardous and toxic chemicals and preventing accidents. Four sets of rules have been notified under the Environment (Protection) Act: the Manufacture, Storage and Import of Hazardous Chemical Rules, 1989; the Hazardous Waste (Management and Handling) Rules, 1989; the Manufacture, Use, Import, Export and Storage of Hazardous Micro-organisms/Genetically Engineered Organisms or Cells Rules, 1989; and the Chemical Accident (Emergencies Planning, Preparedness and Responses) Rules, 1996. Legal provisions exist for the strict control of chemical poisons under the Insecticides Act, 1968; the Poison Act, 1990; and the Hazardous Chemicals Rules, 1989.

There is a well established procedure under the Import and Export (Control) Act, 1947, implemented by the Director General of Foreign Trade, regulating the export and import of various products. The import and export of many products are also covered under the Environment (Protection) Act. After the Bhopal disaster of 1984, the Government took steps, both regulatory and non-regulatory, to reduce the environmental risk from exposure to chemicals. The Environment (Protection) Act was the first step. The Public Liability Insurance Act, 1991 was enacted to provide relief to chemical accident victims. Steps have been taken to phase out, for example, benzidine and benzidine based dyes through this instrument. Analogous provisions exist in the Insecticide Act and the Prevention of Food Adulteration Act.

For prevention and control of major chemical hazards, legal safeguards have been framed under the Hazardous Chemicals Rules. Specific requirements have been prescribed for the safe transportation of hazardous chemicals. Exposure limits for chemicals and toxic chemicals have also been established. Recently, environmental audits have been made mandatory, one of the aims being to reduce environmental risk. Government is also encouraging the use of Cleaner Production Technologies by providing fiscal benefits. The award of the Ecomark on environment friendly consumer products also encourages the use of safer chemicals and technologies.

To limit the discharge of pollutants into water and into the air, standards have been laid down under the relevant Acts. The "Polluter Pays Principle" has also been adopted. Environmental impact assessment has been made mandatory for specified projects. Where feasible, such assessment is also recommended for less toxic chemicals, prior to the sanction of environmental clearance.

Several work programmes for the promotion of safety in the handling of hazardous substances have been planned and implemented. Risk assessment of chemicals is time and resource intensive. At the National level, the following efforts are underway: a) a centrally sponsored scheme to create infrastructure in certain regulatory organizations; b) hazard analysis and off-site emergency plans in sensitive industrial pockets; c) the establishment of emergency response centres; d) the establishment of poison control centres at select places with some available infrastructure; and e) the promotion of epidemiological studies in areas of high risk involving the collection of data from hazardous installations and relating this to the pollution status.

To complement the legislation listed above, there is a need in view of the anticipated rise in the number of cases of chemical poisoning for institutions with qualified staff that would treat poison cases, using the latest information and detection methods. The Ministry of Environment and Forests, and the Ministry of Health and Family Welfare have felt the need for setting up a National Poison Control Centre with a network of Regional Centres. A Poison Control Centre has been set up at the All India Institute of Medical Sciences (AIIMS), New Delhi to provide a full range of clinical, analytical, toxicological and information services to provide quick response against the effects of chemicals on human health.

The Ministry of Environment and Forests has set up a Central Crisis Group Alert System with a Central Control Room for the management of emergencies due to hazardous chemicals. The Ministry has also established the National Register for Potentially Toxic Chemicals (NRPTC) for the collection, collation, analysis, and dissemination of existing National and international information on the lines of the International Register of Potentially Toxic Chemicals (IRPTC). However, the Centre requires a widespread network throughout the country to facilitate coordination with other organizations. An effort in this direction has been made with the establishment of Regional Registers in three regions.

There is increasing concern over the movements of products across the boundaries of developing countries completed in contravention of internationally adopted guidelines and principles. This is especially true of developing countries which do not have the adequate infrastructure to determine the risks associated with such products or to adequately monitor their ingress and egress. India participates regularly in the meetings of the London Guidelines for the Exchange of Information on Chemicals in International Trade. Modalities for strengthening the legal basis of these guidelines are being considered. A voluntary code of ethics on international trade in chemicals has also been finalized in consultation with representatives of the chemical industry. India is a member of International Programme on Chemical Safety (IPCS) and the IRPTC.

Desertification and Draught

About 10% of the 329 million ha of land area in India is arid. This zone is located in the western region. Rajasthan accounts for 61% of the arid area, and a further 20% is located in the adjoining State of Gujarat. Cold deserts located in the High Himalayas of the North West account for the rest. Semi-arid areas account for 30.56% of the area and are located in 127 districts of 10 States. There is a well defined desert region consisting of the great desert and little desert. The great desert extends from Rann of Kutch beyond Luni river northwards. The little desert is located between Jodhpur and Jaisalmer and the two are divided by a zone of sterile rocky land cut up by limestone ridges. There is evidence that the arid area once had dense forest cover. Large scale migrations through the North Western Himalayan passes resulted in clearance of natural vegetation for settled agriculture. As arid areas are located on migration routes, the delicate balance of water and nutrient recycling was lost with the indiscriminate spread of agriculture which started around three thousand years ago. The river "Saraswati" of Indian mythology vanished altogether while other rivers merged into the sand dunes.

The semi-arid regions abutting the arid zone on the North and North East have a better water regime as a number of perennial rivers fed by Himalayan snow traverse this area. A well knit irrigation system makes the area the most productive part of the country. In the East and South, however, agriculture is mainly rain-fed particularly in the plateau region. Periodic cycles of drought due to monsoon failure is a common feature. In the National Conservation Strategy particular attention has been paid to arid and semi-arid areas. The strategy, inter alia, includes classification, zoning, and apportionment of land for designated uses; enactment of laws for appropriate land uses to protect the soil from erosion; pollution and degradation measures for runoff and wind erosion; development of suitable agro-silvipastoral techniques; measures for water conservation, recycling and optimal conjunctive use of surface and ground water; and encouragement for and improvement in traditional methods of rain water harvesting.

The Desert Development Programme (DDP) was initiated in 1977-78. It covers both the hot desert regions of Gujarat, Rajasthan, and Haryana and the cold desert areas in Jammu, Kashmir, and Himachal Pradesh. It is functional in 131 blocks of 21 districts in 5 States covering an area of about 0.362 million km2 and a population of 15 million. The objectives of the programme include controlling the process of desertification, mitigating the effects of drought, restoring the ecological balance, and raising the productivity of land, water, livestock, and human resources. At least 75% of the allocation is earmarked for activities which would contribute towards combating the process of desertification. The programme is implemented with 100% central assistance. The Programme Evaluation Organization of the Planning Commission has the task of evaluating this programme in order to assess its impact on the control of desertification, and on improvements in productivity and income for the people living in these areas. From 1990 to 1993, Rs. 1,485 million has been spent under the scheme, developing an area of 90,412 ha.

The Drought Prone Area Programme (DPAP) was launched in 1973 in arid and semi-arid areas with poor natural resource endowments. The objective is to promote more productive dryland agriculture by better soil and moisture conservation, more scientific use of water resources, afforestation, and livestock development through development of fodder and pasture resource, and in the long run to restore the ecological balance. The DPAP covers 615 blocks of 91 districts in 13 States. This is a Centrally sponsored scheme where the allocations are shared between the Centre and States on a 50:50 basis. Preparation of development plans on a watershed basis, participation of people in planning and implementation of the programme, and developing effective liaison between research agencies and implementing agencies are some of the priority areas of the programme which is being implemented under the Eighth Five Year Plan with renewed thrust. From 1990 to 1993, Rs. 3,066.9 million has been spent by the scheme, developing an area of 571,633 ha. In order to integrate and intensify the activities aimed at combating desertification, a comprehensive plan for control of desertification under the National Forestry Action Programme has been proposed. The plan would evaluate the present status of deserts in the country, assess the implementation of ongoing programmes for development of deserts and desert prone areas, formulate broad policy guidelines and action plans for implementation aimed at control of desertification, develop strategies involving people in desert control through various means, and include appropriate measures related to research and training in desert control.

The basic objective of the integrated Wastelands Development Project is to facilitate pilot projects using an integrated approach to wasteland development by initiating area-specific projects taking into account land capabilities, site condition and local needs, and ultimately aiming to promote optimal land use for both ecological and socioeconomic needs. The different types of problem lands for which projects are prepared include saline/alkaline lands, arid/sandy areas, ravine areas, and Aravallis. The activities covert soil and water conservation, afforestation, silvi-pasture development, grazing management, etc.

The main objective of the Afforestation Project for the Aravalli (Rajasthan) is to check desertification and restore ecological status by re-afforestation and also to increase the production of fuel wood, fodder, timber, and non-wood forest products to meet local needs. The project started in April 1992 and the project period is 5 years. Rehabilitation of common lands in Aravallis (Haryana) is being implemented in the four southern districts of Haryana, that is Bhiwani, Mahendragarh, Gurgaon, and Faridabad since 1990. The project outlay is Rs. 480 million and covers environmental protection, restoration of green cover in the semi-arid Aravalli Hills, and improvement in the living conditions of the local people through meeting their biomass needs.

Research activities pertaining to various aspects of arid zones are being conducted at the Central Arid Zone Research Institute (CAZRI). The majority of these activities are oriented towards agriculture and soil conservation. CAZRI, located in Jodhpur, was established in 1988 under the auspices of Indian Council of Forestry Research and Education (ICFRE) with the prime objective to complete research into sand-dune stabilization, afforestation of the arid saline land of Rann of Kutch, Aravalli Hills, and the Indira Gandhi Nahar Project (IGNP) command area, appropriate land use systems, silviculture of important shrubs and trees with emphasis on selection and tree improvement, vegetative propagation, etc.

Important studies that have been conducted include the identification of species most suitable for restricting the movement of sand-dunes and checking the advance of the desert, the influence of moisture conservation practices in the establishment of plantations in arid and semi-arid areas, investigation of the influence of farm yard manure and nitrogen and potassium fertilizers on the establishment and growth of Prosopis cineraria and Tecomella undulata, irrigation management in forestry plantations in the IGNP command area of the Indian Desert, and the Combined Production System (Agri-silvi-pastoral) in arid regions.

India has built up some degree of expertise in matters relevant to desertification. These include long range weather forecasting, remote sensing, research in arid zone agriculture, forestry and pastures, and dry land farming. The International Convention to Combat Desertification in Countries Experiencing Drought and/or Desertification Particularly in Africa was signed by India on December 26, 1996. India has been participating regularly in the Inter-governmental Negotiating Committee to Combat Desertification (INCD) process. In collaboration with the Interim Secretariat of the United Nations Convention to Combat Desertification, the Government of India hosted a Regional Conference on the Implementation of the UN Convention to Combat Desertification and Drought in Asia from August 21-23, 1996 at New Delhi. At the meeting, the countries resolved to initiate consultations among themselves to identify specific programmes for regional cooperation.

Strategies for Pollution Control

In India, the National Committee of Environmental Planning and Co-ordination (NCEPC) was set up in 1972 under the Department of Science and Technology. A separate Empowered Committee was set up in 1980 for reviewing the existing legislative measures and administrative machinery for ensuring environmental protection and for recommending ways to strengthen them. On the recommendations of this Empowered Committee, a separate Department of Environment was set up in 1980 which was subsequently upgraded to a full-fledged Ministry of Environment and Forests in 1985 to serve as the focal point in the administrative structure of the Government of India for the planning, promotion and co-ordination of environ-mental and forestry programmes. Other Government partners in carrying out environmental protection activities include:

— The State departments of environment;

— Central and State Pollution Control Boards;

— the Botanical and Zoological Survey of India;

— the Forest Survey of India;

— the National River Conservation Authority;

— the National Afforestation and Eco-development Board;

— the Indian Council for Forestry Research and Education; and

— the Wildlife Institute of India and the National Museum for Natural History.

The Government of India has entrusted the work relating to Ozone layer Protection and phase out of the Ozone depleting substances programme under the Montreal Protocol to the Ministry of Environment and Forests. There are several inter ministerial committees and working groups to coordinate issues relating to policy and legislation. In case of implementation of the Montreal Protocol the Empowered Steering Committee consists of members from the Ministry of Science and Technology and other line Ministries. The Ministry of Environment and Forests has set up an Ozone Cell as a national unit to implement the Protocol and the Ozone Depleting Substances phase out programme in India. The decisions related to Ozone Depleting Substances phase-out and protection of Ozone Layer are being taken at the Central Government level. The Government of India frequently consults NGO's research organizations and regional expertise as and when needed. India's approach towards implementation of the UNFCC and associated environmental parameters is covered within policy declarations:

— the National Conservation Strategy and policy statement on Environment and development and the policy statement on abatement of pollution for regulating various environmental parameters;

— In addition various other enactments such as Air pollution (prevention and control) Act 1981 amended in 1987 and Motor Vehicles Act 1939, amended in 1988;

— the Forest Conservation Act amended in 1988 contribute significantly towards minimizing the causes of climate change.

— The Environmental Protection Act 1986 is an umbrella legislation and it also empowers the government to formulate statutory rules for fulfilling various requirements.

— Further EIA has been made statutory for various developmental activities and the Coastal Resource Zones notification provides guidelines for protection and management of coastal zones.

India has taken a series of fiscal and regulatory measures to facilitate Ozone Deleting Substances (ODS) phase out in the country. Trade in ODS with non-Parties to the Montreal Protocol has been banned. Harmonized classifications of commodity codes consistent with the international system have been introduced. Controlled substances under the Protocol have been brought under the ambit of licenses for the purpose of export and import. The Ozone Depleting Substances (Regulation and

Control) Rules, 2000 under the Environment Protection Act 1986 have been notified to Control and phase out production and consumption of Ozone Depleting Substances in order to comply with the Montreal Protocol. The Government decided in 1995 to fully exempt payment of Customs and Excise Duties on capital goods required to implement ODS phase out projects funded by the multi lateral funding(MLF). This benefit was later extended for all MLF eligible projects whether or not MLF assistance was requested/available at the time of implementation of ODS phase out project. The Reserve Bank of India advised all commercial banks in September 1997 not to finance/refinance new investments with ODS technologies.

In 1992, India adopted the policy statement on Abatement of Pollution, which provides instruments in the form of legislation and regulation, fiscal incentives, voluntary agreements, educational programmes and information campaigns to prevent and control pollution of water, air and land. Since the adoption of the policy statement, the focus of activities has been on issues such as promotion of clean and low waste technologies, waste water minimization, reuse/recycling, improvement of water quality, environment audit, natural resource accounting, development of mass-based standards as well as institutional and human resource development.

The issue of pollution prevention and control entails a combination of command and control methods; voluntary regulatory and fiscal measures; promotion of awareness and involvement of public. To facilitate industries in preparing environmental statements, sector-specific environmental audit manuals have been prepared. A software package, *Paryavaran,* along with a user manual has been prepared for analysis of information submitted in these environmental statements and distributed to all the State Pollution Control Boards (SPCB).

Training programmes are also being organized for officials of Central Pollution Control Boards (CPCB) and SPCB to enable them to use the software. An "Eco-mark" label has been introduced to label consumer products that are environment-friendly. Nineteen products have been identified for labeling and 18 notifications have been issued so far on different products criteria. The Bureau of India Standards (BIS)/Directorate of Marketing and Inspection (DMI) is the implementing agency for this scheme. So far one license has been granted by the BIS to a product under the soaps category.

Under the scheme for adoption of clean technology in small-scale industries and for extending necessary technical support, training and awareness programmes for personnel in Small Industry Development Organization and for entrepreneurs are being organized. 'From Waste to Profits', a manual giving guidelines for waste minimization, has been prepared. Sector-specific manuals on waste minimization in the areas of pulp and paper, pesticides formulations and textiles, dyeing and printing and electroplating, have also been prepared. Waste Minimization Circles (WMCs) are being established to promote group efforts in increasing productivity and improving the environmental conditions in small and medium-scale industries through adoption of waste minimization techniques. Fifteen Waste Minimisation Circles have been established so far in different industrial clusters across the country. An Indian Centre for the Promotion of Cleaner Technologies (ICPC) with a network of institutions including industries, academic institutions and other user agencies is being set up for which the World Bank has provided $2 million as grant-in-aid. The Centre will provide evaluated and ranked technology options to entrepreneurs.

Indian Forestry policy

India adopted its forest policy in 1894. It was revised in 1952 and again in 1988. The main plank of the Forestry Policy of 1988 is protection, conservation and development of forest. Its aims are:

i) maintenance of environmental stability through preservation and restoration of ecological balance;

ii) conservation of natural heritage;

iii) check soil erosion and denudation in catchments area of rivers, lakes and reservoirs;

iv) check extension of sand dunes in desert areas of Rajasthan and along coastal tracts;

v) substantial increase in forest tree cover through afforestation and social forestry programmes;

vi) steps to meet requirements of fuel wood, fodder, minor forest produce and soil timber of rural and tribal populations;

vii) increase in productivity of forest to meet the national needs;

viii) encouragement of efficient utilization of forest produce and optimum substitution of wood and

ix) steps to create massive people's movement with involvement of women to achieve the objectives and minimize pressure on existing forests.

The entire gamut of forest activities are being given a new orientation in the light of the National Forest Policy of 1988. In order to operationalise the National Forest Policy 1988, a National Forestry Action Programme (NFAP) is being prepared. As a part of this exercise State Forestry Action Programmes are also being prepared for each State. Under the provisions of the Forest (Conservation) Act, 1980, prior approval of the Central government is required for diversion of forest lands for non-forest purposes. Since the enactment of the Act, the rate of diversion of forest land has come down to around 25,000 hectares per annum from 0.143 million hectares per annum, before1980. During 1998, 851 proposals from various State and UT governments were processed under this Act. A scheme titled 'Association of Scheduled Tribes and Rural Poor in Regeneration of Degraded Forests on Usufruct Sharing Basis' is under implementation in nine States of the country. Besides improving the forest cover, the scheme also aims at providing wage employment and usufructs to the tribal people. Joint Forest Management (JFM) is being practiced in 21 States of the country. About 7 million hectares of degraded forests in the country are being managed and protected through approximately 35,000 village Forest Protection Committees.

Central Pollution Control Board

The Central Pollution Control Board (CPCB) is the national apex body for assessment, monitoring and control of water and air pollution. The executive responsibilities for enforcement of the Acts for Prevention and Control of Pollution of Water (1974) and Air (1981) and also of the Water (Cess) Act, 1977 are carried out through the Board. The CPCB advises the Central Government in all matters concerning the prevention and control of air, water and noise pollution and provides technical services to the Ministry of Environment and forests for implementing the provisions of the Environment (Protection) Act, 1986. Under this Act, effluent and emission standards in respect of 61 categories of industries have been notified. Seventeen categories of heavily polluting industries have been identified. They are: cement, thermal power plant, distilleries, sugar, fertilizer, integrated iron and steel, oil refineries, pulp and paper, petrochemicals, pesticides, tanneries, basic drugs and pharmaceuticals, dye and dye intermediates, caustic soda, zinc smelter, copper smelter and aluminum smelter. Out of a total of 1,551 units identified under these 17 categories, 1,266 units have installed adequate facilities for pollution control and 130 units have been closed down.

The Central Pollution Control Board, in consultation with State Pollution Control Boards, has identified critically polluted areas in the country which need special attention for control of pollution. These are: Vapi (Gujarat), Singrauli (Uttar Pradesh), Korba, Ratlam, Nagda (Madhya Pradesh), Digboi (Assam), Talcher (Orissa), Bhadravati (Karnataka), Howrah (West Bengal), Dhanbad (Bihar), Pali and Jodhpur (Rajasthan), Manali and North Arcot (Tamil Nadu), Visakhapatnam and Patancheru, (AndhraPradesh), Chembur (Maharashtra), Najafgarh (Delhi), Govindgarh (Punjab), Udyog Mandal (Kerala) and Parwanoo and Kala Amb (Himachal Pradesh).

The CPCB in collaboration with the SPCBs monitors the quality of fresh water resources of the country through a network of 480 monitoring stations located all over the country. Based on such monitoring, 13 heavily polluted and 26 medium-polluted river stretches have been identified. Under the National Ambient Air Quality Monitoring programme, 290 stations covering over 90 towns/cities monitor the ambient air quality of the country.

The Central and State Pollution Control Boards regularly conduct surveys in different cities of the country pertaining to vehicular and noise pollution, sanitation status, status of solid waste, etc. A survey on the status of solid waste conducted in 299 Class I cities of the country indicates that 62 per cent of the total solid waste generated in the country comes from the 23 metro cities of the country. The average per capita generation of solid waste for Class I cities is about 376 gms per person per day. A total of 1,532 grossly polluting industries in 24 States/Union Territories have been identified under the National River Action Plan. Comprehensive River Basin Documents for the rivers Ulhas, Brahmaputra, Pennar, Indus Part II, Rishkulya and Chaliyar are being prepared by the Board.

The Central Pollution Control Board has a NGO Cell for interacting with NGOs. Simple water-testing kits are distributed free of cost to selected NGOs and financial assistance provided to them for conducting mass awareness programmes relating to prevention and control of pollution. The White Paper on status of pollution in Delhi with an Action Plan for its control prepared earlier is being implemented. The Action Plan contains specific measures for control of pollution relating to vehicular pollution, water pollution, industrial air pollution, solid waste, hospital wastes, industrial hazardous wastes, noise pollution and people's participation in making Delhi a cleaner city. Directions have been issued by the National Capital Territory of Delhi for imposing restrictions on all commercial vehicles in Delhi in a time-bound programme beginning from April 1998. Based on the recommendations of a National Level Committee on Noise Pollution, directions have been issued to the State governments to check noise pollution from bursting of crackers. There is also a plan to introduce higher parking fees, to augment parking spaces in the city of Delhi and to introduce no traffic zones.

A detailed India Country Programme for phase out of Ozone Depicting Substances (ODS) was prepared in 1993 to ensure the phase out of ODS according to the national industrial development strategy, without undue burden to the consumers and the industry and for accessing the Protocol's financial mechanism in accordance with the requirements stipulated in the Montreal Protocol. At present, an exercise is underway in consultation with CII to update the country programme. The main objectives of the Country Programme has been to minimize economic dislocation as a result of conversion to non-ODS technology, maximize indigenous production, give preference to one-time replacement, emphasize decentralized management and minimize obsolescence.

Environmental Impact Assessment

Impact assessment is a pointer to the environmental compatibility of the projects in terms of their location, suitability of technology, efficiency in resource utilization, recycling and so on. Impact assessment was introduced in India in 1978 and now covers projects such as:

a) river valley, thermal power, mining, industries, atomic power, rail, road, highways, bridges, ports and harbors, airports, new towns, communication projects, etc.

b) those which require the approval of the Public Investment Board/Planning Commission/Central Electricity Authority;

c) those referred to the Ministry of Environment and Forests by other ministries;

d) those which are sensitive and located in environmentally degraded areas; and

e) public sector undertakings of the Centre where the project cost is more than Rs 500 million.

A notification issued in January 1994 makes Environ-mental Impact Assessment statutory for 29 categories of developmental projects under various sectors such as industrial, mining, irrigation, power, transport, tourism, communication, etc. The Environmental Impact Assessment (EIA) Notification was amended in 1997 to provide for public hearing as well as for empowering State governments for according environmental clearance in respect of certain Thermal Power Projects. As per the provisions of the EIA Notification 1994, mining projects are subject to environmental clearance. However, it has been now decided to exempt prospecting through aerial survey and/ or test drilling in smaller areas from mandatory clearances.

Applications complete in every material aspect are normally examined and decision conveyed to the applicants within 30 days in cases of site clearance and 120 days in cases of environmental clearance of projects. Once an application has been submitted by the project authority, the preliminary scrutiny of the project is done by the respective technical divisions and the overall appraisal of the projects is undertaken by specially constituted environmental appraisal committees of experts. In addition, special groups/committees and task forces are constituted as and when needed for expert inputs on major projects. After detailed scrutiny and assessment, the appraisal committee makes its recommendations for approval or rejection of the project. Depending on the nature of the project, certain safeguards are recommended. For monitoring and timely implementation of safeguards suggested, six regional offices of the Ministry have been set up at Shillong, Bhubaneswar, Chandigarh, Bangalore, Lucknow and Bhopal.

Ozone Cell

To meet the country's commitment on ODS phase-out under the protocol and to disseminate information on ozone and ODS, the Ministry of Environment and Forests has established an Ozone Cell. A newsletter on ozone issues is being published by the Cell every two months and a number of workshops and seminars are also conducted to create awareness about ozone among industries. UNEP-IE Ozone Action Programme, Paris held its first south-Asia ODS officers Network Meeting in Delhi. The Government provides custom/excise duty exemption for ODS phase-out projects and detailed guidelines/procedures have been finalized to grant duty exemption for new investments with non-ODS technologies. A policy to issue licenses for import of ODS has been implemented and the Reserve Bank of India, on the recommendation of the Ministry, has issued instructions to all commercial banks prohibiting finance or refinance of new investments with ODS technologies. One hundred seventy seven projects worth about US $ 49 million have been approved for India by the Multilateral Fund under the convention. Trade in ODS with non-

Parties has been banned. Imports and exports of ODS have been licensed. Exports of Chloro Fluro Carbons (CFCs) to developed countries has been stopped. Rules on Ozone Depleting Substances (ODS) phase-out were published on 9 May 1998 in the Gazette of India. The Policy to issue licenses for imports of ODS has been implemented. The country thus has a strategy to phase out ODS by 2010 with minimum economic dislocation, and give preference to one-time replacement.

Fiscal measures have been taken by extending full exemption of duties (Customs and Excise) on goods required substitution of ODS and for establishment of new capacity with non-ODS technology. The Ozone Depleting Substances (Regulation and Control) Rules, 2000 have been notified. 225 ODS phase out projects have been approved by the Multilateral Fund to phase out 8600 ODP tones in India. Funding has also been approved for gradual phase out of production of CFCs.

The National Conservation Strategy and Policy Statement on Environment and Development, adopted by the Government of India in June 1992, lays down strategies and actions for integration of environmental considerations in the development activities of various sectors of the country, thus paving the way for achieving sustainable development. The action points pertaining to individual ministries/departments ensure that they take action for reorienting their policies and programmes in conformity with the strategy.

Environmental Education

Priority is accorded by the Ministry of Environment and Forests to promote environmental education, create environmental awareness among various age-groups and to disseminate information through Environmental Information System (ENVIS) network to all concerned. A major initiative to include environment education as a separate and compulsory subject in the educational curricula has been taken by the Ministry at all levels of formal education, i.e., secondary, senior secondary and tertiary levels. A discussion paper prepared on strengthening environment education was presented by the Minister for Environment and Forests at the State Education Ministers' Conference held from 22 to 24 October 1998. The paper was adopted by the Conference. The Chief Ministers were urged to introduce environment education in the school curricula from the 1999-2000 academic session. Maharashtra is the first State to introduce the subject in the school curriculum.

Paryavaran Vahinis (environment launch-vehicle) are proposed to be constituted in 194 selected districts all over the country which have a high incidence of pollution and density of tribal and forest population. The Vahinis also play a watch-dog role by reporting instances of environmental pollution, deforestation and poaching. They function under the charge of District Collectors, with the active cooperation of the State/Union Territory governments. This scheme is entirely financed by the Ministry of Environment and Forests. Seven Centres of Excellence have been set up by the Ministry to strengthen awareness, research and training in priority areas of Environmental Science and Management. These are: Centre for Ecological Sciences, Bangalore; Centre for Mining Environment, Dhanbad; Centre for Environmental Education, Ahmedabad; CPR Environmental Education Centre, Chennai; Salim Ali Centre for Ornithology and Natural History, Coimbatore; the Centre for Environmental Management of Degraded Ecosystems,

Delhi, and the Tropical Botanical Garden and Research Institute, Thiruvananthapuram, Kerala.

The National Museum of Natural History (NMNH) set up in New Delhi in 1978,is concerned with the promotion of non-formal education in the area of environment and conservation. Besides permanent exhibit galleries on various aspects of environment, the museum also conducts temporary exhibitions and a large number of educational programmes and activities for school children, college youth and the general public. Three Regional Museums of Natural History have been established at Mysore, Bhopal and Bhubaneswar.

The Indian Council for Forestry Research and Education is the focal point for forestry education and extension development in the country. The Indira Gandhi National Forest Academy, Dehra Dun, imparts in-service professional training to Indian Forest Service (IFS) professionals. State forest service colleges provide training to the officers of the State Forest Service (SFS). The Indian Plywood Industries Research and Training Institute, Bangalore, organizes short-term courses in the area of wood science.

The Indian Institute of Forest Management, Bhopal, also provides training in forest management and allied subjects to persons from the Indian Forest Service, forest development corporations, and forest-related industries to develop forestry programmes. The Wildlife Institute of India, Dehradun, provides in-service training to forest officers, wildlife ecologists and other professionals for conservation and management of the wildlife resources of the country.

Information dissemination package for school teachers and NGOs prepared by Centre for Environment

Education was launched on 16th September, 1998 and distributed in four workshops organized in Calcutta, Delhi, Pune and Chennai in November-December, 1998. This kit has been developed in consultation with the UNEP-DTIE office in Paris. Painting Competitions are being organized by the Ozone Cell. An Indian entry won the prize in the international competition organized by UNEP in 1999. A National Painting Competition has been organized on the occasion of Sixty International Ozone Day, 16th September, 2000. Ozone-friendly equipment and products are being exhibited during 16-18th September every year. A similar exhibition is being held on the occasion of the International Ozone Day, 2000. An information kit on Ozone Science and Ozone layer has been prepared by Centre for Environment Education, Ahmedabad. Chapters on pollution and environmental issues are part of the curriculum. Several training programmes are being organized on a regular basis. India is a member of WMO and is participating in various international research programmes on systematic observation atmosphere and ocean through IMD/ DST New Delhi.

The Indian Meteorological Department (IMD) is the principal government agency in all matters relating to meteorology, seismology and allied subjects. The Department has units all over the country engaged in collecting meteorological and seismological data besides providing various meteorological services. Its main objective is to provide meteorological information for weather sensitive activities like aviation, shipping, agriculture, irrigation, off-shore oil exploration and industries. The Department also issues warnings against severe weather phenomena like cyclones, dust-storms, heavy rains, cold and heat waves that cause destruction of life and property. Besides, it also provides climatological information, records earthquakes and promotes research in meteorology. The Department maintains an extensive network of modern observatories and communication links all over the country. Observations received through high power radars and weather satellites are extensively used these days for analysis and prediction of weather.

INSAT Meteorological Data Processing System is being upgraded to handle reception, processing of data from INSAT 2E Satellite. This satellite is similar to INSAT 2B but has got additional capability of providing imagery in water-vapor band and higher resolution imagery in visible, near IR and short wave IR bands, using charge coupled devices. Current satellites provide imagery in Visible and IR bands. A satellite based wide area network (WAN) using Very Small Aperture Terminals (VSATs) is being established for speedy dissemination of forecast products to various user agencies, particularly to AAS units. The plan is being implemented by installing VSATs in 127 locations out of which 47 have been installed. Scientific campaigns such as GAME-India (Global Energy Water Cycle Asian Monsoon Experiment), I-STEP (Indian Solar Terrestrial Energy Programme), OCEANSAT (IRS P4), Indo-US Agreement on Satellite Data Utilization, and INDOEX are being carried out.

The Ozone measurement is being carried out at 5 stations by Indian Meteorological Department. These stations are at Srinagar, New Delhi, Varanasi, Pune and Kodaikenal. The total Ozone data and Umkehr data (vertical profile of Ozone) are being regularly sent in WMO format to the World Ozone Data Centre, Canada and are being regularly published by the Centre. India developed ozonesonde in 1963. Since 1970, vertical Ozone distributions are being measured at 5 stations at New Delhi, Pune, Thiruvananthapuram, Dakshni Gangtri and Maitri.

Scientific data and information on the protection of atmosphere and ozone Layer are made available to potential users at national level via internet and other modes of information dissemination. Information on Ozone Science and non-ODS technology has been provided by UNEP DTIE Ozone Action Programme through its clearing housing mechanism and they send information directly to users. There are several programmes for awareness and information dissemination and websites exist for access to information.

The Indian Government is making several efforts for developing new environmental friendly technologies for example, Dobson and Brewer Spectrophotometers are used to monitor total ozone measurement. It is disappointed by the non implementation of commitments made by the developed countries on providing new and additional financial resources as well as technology for promoting ecologically sustainable development. In order to implement measures to protect the atmosphere, India need the following new technologies:

— IGCC and other advanced clean coal technologies;

— state of art power generation technologies;

— Solar photovoltaic (advanced systems);

— Mass rapid transport system for urban transport; New non-ODS technology for refrigeration, aerosol, foam fire extinguisher and solvent sector; and

— Technology for manufacturing ODS substitutes.

Producers of CFCs, and the Government of India jointly supported research programmes to develop technology to produce HFC 134a at the Indian Institute of Chemical Technology, Hyderabad. The pilot plant has been set up. Commercial production of HFC-134a is envisaged. Both Government and voluntary organizations are involved in climate change research in India with the former supporting a wide variety of projects in the area of global change research. The India Meteorological Department (IMD) monitors climate to detect change, predict climate change, determine the effects of climate change, and contribute to global observational efforts. Since 1983, IMD has maintained a meteorological observatory at the Indian permanent station in Antarctica. The Department has actively participated in various international and National observational efforts. A National Climate Centre (NCC) has been established at IMD's research wing in Pune to undertakes climate research, applications, data collection and management, and impact awareness studies. Data collected from the extensive network of observations are archived at the Department's National Data Centre in Pune. The Centre holds over 60 million records in its archives. About 2.5 million records are currently being added to the archives.

Through the Department of Science and Technology (DST) the Government has undertaken several projects to promote technologies that will reduce pollution of the atmosphere. Technologies that use compressed natural gas (CNG) as fuel in internal combustion engines have been developed for generating electricity in remote hilly areas. To help promote waste reduction, the production of fuel pellets from waste has been successfully demonstrated to industrial users in Mumbai. DST supports R&D efforts to promote environmental conservation conducted by several autonomous institutions and service organizations. Considerable research work has been completed on climate modeling, air pollution, and atmospheric ozone at the Institute of Tropical Meteorology, Pune, which has climate change as one of its major thrust areas.

Activities concerning protection of Atmosphere cut across several government departments and the main source is public funding. Despite lack of external funding India has made big strides in protecting the atmosphere. Climate change/ protection of atmosphere considerations have been in built into the five year plan process in the country and an adequate thrust has been accorded to it by GOI Ozone regulations and Market forces are driving the industries to invest money in non-ODS technologies.

The Ministry of Environment and Forests functions as a nodal agency for United Nations Environment Programme (UNEP), South Asia Co-operation Environment Programme (SACEP), and International Centre for Integrated Mountain and Development (ICIMOD), International Union for Conservation of Nature and Natural Resources (IUCN) and various international agencies, regional bodies and multilateral institutions. India is signatory to the following important international treaties/ agreements in the field of environment:

i) International Convention for the regulation of Whaling;

ii) International Plant Protection Convention;

iii) The Antarctic Treaty;

iv) Convention on Wetlands of international importance;

v) Convention on International trade in Endangered Species of Wild Flora and Fauna;

vi) Protocol of 1978 relating to the international convention for the prevention of pollution from ships;

vii) Vienna Convention for the protection of the Ozone Layer;

viii) Convention on Migratory Species;

ix) Basel Convention on Trans-boundary movement of hazardous substances;

x) Framework Convention on Climate Change;

xi) Convention on conservation of bio-diversity;

xii) Montreal Protocol on the substances that deplete the ozone layer; and

xiii) International Convention for Combating Desertification.

The Ministry and its agencies cooperate with various countries such as Sweden, Netherlands, Norway, Denmark, Australia, U.K., U.S.A., Canada, Japan, FRG, etc., on bilateral basis and with several UN and other multilateral agencies such as UNDP, World Bank, Asian Development Bank, OECF (Japan) and ODA (U.K.) for various environmental and forestry projects.

India is a party to GEF and has following UNDP/ GEF projects

i) GHG stabilization in India

ii) Enabling activities for preparation of an initial national communication

The Article 3 of the Vienna Convention for protection of the Ozone Layer provide for conducting research and scientific assessment. India is a party to UNFCCC. It was among the first fifty countries to bring it into force w.e.f March 21,1994. India ratified the Montreal Protocol along with its London Amendment in 1992. India is yet to ratify the Kyoto Protocol. The Montreal Protocol under its article 10 has the provision to provide financial assistance to the developing countries. A multilateral Fund has been set up in 1992. Developed countries replenish the Fund by their annual contribution. This may continue till 2010.

The Government of India is disappointed at the non implementation of two important / seminal commitments by the developed countries at UNCED 1992 relating to New and additional financial resources Transfer of EST's. It is a matter of regret there is no progress on transfer of EST's to developing countries. Technology for development of ODS substitute chemical is need to be transferred in fair and favorable terms. The policies adopted by the Executive Committee of the Montreal Protocol do not address the special needs of small and medium enterprises. It is, therefore, special funding wind with differentiated cost effectiveness for all sectors in SMEs is need to be established.

Pakistan

Pakistan is an agricultural country, and more than 50% of its population is employed in the agricultural sector. Less than 20% of Pakistan's land can be intensively farmed, nearly all of which is cultivated. In 1990, 209,400 km2 were in use as farmland. In general, farmers lack knowledge of operating characteristics and full capabilities of technologies within the agricultural sector. The decision for intensification of farm lands in Pakistan stems from demographic reality. In rough terms, one hectare of cultivated land supported an average 5 people in 1993; by the year 2010, it is estimated that the same land must support nearly 10. Pakistan has developed strategies to ensure food security by 1998, which also includes the agricultural sector.

Local communities and NGOs are taken into consideration to review international trade relations and agricultural production. Women, youth, indigenous people, and local communities are also involved through workshops in developing and strengthening institutional capacity for plant genetic resources. In 1981-82, a programme called "Matching Grants Programme" (MGP) focuses on the development of infrastructure in rural areas, and is based on community participation. To date, about 22,000 schemes have been implemented in 26.500 villages.

Pakistan is faced with some common problems in both irrigated and rainfed areas used for agriculture. These problems can be summarized as erosion of soil, underuse of organic fertilizers and overuse of synthetic chemicals. A National Rural Support Programme was established to promote education and health, based on community participation.

In 1993, this programme was supported by the Government with Rs.1,000,000. MGP is structured so that the local councillor is normally the leader of the Project Committee which approves the projects. The councillor is responsible for collecting community finance.

The Pakistan Environment Protection Council (PEPC) has jurisdiction in this area, and it has established National Environmental Quality Standards (NEQS). Protection of the atmosphere is one of the fourteen core issues in the National Conservation Strategy of Pakistan.

PEPC has established a Committee on Clean Fuels, which has the mandate to make recommendations for the alleviation of atmospheric pollution. An incentive reduction scheme has been recommended in relation to the emissions from Compressed Natural Gas and Liquid Petroleum Gas powered buses, trucks, and urban public services, and a mandatory introduction of catalytic converters in two-stroke engines by July 1997 has been suggested.

The Energy Conservation Centre (ENERCON) has put together some programmes to reduce the output of greenhouse gases. These programmes involve:

— setting up tuning demonstration centres in nine cities;

— training 1,000 mechanics and workshop owners;

— providing funding for 100 tuning centres;

— conducting surveys that will lead to new policies and projects.

The diesel and furnace oil being marketed in Pakistan have a high sulphur (SO2) content. Pakistan is also facing numerous problems from the lack of efficient fuel burning, abnormal exhaust emissions from automobiles, inadequate tuning of engines, and improper repairs and maintenance. These problems mainly affect the larger cities where breathing difficulties can occur during peak-hours.

Air quality clashing with the WHO standards is costing Pakistan about Rs. 25 billion a year from adverse health and other effects. The number of vehicles in the country increased from 0.85 million in 1982 to 2.8 million in 1995, showing an overall increase of 229%. It is envisaged that, with the present rate of growth, the number of vehicles will increase to 4.5 million by the year 2000, thereby adding to quantum green house gases. Pakistan has developed a system of inventory of all green gases not controlled by the Montreal Protocol, which is periodically updated.

The United Nations Framework Convention on Climate Change was ratified on 1 June 1994 and entered into force on 30 August, 1994. The United Nations has extended major support to this project through UNDP. Support for phasing out Ozone Depletion Substances is provided through cooperation with UNDP, the World Bank and UNIDO.

The Ministry of Environment, Local Government and Rural Development is responsible for the implementation of this sector. The Ministry is involved in national decision-making. Pakistan has initiated preparation of a Biodiversity Action Plan (BAP) which should be completed in its first phase by the time that CSD V is convened. Pakistan has 15 National Parks, 86 Wildlife Sanctuaries and an equal number of Game Reserves. Management Plans have been prepared for 3 National Parks.

The implementation of the management plans of these National Parks and preparation of the management plans for the remaining National Parks is required immediately. Similarly, many species are endangered and plans for their recovery are to be made immediately. The Provincial Wildlife Departments need to have permanent resource persons to make inventories in the protected areas, since the inventories that are made for PAs are not sufficient for policy formulation.

The protected areas need well-equipped staff for checking the poaching of wildlife. Pakistan has many wetlands of international importance, but so far, few could be identified for listing in the Wetlands Conventions. This Convention also does not have an effective funding mechanism. The Monitoring procedure of the Wetlands Convention could not assist Pakistan in developing its Wetlands and Coastal Areas, and there is a great need for such a mechanism to be strengthened. Pakistan has many sites which could qualify for designation as sites for the World Heritage Convention. The search for an outstanding site which may qualify needs special attention.

Forest Officers are posted in the National Parks as Park Managers, but they can be transferred wherever needed to other forest areas without the consideration of the needs of the specific National Park or Protected Area. The reason for this is because of financial constraints, as the Provincial Forests Departments cannot afford to place separate Wildlife Managers. There is a great need for capacity-building in all of the relevant institutions in Pakistan in all of the components of biodiversity. For example, the conservation of species and protected areas management requires the capacity of the provincial wildlife departments.

Pakistan has been successful in implementing the above-mentioned Conventions and this has resulted in a new lease on life for wild animals and the conservation of protected areas, including wetlands, and coastal areas. There is a great need to develop a mechanism for the implementation of all the Conventions.

CITES, for example, can only be made effective if the Management and Scientific Authorities in the developing countries under CITES are made strong by increasing their capacity both in terms of finance, technology and staffing. Their research capabilities need to be extended.

Rescue centres, which are required to be designated by the Parties, do not have the capacity to host confiscated species, and therefore specific funding for this is required, particularly for Authorities and Custom Officers. Training of Customs Officers as well as Enforcement Officers is needed and which also requires funding in developing countries. Through the funding of US$ 313,000 being provided through the Global Environment Fund, Pakistan initiated the preparation of a Biodiversity Action Plan (BAP), to be completed by the first quarter of 1997.

However, this is a continuous activity and the BAP is likely to require further funding for its second phase. An investment proposal is also being prepared for the management and development of three selected Protected Areas of Pakistan through possible funding by the GEF. A project entitled "Maintaining Biodiversity in Pakistan with Rural Community Development" is being funded by the GEF through UNDP at a cost of US$2.5 million. Upon the successful completion of the project, it is likely that Pakistan may receive another 3.5 million US$ from GEF through UNDP. Only the Convention on Biological Diversity has a funding mechanism, while other Conventions do not. The governments, especially developing country parties, have to bear the costs of implementation of the obligations of the Conventions.

Therefore, there is a great need for all of the Conventions to be technically and financially supported through the GEF mechanism and extended to all developing country parties. CSD should ensure that the funding of the developing country Parties is made obligatory, without which the world's heritage is not likely to be conserved on a sustainable basis. Pakistan is a Party to the Convention on Biological Diversity and has taken up many measures before becoming a Party to this Convention.

Pakistan is also a party to a number of nature conservation Conventions which include :

— The Convention on International Trade in Endangered Species of Wild Fauna and Flora (CITES)

— The Convention on Conservation of Migratory Species (CMS) - Bonn Convention

— The Convention on Wetlands of international Importance Especially as Waterfowl Habitat

— World Heritage Convention

— The Convention on Biological Diversity (CBD)

— The Framework Convention on Climate Change

— The Convention to Combat Desertification in Countries Experiencing Drought and/or Desertification, Particularly in Africa (CCD).

Current land use knowledge in Pakistan is based on Satellite Imagery Interpretation. Land degradation and human impact assessment have not yet been covered, although some surveys were done dating back to 1988. The International Convention to Combat Desertification in Countries Experiencing Drought and/or Desertification, Particularly in Africa was signed 15 October 1994 and ratified 24 February 1997. The United Nations Environment Programme is providing financial assistance of US$60,000 for the preparation of the National Plan for Combatting Desertification, a plan which will soon become operational.

Pakistan has the objective of doubling its forest area, from the existing 5% to 10% of total land area. In order to meet this target, the Government has initiated various projects in an umbrella campaign of a Massive Afforestation Programme (MAP). This programme has five main components:

i) Mobilization of resources;

ii) Nursery development;

iii) Procurement of large forest lands;

iv) Ensuring adequate technical capacity; and

v) Monitoring plantations.

In Pakistan, forests are divided on the basis of whether they are state-owned or private-owned forests. The state-owned forests are again divided into four categories: reserved, protected, unclassified and resumed lands. Two-thirds of the public forest are non-commercial. The remaining one-third, located mostly on steep and unstable slopes of the Himalayas, is harvested. Production of timber from commercial forests is about 0.5 million m3.

The Rawal Lake has been selected for special attention concerning unsustainable activities, such as building latrines at specific locations and construction of septic tanks in the existing settlements. In addition, three projects have been recommended, concerning improvement of catchment areas and the provision of septic tanks and watershed management. A pilot project in Karachi has been cleared for implementation. The concept of the project is to recycle waste water by sewage collection and by conveying the waste water to irrigate areas via underground pipes.

Surface water from rivers is the primary source of water in Pakistan. Infiltration from rivers, canals, watercourses, and fields is the main source of groundwater, which is a secondary resource. The limitation on some of the water available cannot be facilitated through storage dams.

Pakistan is struggling with the fact that only 30% of the diverted water at canal heads reaches crop roots. In general, Pakistan needs much integrated water and soil improvement. The Kabul and Ravi Rivers provide food, directly through fishing and indirectly through irrigation, as well as water for both drinking and industry.

In general, Pakistan needs to address a vast array of problems regarding water usage since, for example forty percent of urban deaths are caused by water-borne diseases. Special focus is also needed in terms of sodicity, water mining and the accumulation of salt in commercial crop roots. Pakistan also has an on-going research-project which aims at assessing the water requirements of different species. The idea is to use the information for various forest extension projects.

The Asian Development Bank has worked with the Ministry of Environment, Urban Affairs, Forestry and Wildlife, under an Umbrella Technical Assistance Agreement, to study Rivers Kabul and Ravi and their environmental state. The initial study on River Kabul was conducted with the assistance of the International Union for Conservation of Nature (IUCN).

Pakistan faces a general lack of capacity of institutions to promote an integrated approach to the planning and management of land resources. The institutions responsible for mountain issues are the Governments of Azad Jammu & Kashmir; North West Frontier Province; Northern Area; Punjab and Sindh.

Pakistan is troubled by the lack of land-use planning and land-use control, uncertain land tenure and an inadequate policy on sustainable development in mountain areas. The mountain areas which are cultivated suffer from soil and water erosion, as well as limited infrastructure and marketing facilities. These problems lead to a need for sustainable economic diversification, especially since, despite intensification of the use of farmlands in the mountain areas, these lands will never be able to accommodate the additional population growth expected and already apparent.

The environmentally sound management of toxic chemicals is a core issue of the National Conservation Strategy. Management of this type of waste has not yet been achieved. This committee is collaborating with the Ministry of Environment, Urban Affairs, Forestry and Wildlife, and they have launched a joint action plan.

The joint action plan to deal with medical wastes underlines the need for more training and education of relevant personnel, identification and strengthening of the proper institutions, and an initiative to raise awareness of problems. The projects aiming at reducing pollution from the industries, address toxic effluent reduction by using appropriate technology transfer, recycling chrome recovery, establishing institutions for in-house pollution control in the tanneries, and by establishing industrial complexes which provide the leather industry with the infrastructure and utilities required.

Pakistan is suffering from the adverse soil, air and occupational effects caused by the use of chemicals in the textile and leather industries. The privatization of solid waste management was initiated by the Ministry of

Environment, Urban Affairs, Forestry and Wildlife. The Ministry is also responsible for the proposals in connection with the recycling of paper in Federal Government Offices.

The National Environment Quality Standards have been implemented for issues related to this sector. This has led to some concrete measures; for example the waste problems of cement factories are being addressed by installing anti-pollution technology. The environmentally sound management of sewerage and solid waste is a core issue in the National Conservation Strategy of Pakistan. There is practically no solid waste management in Pakistan. Around 40% of the waste is discarded in the streets or at collection sites. Only half of the urban wastes is disposed in sewers, with most remaining untreated.

Solid waste treatment has been privatized in order to keep up with the demand for solid waste treatment services. Only Karachi and Islamabad have sewage treatment plants. Communities are being encouraged to participate in enhancing solid waste treatment capacities.

The industrialization of Pakistan has had an effect on the environment, especially since the discharging of waste is being done without consideration of the treatment facilities that are required to maintain sustainability. Pakistan has implemented a Pollution Release Project to monitor select industries in the Province of Punjab.

Bangladesh

In 1990s, Bangladesh signed the Montreal Protocol. A country study on climate change has just been completed under the United States Country Study Programme.

Training programmes are undertaken for capacity-building in GHG Inventory analysis and for the application of new technology. The Convention on Biological Diversity was signed by Bangladesh in 1992 and ratified in 1994. The Convention on International Trade in Endangered Species of Wild Fauna and Flora was signed by Bangladesh in 1973. Bangladesh is also a party to the Ramsar Convention and the World Heritage Convention.

Conservation and sustainable use of biological diversity are applied to the following areas:

— terrestrial biological diversity,

— agricultural biological diversity,

— freshwater biological diversity and

— coastal and marine biological diversity.

Bangladesh signed The International Convention to Combat Desertification in Countries Experiencing Drought and/or Desertification Particularly in Africa in 1994 and ratified it in 1995. Programmes for human resource development and transfer of appropriate technologies are required for managing fragile eco-systems. Cooperation with international development financing agencies and development partners is needed. Financial and technical assistance is required from these international development agencies and development partners. Managerial and technical decisions needed for effective forest management are drafted and initiated by the Forest Department. After the approval of the Ministry of Environment and Forests, the Forest Department executes the decisions. Major financial and administrative decisions are taken by the concerned Ministries of the Government. The Government of Bangladesh imposed a moratorium on tree felling in 1989 and declared that it would increase the protected area from 5% of total forest area to 10%. It envisages raising forest area to 20% within the next 15 years. Further policy and legal measures are under consideration in the Government in order to arrest the deforestation trend in the country.

Institutional strengthening in the forestry sector is a major issue, and the modalities for institutional restructuring are under consideration in the Government in accordance with the guidelines provided by the 20-year Forestry Sector Master Plan. Government agencies such as the Environment Directorate, LGED, NGOs and major international development organizations are involved. Local people, including indigenous people, are also stakeholders in the afforestation programmes of the Government as well as the NGOs.

The Forest Department (FD) takes up afforestation programmes covering the whole country and all forest types through participatory mechanisms in every year. Between 1974 and 1995, Bangladesh raised a total of 321,254 ha of plantations of various types. Among these were 165,954 ha of hill forests, 28,208 ha of plain land Sal Forests, and 127,092 ha of littoral plantations. By using a social forestry approach, the Forest Department is mobilizing a movement involving people from all walks of life to plant trees.

The Forest Department is presently pursuing the identified issues of human resource development through recruitment and training, infrastructure and logistics development, genetic improvement of trees through tissue culture and clonal propagation, computerized database development, appropriate technology for in situ and ex situ conservation, etc.

The Forest Department is carrying out an inventory of the Sundarban and Coastal plantations by using the Resource Information Management System (RIMS) facilities. This information will be used to implement the strategies identified under the Integrated Resource Management of Sundarban.

RIMS will also be used in the subsequent inventory programmes of the hill forest and plain land Sal Forests. Being a computer-based facility RIMS will also enable the monitoring of changes in the forest resources of the country. The Forest Department is putting a special emphasis on genetic research to meet the growing demand of forest products as quickly as possible.

In Bangladesh, National Water Council (NWC), chaired by the Prime Minister, takes decisions and provides policy guidance on key national issues relating to water resources. Decisions are also taken in the interministerial meetings where different agencies involved in water-related projects are represented. In 1983, the National Water Plan, started in 1983, focused on the assessment of water resources and demand by different users. It assembled a substantial amount of information, developed a range of planning models and analytical tools and recommended strategies and programmes, many of which were adopted by the Government.

The Plan also produced a water policy and other proposals to institutionalize the process of water planning and long-term water resources management. Despite these achievements the Plan fell short of a comprehensive national water plan. It was inadequate for evaluating large-scale programmes, impacts and requirements; failed to evaluate properly and integrate a number of major projects and programmes within the sector: inadequately addressed requirements in other Ministries, viz. fisheries, navigation, public health, industries, municipalities, etc.

Under the Flood Action Plan (FAP), a number of projects were evaluated at the prefeasibility level, and possible flood mitigation projects have been identified within a regional context. Implementation of a few priority projects are either under way or ready to commence. Amongst the considerable achievements have been the formulation of standard guidelines for project assessment, participatory planning and environmental impact assessment. On the basis of the FAP studies, a strategy for the development of water resources and the management of water and floods was approved by the Government of Bangladesh in 1995.

The major water user groups are farmers (marginal, landless), fishermen, boatmen, women, indigenous people and local communities. The groups' activities are organized by the local governmental agencies and NGOs. Participatory planning helps address issues of all Project-Affected People (PAP). However, significant use is required for salinity management in the coastal belt, where considerable fresh upland flow is needed during the dry season.

In Bangladesh, land-based activities affecting oceans and coasts and needing to be implemented by Bangladesh include:

(i) alternatives for pesticides and insecticides for agriculture;

(ii) industries to be provided with waste recycling equipment;

(iii) new industrial machineries to be designed for producing minimum wastes;

(iv) facilities for storage, recycling and treatment of harmful wastes are to be built.

The Local Government Engineering Department (LGED) has been engaged in various Urban Services Projects with components of solid waste disposal, health and sanitation with other services. The projects through which these services are provided are the Secondary Towns Infrastructure Development Project (STIDP), the Secondary Towns Integrated Flood Protection Project (STIFPP), the Slum Improvement Project (SIP), the Municipal Services Project (MSP), the Urban Poor Reduction Project (UPRP) and the Urban Basic Services Project (UBSP).

Technology is needed for recycling, transportation, disposal design improvement, and equipment. Capacity-building will be required at the following levels:

(i) Executive agency level: technical/technological issues, support to local governmental bodies, NGOs/CBOs, beneficiaries;

(ii) Local governmental bodies: technical/technological issues, equipment, linkage with governmental agencies and support to NGOs/CBOs.

Human resource development in the management of hazardous wastes and equipment for detection is necessary. Financial assistance from international development financing agencies and development partners is required for environmentally sound management of hazardous wastes.

The Bangladesh Atomic Energy Commission (BAEC) is, in principle, responsible for developing and implementing a national strategy and the necessary infrastructure for the collection, handling, treatment, conditioning, transportation, storage and disposal of radioactive wastes in compliance with the regulatory requirements, duly considering local and socio-economic conditions of the country. Wastes are temporarily stored in the respective places of origin. The proposed waste processing and storage facility will be constructed at AERE, Savar, to meet the current national needs on approval by the competent authority.

Nepal

Nepal is a Himalayan terrain with hills and mountains covering three quarters of the country's total land area. Because of the pronounced steepness and fragility of the land, there are landslide and erosion problems which limit its productivity. Migration from the hills and mountains to the Terai is likely to continue as new infrastructure increasingly opens up in the south, and as the disparity between incomes in upland and lowland regions continues to grow. The hills and mountains need to be developed in an ecologically sustainable way with the development of watersheds and by providing hydropower to industrial establishments.

Growing urbanization, markets and employment accelerate the economy in the hinterlands. This is still a matter of operational research and cautious practices. The ecologically and economically strained hills and mountains have to develop their unique but intrinsic potential to support the population growth.

In Nepal, the National Planning Commission (NPC) is the apex body formulating and monitoring the national plans on sustainable development. People, including farmers, NGOs, and the private sector are involved in this field. This is consistent with the efforts of Nepal which, after restoring a multi-party democracy, has been trying to practice decentralization through participatory decision-making. Agriculture is very important to Nepal as it alone contributes to about 60% of the GDP, and provides employment to nearly 80% of the entire population.

The percentages of the total land area used for agriculture are 9.3% in the mountains, 43.1% in the hills and 47.6% in the Terai. Nepal has to integrate a developmental dimension into land productivity within the Rural Development Programme as well as open up off-farm economic opportunities for industrial development based on the resources available in the mountain terrain.

Some studies indicate that the pre- and post-harvest losses in food crops caused by pests and diseases range from 20 to 35%. In 1996, a severe outbreak of rice hopper affecting an area of about 2,000 ha was recorded in the main rice growing belt of the south causing a loss of an estimated NRs 50 million.

Nepal may be among the few countries in the world where farmers use traditional botanicalpesticides with considerable success in crop protection. Exploiting these skills, His Majesty's Government of Nepal (HMG/N) has launched an Integrated Pest Management (IPM) Programme in the Kingdom, and IPM has now been endorsed as the national policy. HGM/N is in the process of establishing a National Steering Committee for the effective launching of the IPM Programme. HMG/N has established Regional Plant Protection Laboratories in five different development regions, though there is still a lack of human resources, equipment and infrastructural support.

Nepal is trying to become a member of the International Plant Protection Convention (IPPC), the Asian Plant Protection Convention (APPC) and similar international/regional agencies. Nepal is going to become a member of the WTO for which the Ministry of Agriculture has consituted a core group.

The protection of the atmosphere is a worldwide concern and Nepal, as a Least Developed Country, cannot afford to invest in this issue without compromising its economic growth and development. With regard to the import and export of substances and products affecting the atmosphere, such as fossil fuels, industrial goods, agricultural chemicals and so forth, different governmental and non-governmental organizations make their own decisions depending on the national policies. There are no institutions or research groups with specific technology for improving the state of the environment.

The Department of Hydrology and Meteorology has, to some extent, been supported by the US Government in assessing the nation's vulnerability to the impacts of climate change, and in preparing the national inventory of greenhouse gases. The Government of Nepal has actively promoted the development of greenhouse gas-free hydropower energy. It is estimated that Nepal has a theoretical hydropower potential of 83,000MW, of which 42,000 MW can be generated according to the economic feasibility studies.

The installed hydropower generation capacity in the country is around 233 MW which is less than 0.3% of the total theoretical potential. The Government policy for the massive production of hydropower energy in Nepal has largely been targeted to the vast village communities which otherwise depend on the already dwindling forests and woods which are also the potential carbon dioxide sinks.

Nepal signed the Montreal Protocol (1987) on 6 July 1994 and the London Amendment (1990) signed in 6 July 1994. It signed the United Nations Framework Convention on Climate Change on 2 May 1994. Nepal is trying to develop an innovative, decentralized decision-making process involving the Department for National Parks and Wildlife Conservation (DNPWC), national NGOs, and international NGOs. The DNPWC needs to expand its staffing and training activities for effective conservation and management. Training of professional, technical as well as administrative staff is necessary in order to strengthen DNPWC's capacity.

Nepal signed the Convention on Biological Diversity in 1992, and ratified it in 1993. The Convention on International Trade in Endangeredof Wild Fauna and Flora was signed by Nepal in 1975, and the latest report was submitted in 1995.

In Nepal, the Ministry of Forests and Soil Conservation, the National Planning Commission, the Ministry of Finance (MOF), and the Ministry of Population and Environment; at the district level, District D C and District Soil Conservation Offices; and at the community level, user groups. NGOs, and GOs. Active participation of local people is important in land-use planning, forest management, and watershed development. Ecological rehabilitation and specific measures on land and resources have been the appropriate base for sustainable development. Experiences to date show that planning, decision-making and implementation efficiency is to grow from the grassroots level.

Policies for resource management, ecological balance and industrial growth prevail in a broader sphere of human undertakings. Updating policy formulations need to be in terms of achieving the objectives through ensured implementation and of strengthening regional cooperation in specific issues of concern. National and regional activities need to be active simultaneously and be directed towards providing capacity for resource management. The Department of Soil Conservation is planning, implementing and monitoring the Soil Conservation and Watershed Management (SCWM) Programme through its District Soil Conservation Offices in 45 of 75 districts

The SCWM Programme includes land-use development and improvement, land productivity conservation, erosion hazard prevention, infrastructural protection, and community soil conservation and income generation activities. Nepal needs capacity-building for the technical and professional staff and, at the local level, awareness-building and transfer of technology.

Nepal signed the International Convention to Combat Desertification in Countries Experiencing Drought and/or Desertification Particularly in Africa in 1994, and ratified it in 1996. Nepal took an active part in the UN Conference on Desertification, and in the formulation of the UN Plan of Action to Combat Desertification.

For Nepal, being a mountainous country, combating desertification is a matter of great concern both in developmental activities as well as in regional cooperation.

Thirty-seven percent (5.4 million ha) of the total land area of Nepal is covered by natural forests, and another 16% is potentially suitable for forest development or for rangeland. Forests are the main natural resources of Nepal.

Various programmes have been launched to develop the forestry sector, including forest management programmes under which, for example community groups have been formed. Other programmes have been designed for the production of saplings, for afforestation, and for the implementation of national and leasehold forestry programmes. Programmes related to forests, soil and watershed conservation, and to the production and processing of medicinal herbs, have also been undertaken.

Strengthening the capacities of both the governmental and semi-governmental organizations at all levels, from central to local level, is essential for the successful implementation of these programmes. Similarly, relevant laws and regulations are being reviewed and revised to meet operational needs. People are also more aware of the programme objectives and take more interest in the community forest management and in informing user groups.

Nepal's water supply and sanitation authorities have not mobilized enough financial resources to enable them to operate and maintain their systems properly, much less contribute to investments. To make land use and environmental information effective, an appropriate institutional system will be developed under the National Planning Commission by integrating scattered units into a single unit. Management of land resources has been deemed critical from the point of view of sustainable agricultural production. Improved agricultural output is the only way towards economic growth and poverty alleviation.

Soil fertility is a crucial element in determining the productivity of the land. It has been noted that soil fertility is declining in many parts of Nepal, having a negative impact on the yield of the key crops. Changes in farming practices are needed to reverse this trend, and institutional improvements are imperative for agricultural research and extension. Agricultural policies must be flexible in order to conform to the features of different agro-ecological zones and thus take maximum advantage of the diversity of natural resources.

As Nepal adjusts to these essential requirements, the production of food grains, fruit farming and livestock farming will be gradually expanded. In addition, district level planning will have a significant role. Therefore, a mapping system for districts will be developed taking into account different agro-ecological zones. There is a great diversity in the nature of different geographical regions of Nepal. The Terai occupies 23.11%, whereas hills and mountains cover 35.21% and 41.68%, respectively, of the country's total land area. Eighteeen percent of Nepal's land area is not in use, including barren land, land-slide affected areas, snow-covered land, etc. Of the remaining 82%, 20% is reserved for agricultural purposes. Appropriate programmes relating to mountaineering and other associated arrangements under the Development of Mountain Tourism Programme will be undertaken with the objective of protecting the environment and increasing local employment.

Chemical manufacturing industries are now required to obtain a permit. The proponents need to submit IEE or EIA reports depending upon their annual production capacity. Importation of toxic chemicals also requires a permit from the Ministry of Home Affairs. Among industrial users, to date, very little pollution abatement equipment has been used by industries in Nepal. Investors wishing to maximise profits have opted for the cheapest technology, which, unfortunately, often turns out to be the most polluting one as well. It is the people in general who have to face the consequences of such decisions.

Therefore, industries need to adopt less polluting technologies, and for that, His Majesty's Government of Nepal (HMG/N) may need to offer a limited range of subsidies as well as provide the technologies directly. Research has already been carried out in Nepal to identify pollution prone industries. The cement, leather and tanning, paper and pulp, soap and chemicals, sugar and textile industries have all been identified as major sources of various kinds of pollution. HMG adopted the Pesticides Act in 1991, and Pesticides Regulation in 1993.

In accordance with these laws, Nepal has established the Nepal Pesticide Board which will assist the Government in formulating pesticide policies and in adopting regulatory measures for the safe use of these. There are about 10 major importers of pesticides in the country and nearly 100 domestic retail outlets. The predominant users of toxic chemicals, especially pesticides, are farmers who are also over 90% of the Nepalese population.

Due to the lack of appropriate Integrated Pest Management technologies, farmers have been largely dependent on using these chemicals for pest control to obtain the expected yield. This has, in isolated cases, begun to cause health and environmental hazards. Nepal has already prohibited some toxic chemicals like DINOSEB and dinoseb salts, fluoroacetamide, chlordane, chlordimeform, cyhexatine, edb, heptachlor, and mercury compounds.

In Nepal, the National Council for Solid Waste Management is responsible for policy formulation at the national level and the Solid Waste Management and Resource Mobilization Center (SWMRMC) is responsible for landfill management in Kathmandu Valley. Local bodies are responsible in the field. The responsibility for public sanitation is divided among several institutions:

— municipalities (for drainage, sanitation and solid wastes);

— Department of Water Supply and Sanitation (for drainage and sewerage, although the Department does not actually have any sewerage operations);

— Nepal Water Supply Cooperation (for sanitary sewers)

— Department of Roads (for roadside drains).

Nepal has a programme on waste management concentrating on street cleaning, waste collection, transport and landfill deposit activities. In urban and suburban areas, solid wastes have been identified as problematic. In 1987, an act was adopted with a view to systematizing waste management in Kathmandu and to seek possibilities of recycling solid wastes into economic resources.

In accordance with the act, the Solid Waste Management and Resources Mobilization Center was established. Composting activities were carried out by the Center with successful results, but were dropped for various reasons after 3-4 years. At present, the Center is responsible for the management of sanitary landfill sites, and the rest of the waste management activities are undertaken by municipalities. His Majesty's Government (HMG) adopted a national policy for solid waste management in order to set standards for waste disposal, recycling and reuse. A National Council for Solid Waste Management has been set up under the chairmanship of the Ministry of Local Development.

In addition, the Ministry undertakes major activities in this field. The role of local governments needs to be strengthened as self-contained and active agencies in waste management. The Ministry of Population and Environment is responsible for decision-making on hazardous wastes. At present, Nepal does not perceive itself to have a hazardous waste problem. In the future, activities will be regulated in accordance with the Basel Convention.

In November 1996, the Ministry of Population and Environment organized a one-day workshop on the Basel Convention and management of solid wastes in Kathmandu Valley. In the workshop, environmental experts and concerned officials from different governmental and non-governmental organizations discussed national policies and programmes for the control of transboundary movement of hazardous wastes and their disposal. In the conclusions of the workshop it was stressed that national policies need to be revised in accordance with the convention, and that the nature of toxic wastes should be identified so as to minimize their potential risks.

Wastes from hospitals, laboratories, pathological clinics, and the leather industry cause massive harm to human health. In addition, the experts stressed that it is important to see the issue of hazardous waste in a global context as well as a domestic context and to integrate this issue into overall sustainable decision-making.

Sri Lanka

Sri Lankan National Development Council has appointed a Task Force to recommend policy changes to address issues such as agriculture research, extension, marketing, pricing and the role of the State in providing services and inputs and the role of the private sector in providing inputs, and multiplication and distribution of seeds. Farmers' organizations have been established to strengthen their bargaining power. By the end of 1996, a total of 12,934 farmers' organizations had been established. Farmers' organizations and Samurdhi Animators focus on mobilizing the rural poor to upgrade their skills and create employment opportunities.

The Ministry of Agriculture launched an island-wide food drive called 'Vaga Lanka' which aims at combining modern and traditional methods of agriculture. This involves agriculture and the adoption of integrated farming techniques. The emphasis placed on integrated pest management contributed to a reduction in the use of pesticides in 1996. During this year, the Department of Agriculture conducted Farmer Field Schools for integrated pest management (IPM) in 21 districts and 3 Mahaveli Systems; 800 field-level IPM demonstrations have been conducted in selected areas.

Rural credit schemes have provided agricultural loans. A number of policy measures are directed to give an impetus to agricultural exports. Plantation Sector Reforms (privatization) are expected to improve the productivity and efficiency of the Tree Crop Sector. Agriculture continues to be an important sector in the economy of Sri Lanka, contributing 20 percent of the GNP. Between 1991 and 1995, the agriculture sector was able to absorb 89 percent of the public investments per annum. The Government implemented large irrigation projects, like the Mahaveli Programme, to increase food production and employment opportunities for the rural poor.

The Ministry of Environment is the focal point for both Conventions. Interministerial committees have been set up to consider relevant issues and make recommendations. Important decisions need ratification by the Cabinet Ministers. Government Ministries, Departments Statutory Corporations, Universities and NGO groups, are involved in implementing the Montreal Protocol and the UNFCCC.

There was a regional programme on the impact of climate change under SAARC in 1992. Sri Lanka was also a participant in the Regional Study on Global Environmental Issues, funded by the Asian Development Bank in 1992-1993.

Sri Lanka signed the Convention on Biological Diversity in June 1992 and ratified it in March 1994. Sri Lanka ratified the Convention on International Trade in Endangered Species of Wild Fauna and Flora on 4 May 1979, and the Convention on the Conservation of Migratory Species of Wild Animals entered into force on 1 September 1990. Major legislative enactments on the biological resources of Sri Lanka are the National Environmental Act 1980, Forest Ordinance, The Flora and

Fauna Protection Ordinance, National Heritage Wilderness Areas Act, Botanic Gardens Ordinance, Fisheries and Aquatic Resources Act, the Plant Protection Ordinance, and the Customs Ordinance.

The preparation of the Biodiversity Action Plan was undertaken in response to Article 6 of the Convention (CITES). While consolidating the ongoing efforts of conservation and sustainable use of biological diversity, the Action Plan aims at establishing a policy and programme regime, which brings national action to various aspects of the subject, including capacity-building and bio-safety measures, in tune with the articles of the Convention. The Government is to adopt this National Biodiversity Action Plan for the conservation and sustainable use of these resources in the near future.

Wildlife preservation, in the form of zoos and national farms, is used for the ex-situ preservation of wildlife. Also, efforts are being made to strengthen the legislative framework to derive maximum benefit from biotechnology while minimizing its risks. The lack of technology and technical capacity, as well as financial constraints, have weakened the national efforts to protect biodiversity. A network of over 100 NGOs has been built up, and biodiversity focal points have been established in development ministries and agencies for environmental advocacy in formulating biodiversity policies.

Topographically the island consists of a south central mountainous region which rises to an elevation of 2,502 m and is surrounded by broad lowland plains at an elevation of 0-75 m above sea level. From the mountainous regions nine major rivers and 94 other rivers flow across the lowlands into the Indian Ocean. Sri Lanka is one of the few countries in South Asia having a wealth of biodiversity. Within a land area of 25,000 sq. miles, this rich biodiversity is distributed within a wide range of eco-systems varying from rainforests to grasslands, freshwater bodies, wetlands and rivers, and coastal and marine eco-systems.

An important feature of the climate is that there are two basic eco-zones: a wet zone and a dry zone. Since these two zones are not sharply distinct, there is also what may be termed, an "intermediate" zone gradually merging into the wet and the dry zones.

These climatic conditions and the panorama of natural eco-systems in the country support over 3,800 species of flowering plants, of which 23% are endemic, 314 species of fern and derivatives of the fern family. Species diversity is also high among mosses and fungi. In addition, the country has a high faunal diversity.

The diversity of the country's biological resources has not yet been fully surveyed. Conservation and sustainable use of these resources based on the indigenous knowledge systems and practices is ingrained in Sri Lanka's ethos and way of life.

The developed countries should ensure that benefits of biotechnology accrue to the country of origin of the biological resources; these benefits to include royalty payments and transfer of technologies to the countries of origin of the biological resources in accordance with the provisions of the Convention.

The capacities of biodiversity-rich countries should be built up to enable them to carry out bio-prospecting and undertake technology assessment for protection of their resources. The introduction of transgenic and alien species should be only with the requisite safeguards. Sri

Lanka is trying to build up a bio-technology information network and capacity in the area of taxonomy. The facilities for cryo-preservation of germ plasma in the country are very limited.

The Plant Genetic Resource Centre at Peradeniya is the only institution with such facilities and only a fraction of the range of the agricultural germ plasma available in the country is stored at this centre. It is necessary to build capacities and develop programmes for gaining a better understanding of the different components of the country's biodiversity. The country's capacity in the area of taxonomy needs to be built up. The opportunities available for training in this area are limited.

The SAARC countries cooperate in identifying regional issues and taking regional and international measures for the conservation and sustainable use of biological resources. However, national action regarding conservation and sustainable use of biodiversity and an equitable share of benefits, demands contributory action on the part of the international community, particularly the developed countries.

Sri Lanka has not signed the International Convention to Combat Desertification in Countries Experiencing Drought and/or Desertification Particularly in Africa. The process of development and increase in the number of households is increasing the consumption of energy. It should be emphasized that the consumption of energy by an individual in South Asia is about one-twentieth that of a person in a developed economy.

The Ministry of Forestry and Environment lays down policy in consultation with the Department of Forests. The Chief Conservator of Forests implements the programmes. The Cabinet approves major policies and investments on the recommendation of the Ministry. The Government's efforts to arrest deforestation through the enforcement of stringent laws, such as the Forestry Ordinance and the Wild Life Conservation Act, have resulted in limited success. A forestry sector Master Plan was prepared and it was revised in 1993, with the aim to protect and develop forest cover.

NGOs are involved in developing forestry development plans and they contributed in preparing the 5-year forestry development programme which commenced in 1997 with ADB assistance. Environmental groups exercise vigilance and assist law enforcement authorities in the prevention of illicit logging. Deforestation is one of the critical environmental problems in Sri Lanka.

Forest cover which stood at 44% of the land area in 1956, declined to 27% by 1981, and the present forest cover is estimated at approximately 23% of the land area. This situation was brought about by both poverty and affluence. Nearly 70% of the people are rural and agriculture-dependent. The rural poor destroy forests for cultivation and to meet energy needs. The affluent and the entrepreneurs use more and more timber without replacing the forests. The development process has also contributed to deforestation.

Sri Lankan national tree planting campaigns are carried out by the Ministry of Forestry and Environment to increase the forest cover in urban areas and to mobilize the energies of school children and youth in promoting reforestation. The Department of Forests trains officials in forestry management. Youth and NGOs participate in tree-planting campaigns.

Sri Lankan Water Resources Council is a coordinating body which was established to plan the water resources at the macro level. Decisions are made by respective agencies, and they follow a hierarchical order. All related agencies are represented in the Council and an integrated approach has been adopted for the protection of the quality and supply of freshwater resources. The Central Environmental Authority (CEA) has published water quality standards as well as standards for industrial effluent that could be discharged into water bodies. Other agencies, such as the Department of Irrigation and the Department of Agrarian Services, have been alerted to ensure quality water.

The Water Resources Board is most concerned about the underground water supply and studies are being undertaken to ascertain the volume of water supplies. The main supplier of drinking water for the urban centres, namely, the National Water and Drainage Board, has a strong programme to monitor the water quality of the Kelani River, before releasing it for drinking purposes. The Community Water Supply and Sanitation Project is ongoing and has improved the sanitation facilities and raised awareness about the need for maintaining hygienic standards in water supply.

A Land-use Planning Unit has been established in the Ministry of Lands with a view to planning development in a sustainable manner and conserving natural resources. This Unit identifies different types of soil for agricultural purposes. There are coastal development laws in which lands are identified for development projects, such as the construction of hotels, taking into account the need to protect the marine environment.

The Department of Fisheries and Coast Conservation, under the Ministry of Fisheries, is responsible for policy-making and implementation. Sri Lanka signed and ratified UN Convention on the Law of the Sea in 1994. The Government of Sri Lanka has various laws, rules, and regulations for dealing with activities in the coastal zone. Regulations have been developed to prevent over-fishing, and the coastal management plan provides for zones to conserve marine species threatened by indiscriminate fishing and the use of inappropriate fishing techniques.

A Coastal Zone Management Plan has been prepared by the Ministry of Fisheries in order to adopt an integrated approach to the management of coastal resources and to involve local communities in the planning and implementation of programmes for the conservation and sustainable use of marine resources and the conservation of the coastline. The policy on coastal fishing has been oriented towards mitigating the adverse effects on the environment and maximizing the protection of fish in a sustainable manner.

A complete inventory of chemicals in use within the country was completed. The International Register of Potentially Toxic Chemicals (IRPTC) database on chemicals is also to be installed.

The Ministry of Forestry and Environment is the focal point, and the Central Environment Authority is the competent authority for this convention. Decision-making is also the responsibility of the National Co-ordinating Committee for the implementation of the Basel Convention, chaired by the Secretary, Ministry of Forestry and Environment. Sri Lanka ratified the Basel Convention on the Control of Transboundary Movements of Hazardous Wastes and their Disposal in August 1992. The regulations for the internal management of hazardous waste were published in 1996, by the Ministry of Environment. Regulations for the transboundary movement of hazardous waste are being formulated and will be brought into operation under the Import and Export Control Act.

In addition to that, several regulatory measures taken by the Government help indirectly to reduce the pollution caused by high- and medium- polluting industries. Some of the significant regulatory measures are:

— Environmental Protection Licensing Scheme

— Environment Impact Assessment Scheme

— Siting of industries in an industrial estate or park to ensure proper waste disposal.

— Projects to relocate certain hazardous industries, such as tanneries and pesticides, are ongoing.

The capacity of the regulatory bodies are also inadequate to ensure the effective implementation of the new hazardous waste regulations. Sri Lanka lacks financial assistance for the efficient implementation of the Basel Convention. Particularly, financial assistance is essential to build the capacity of the country for hazardous waste management, including establishing hazardous waste disposal facilities.

3

Towards Ecosystem Balance

Protection of the atmosphere is a broad and multi-dimensional endeavour involving various sectors of economic activity. Concern about climate change and climate variability, air pollution and ozone depletion has created new demands for scientific, economic and social information to reduce the remaining uncertainties in these fields. Better understanding and prediction of the various properties of the atmosphere and of the affected ecosystems, as well as health impacts and their interactions with socio-economic factors, are needed.

Governments at the appropriate level, with the cooperation of the relevant United Nations bodies and, as appropriate, intergovernmental and non-governmental organizations, and the private sector, should promote research related to the natural processes affecting and being affected by the atmosphere, as well as the critical linkages between sustainable development and atmospheric changes, including impacts on human health, ecosystems, economic sectors and society. The government also ensure a more balanced geographical coverage of the Global Climate Observing System and its components, including the Global Atmosphere Watch, by facilitating, inter alia, the establishment and operation of additional systematic observation stations, and by contributing to the development, utilization and accessibility of these databases

The US government promote the development of early detection systems concerning changes and fluctuations in the atmosphere. The establishment and improvement of capabilities to predict such changes and fluctuations and to assess the resulting environmental and socio-economic impacts. The government also promote, and cooperate in the building of scientific capacities, the exchange of scientific data and information, and the facilitation of the participation and training of experts and technical staff, particularly of developing countries, in the fields of research, data assembly, collection and assessment, and systematic observation related to the atmosphere.

Energy is essential to economic and social development and improved quality of life. Much of the world's energy, however, is currently produced and consumed in ways that could not be sustained if technology were to remain constant and if overall quantities were to increase substantially. The need to control atmospheric emissions of greenhouse and other gases and substances will increasingly need to be based on efficiency in energy production, transmission, distribution and consumption, and on growing reliance on environmentally sound energy systems, particularly new and renewable sources of energy.

The intergovernmental and non-governmental organizations, and the private sector, should cooperate in identifying and developing economically viable, environmentally sound energy sources to promote the availability of increased energy supplies to support sustainable development efforts, in particular in developing countries. These organisations also promote the development at the national level of appropriate methodologies for making integrated energy, environment and economic policy decisions for sustainable development, inter alia, through environmental impact assessments.

The current energy supply mixes to determine how the contribution of environmentally sound energy systems as a whole, particularly new and renewable energy systems, could be increased in an economically efficient manner, taking into account respective countries' unique social, physical, economic and political characteristics, and examining and implementing, where appropriate, measures to overcome any barriers to their development and use. In accordance with national socio-economic development and environment priorities, evaluate and, as appropriate, promote cost-effective policies or programmes, including administrative, social and economic measures, in order to improve energy efficiency.

The transport sector has an essential and positive role to play in economic and social development, and transportation needs will undoubtedly increase. However, since the transport sector is also a source of atmospheric emissions, there is need for a review of existing transport systems and for more effective design and management of traffic and transport systems. It also develop and promote cost-effective policies or programmes, as appropriate, to limit, reduce or control, as appropriate, harmful emissions into the atmosphere and other adverse environmental effects of the transport sector, taking into account development priorities as well as the specific local and national circumstances and safety aspects.

The transport sector strengthen, as appropriate, their efforts at collecting, analysing and exchanging relevant information on the relation between environment and transport, with particular emphasis on the systematic observation of emissions and the development of a transport database. In accordance with national socio-economic development and environment priorities, evaluate and, as appropriate, promote cost-effective policies or programmes, including administrative, social and economic measures, in order to encourage use of transportation modes that minimize adverse impacts on the atmosphere.

Industry is essential for the production of goods and services and is a major source of employment and income, and industrial development as such is essential for economic growth. At the same time, industry is a major resource and materials user and consequently industrial activities result in emissions into the atmosphere and the environment as a whole.

Protection of the atmosphere can be enhanced, inter alia, by increasing resource and materials efficiency in industry, installing or improving pollution abatement technologies and replacing chlorofluorocarbons (CFCs) and other ozone-depleting substances with appropriate substitutes, as well as by reducing wastes and by-products.

The intergovernmental and non-governmental organizations, and the private sector, should promote cost-effective policies or programmes, including administrative, social and economic measures, in order to minimize industrial pollution and adverse impacts on the atmosphere and encourage industry to increase and strengthen its capacity to develop technologies, products and processes that are safe, less polluting and make more efficient use of all resources and materials, including energy. These organisations are promote efficient use of materials and resources, taking into account the life cycles of products, in order to realize the economic and environmental benefits of using resources more efficiently and producing fewer wastes.

Land-use and resource policies will both affect and be affected by changes in the atmosphere. Certain practices related to terrestrial and marine resources and land use can decrease greenhouse gas sinks and increase atmospheric emissions. The loss of biological diversity may reduce the resilience of ecosystems to climatic variations and air pollution damage.

Atmospheric changes can have important impacts on forests, biodiversity, and freshwater and marine ecosystems, as well as on economic activities, such as agriculture. Policy objectives in different sectors may often diverge and will need to be handled in an integrated manner. The government promote sustainable management and cooperation in the conservation and enhancement, as appropriate, of sinks and reservoirs of greenhouse gases, including biomass, forests and oceans, as well as other terrestrial, coastal and marine ecosystems.

While the 1985 Vienna Convention for the Protection of the Ozone Layer and the 1987 Montreal Protocol on Substances that Deplete the Ozone Layer were important steps in international action, the total chlorine loading of the atmosphere of ozone-depleting substances has continued to rise. This can be changed through compliance with the control measures identified within the Protocol. The objectives defined in the Vienna Convention and the Montreal Protocol and its 1990 amendments, including the consideration in those instruments of the special needs and conditions of the developing countries and the availability to them of alternatives to substances that deplete the ozone layer.

Technologies and natural products that reduce demand for these substances should be encouraged to develop strategies aimed at mitigating the adverse effects of ultraviolet radiation reaching the Earth's surface as a consequence of depletion and modification of the stratospheric ozone layer. Further expansion of the Global Ozone Observing System by facilitating - through bilateral and multilateral funding - the establishment and operation of additional systematic observation stations, especially in the tropical belt in the southern hemisphere.

Transboundary air pollution has adverse health impacts on humans and other detrimental environmental impacts, such as tree and forest loss and the acidification of water bodies. The geographical distribution of atmospheric pollution monitoring networks is uneven, with the developing countries severely underrepresented.

The lack of reliable emissions data outside Europe and North America is a major constraint to measuring transboundary air pollution. There is also insufficient information on the environmental and health effects of air pollution in other regions. The 1979 Convention on Long-range Transboundary Air Pollution, and its protocols, have established a regional regime in Europe and North America, based on a review process and cooperative programmes for systematic observation of air pollution, assessment and information exchange.

Following are the objectives of this programmes:

— To develop and apply pollution control and measurement technologies for stationary and mobile sources of air pollution and to develop alternative environmentally sound technologies;

— To observe and assess systematically the sources and extent of transboundary air pollution resulting from natural processes and anthropogenic activities;

— To strengthen the capabilities, particularly of developing countries, to measure, model and assess the fate and impacts of transboundary air pollution, through, inter alia, exchange of information and training of experts;

— To develop capabilities to assess and mitigate transboundary air pollution resulting from industrial and nuclear accidents, natural disasters and the deliberate and/or accidental destruction of natural resources;

— To encourage the establishment of new and the implementation of existing regional agreements for limiting transboundary air pollution;

— To develop strategies aiming at the reduction of emissions causing transboundary air pollution and their effects.

Planning and Management of Land Resources

The natural resources, the soils, minerals, water and biota that the land comprises are organized in ecosystems which provide a variety of services essential to the maintenance of the integrity of life-support systems and the productive capacity of the environment. Land resources are used in ways that take advantage of all these characteristics. Land is a finite resource, while the natural resources it supports can vary over time and according to management conditions and uses.

Expanding human requirements and economic activities are placing ever increasing pressures on land resources, creating competition and conflicts and resulting in suboptimal use of both land and land resources. If, in the future, human requirements are to be met in a sustainable manner, it is now essential to resolve these conflicts and move towards more effective and efficient use of land and its natural resources. Integrated physical and land-use planning and management is an eminently practical way to achieve this.

By examining all uses of land in an integrated manner, it makes it possible to minimize conflicts, to make the most efficient trade-offs and to link social and economic development with environmental protection and enhancement, thus helping to achieve the objectives of sustainable development. The essence of the integrated approach finds expression in the coordination of the sectoral planning and management activities concerned with the various aspects of land use and land resources. These resources are used for a variety of purposes which interact and may compete with one another; therefore, it is desirable to plan and manage all uses in an integrated manner.

Integration should take place at two levels, considering, on the one hand, all environmental, social and economic factors and, on the other, all environmental and resource components together. Integrated consideration facilitates appropriate choices and tradeoffs, thus maximizing sustainable productivity and use. Opportunities to allocate land to different uses arise in the course of major settlement or development projects or in a sequential fashion as lands become available on the market.

In doing so, environmental, social and economic issues should be taken into consideration. Protected areas, private property rights, the rights of indigenous people and their communities and other local communities and the economic role of women in agriculture and rural development, among other issues, should be taken into account.

Governments at the appropriate level, with the support of regional and international organizations, should review and, if appropiate, revise planning and management systems to facilitate an integrated approach. To do this, they should:

— Adopt planning and management systems that facilitate the integration of environmental components such as air, water, land and other natural resources, using landscape ecological planning (LANDEP) or other approaches that focus on, for example, an ecosystem or a watershed;

— Adopt strategic frameworks that allow the integration of both developmental and environmental goals; examples of these frameworks include sustainable livelihood systems, rural development, the World Conservation Strategy/Caring for the Earth, primary environmental care (PEC) and others;

— Establish a general framework for land-use and physical planning within which specialized and more detailed sectoral plans (e.g., for protected areas, agriculture, forests, human settlements, rural development) can be developed; establish intersectoral consultative bodies to streamline project planning and implementation;

— Strengthen management systems for land and natural resources by including appropriate traditional and indigenous methods;

There are major weaknesses in the policies, methods and mechanisms adopted to support and develop the multiple ecological, economic, social and cultural roles of trees, forests and forest lands. Many developed countries are confronted with the effects of air pollution and fire damage on their forests. More effective measures and approaches are often required at the national level to improve and harmonize policy formulation, planning and programming; legislative measures and instruments; development patterns; participation of the general public, especially women and indigenous people; involvement of youth; roles of the private sector, local organizations, non-governmental organizations and cooperatives; development of technical and multidisciplinary skills and quality of human resources; forestry extension and public education; research capability and support; administrative structures and mechanisms, including intersectoral coordination, decentralization and responsibility and incentive systems; and dissemination of information and public relations.

This is especially important to ensure a rational and holistic approach to the sustainable and environmentally sound development of forests. The need for securing the multiple roles of forests and forest lands through adequate and appropriate institutional strengthening has been repeatedly emphasized in many of the reports, decisions and recommendations of FAO, ITTO, UNEP, the World Bank, IUCN and other organizations.

Forests world wide have been and are being threatened by uncontrolled degradation and conversion to other types of land uses, influenced by increasing human needs; agricultural expansion; and environmentally harmful mismanagement, including, for example, lack of adequate forest-fire control and anti-poaching measures, unsustainable commercial logging, overgrazing and unregulated browsing, harmful effects of airborne pollutants, economic incentives and other measures taken by other sectors of the economy.

The impacts of loss and degradation of forests are in the form of soil erosion; loss of biological diversity, damage to wildlife habitats and degradation of watershed areas, deterioration of the quality of life and reduction of the options for development. The present situation calls for urgent and consistent action for conserving and sustaining forest resources. The greening of suitable areas, in all its component activities, is an effective way of increasing public awareness and participation in protecting and managing forest resources.

The Tropical Forestry Action Programme are currently being implemented in more than 80 countries, with the support of the international community to ensure sustainable management and, where appropriate, conservation of existing and future forest resources and increase the ecological, biological, climatic, socio-cultural and economic contributions of forest resources.

The United Nations Conference on Environment and Development, promote international cooperation on forest management, conservation and sustainable development of all types of forests, including afforestation, reforestation and rehabilitation. Governments should recognize the importance of categorizing forests, within the framework of long-term forest conservation and management policies, into different forest types and setting up sustainable units in every region/watershed with a view to securing the conservation of forests.

Governments, with the participation of the private sector, non-governmental organizations, local community groups, indigenous people, women, local government units and the public at large, should act to maintain and expand the existing vegetative cover wherever ecologically, socially and economically feasible, through technical cooperation and other forms of support. Major activities to be considered include:

— Ensuring the sustainable management of all forest ecosystems and woodlands, through improved proper planning, management and timely implementation of silvicultural operations, including inventory and relevant research, as well as rehabilitation of degraded natural forests to restore productivity and environmental contributions, giving particular attention to human needs for economic and ecological services, wood-based energy, agroforestry, non-timber forest products and services, watershed and soil protection, wildlife management, and forest genetic resources;

— Establishing, expanding and managing, as appropriate to each national context, protected area systems, which includes systems of conservation units for their environmental, social and spiritual functions and values, including conservation of forests in representative ecological systems and landscapes, primary old-growth forests, conservation and management of wildlife, nomination of World Heritage Sites under the World Heritage Convention, as appropriate, conservation of genetic resources, involving in situ and ex situ measures and undertaking supportive measures to ensure sustainable utilization of biological resources and conservation of biological diversity and the traditional forest habitats of indigenous people, forest dwellers and local communities;

— Undertaking and promoting buffer and transition zone management;

— Carrying out revegetation in appropriate mountain areas, highlands, bare lands, degraded farm lands, arid and semi-arid lands and coastal areas for combating desertification and preventing erosion problems and for other protective functions and national programmes for rehabilitation of degraded lands, including community forestry, social forestry, agroforestry and silvipasture, while also taking into account the role of forests as national carbon reservoirs and sinks;

— Developing industrial and non-industrial planted forests in order to support and promote national ecologically sound afforestation and reforestation/ regeneration programmes in suitable sites, including upgrading of existing planted forests of both industrial and non-industrial and commercial purpose to increase their contribution to human needs and to offset pressure on primary/old growth forests. Measures should be taken to promote and provide intermediate yields and to improve the rate of returns on investments in planted forests, through interplanting and underplanting valuable crops;

— Developing/strengthening a national and/or master plan for planted forests as a priority, indicating, inter alia, the location, scope and species, and specifying areas of existing planted forests requiring rehabilitation, taking into account the economic aspect for future planted forest development, giving emphasis to native species;

— Increasing the protection of forests from pollutants, fire, pests and diseases and other human-made interferences such as forest poaching, mining and unmitigated shifting cultivation, the uncontrolled introduction of exotic plant and animal species, as well as developing and accelerating research for a better understanding of problems relating to the management and regeneration of all types of forests; strengthening and/or establishing appropriate measures to assess and/or check inter-border movement of plants and related materials;

— Stimulating development of urban forestry for the greening of urban, peri-urban and rural human settlements for amenity, recreation and production purposes and for protecting trees and groves;

— Launching or improving opportunities for particpation of all people, including youth, women, indigenous people and local communities in the formulation, development and implementation of forest-related programmes and other activities, taking due account of the local needs and cultural values;

— Limiting and aiming to halt destructive shifting cultivation by addressing the underlying social and ecological causes.

The vast potential of forests and forest lands as a major resource for development is not yet fully realized. The improved management of forests can increase the production of goods and services and, in particular, the yield of wood and non-wood forest products, thus helping to generate additional employment and income, additional value through processing and trade of forest products, increased contribution to foreign exchange earnings, and increased return on investment.

Forest resources, being renewable, can be sustainably managed in a manner that is compatible with environmental conservation. The implications of the harvesting of forest resources for the other values of the forest should be taken fully into consideration in the development of forest policies. It is also possible to increase the value of forests through non-damaging uses such as eco-tourism and the managed supply of genetic materials. Concerted action is needed in order to increase people's perception of the value of forests and of the benefits they provide.

Fragile Ecosystems

Fragile ecosystems are important ecosystems, with unique features and resources. Fragile ecosystems include deserts, semi-arid lands, mountains, wetlands, small islands and certain coastal areas. Most of these ecosystems are regional in scope, as they transcend national boundaries.

Desertification is land degradation in arid, semi-arid and dry sub-humid areas resulting from various factors, including climatic variations and human activities. Desertification affects about one sixth of the world's population, 70 per cent of all drylands, amounting to 3.6 billion hectares, and one quarter of the total land area of the world. The most obvious impact of desertification, in addition to widespread poverty, is the degradation of 3.3 billion hectares of the total area of rangeland, constituting 73 per cent of the rangeland with a low potential for human and animal carrying capacity; decline in soil fertility and soil structure on about 47 per cent of the dryland areas constituting marginal rainfed cropland; and the degradation of irrigated cropland, amounting to 30 per cent of the dryland areas with a high population density and agricultural potential.

The priority in combating desertification should be the implementation of preventive measures for lands that are not yet degraded, or which are only slightly degraded. However, the severely degraded areas should not be neglected. In combating desertification and drought, the participation of local communities, rural organizations, national Governments, non-governmental organizations and international and regional organizations is essential. Strengthening the knowledge base and developing information and monitoring systems for regions prone to desertification and drought, including the economic and social aspects of these ecosystems;

— Combating land degradation through, inter alia, intensified soil conservation, afforestation and reforestation activities;

— Developing and strengthening integrated development programmes for the eradication of poverty and promotion of alternative livelihood systems in areas prone to desertification;

— Developing comprehensive anti-desertification programmes and integrating them into national development plans and national environmental planning;

— Developing comprehensive drought preparedness and drought-relief schemes, including self-help arrangements, for drought-prone areas and designing programmes to cope with environmental refugees;

— Encouraging and promoting popular participation and environmental education, focusing on desertification control and management of the effects of drought.

The global assessments of the status and rate of desertification conducted by the United Nations Environment Programme (UNEP) in 1977, 1984 and 1991 have revealed insufficient basic knowledge of desertification processes. Adequate world-wide systematic observation systems are helpful for the development and implementation of effective anti-desertification programmes.

The capacity of existing international, regional and national institutions, particularly in developing countries, to generate and exchange relevant information is limited.

An integrated and coordinated information and systematic observation system based on appropriate technology and embracing global, regional, national and local levels is essential for understanding the dynamics of desertification and drought processes. It is also important for developing adequate measures to deal with desertification and drought and improving socio-economic conditions.

The objectives of this programme area are:

— To promote the establishment and/or strengthening of national environmental information coordination centres that will act as focal points within Governments for sectoral ministries and provide the necessary standardization and back-up services; to ensure also that national environmental information systems on desertification and drought are linked together through a network at subregional, regional and interregional levels;

— To strengthen regional and global systematic observation networks linked to the development of national systems for the observation of land degradation and desertification caused both by climate fluctuations and by human impact, and to identify priority areas for action;

— To establish a permanent system at both national and international levels for monitoring desertification and land degradation with the aim of improving living conditions in the affected areas.

Mountain Ecosystem

Mountains are an important source of water, energy and biological diversity. Furthermore, they are a source of such key resources as minerals, forest products and agricultural products and of recreation. As a major ecosystem representing the complex and interrelated ecology of our planet, mountain environments are essential to the survival of the global ecosystem.

Mountain ecosystems are, however, rapidly changing. They are susceptible to accelerated soil erosion, landslides and rapid loss of habitat and genetic diversity. On the human side, there is widespread poverty among mountain inhabitants and loss of indigenous knowledge. As a result, most global mountain areas are experiencing environmental degradation. Hence, the proper management of mountain resources and socio-economic development of the people deserves immediate action. About 10 per cent of the world's population depends on mountain resources. A much larger percentage draws on other mountain resources, including and especially water. Mountains are a storehouse of biological diversity and endangered species.

Mountains are highly vulnerable to human and natural ecological imbalance. Mountains are the areas most sensitive to all climatic changes in the atmosphere. Specific information on ecology, natural resource potential and socio-economic activities is essential.

Mountain and hillside areas hold a rich variety of ecological systems. Because of their vertical dimensions, mountains create gradients of temperature, precipitation and insolation. A given mountain slope may include several climatic systems - such as tropical, subtropical, temperate and alpine - each of which represents a microcosm of a larger habitat diversity. There is, however, a lack of knowledge of mountain ecosystems. The creation of a global mountain database is therefore vital for launching programmes that contribute to the sustainable development of mountain ecosystems.

Coordinate regional and international cooperation and facilitate an exchange of information and experience among the specialized agencies, the World Bank, IFAD and other international and regional organizations, national Governments, research institutions and non-governmental organizations working on mountain development to encourage regional, national and international networking of people's initiatives and the activities of international, regional and local non-governmental organizations working on mountain development, such as the United Nations University (UNU), the Woodland Mountain Institutes (WMI), the International Center for Integrated Mountain Development (ICIMOD), the International Mountain Society (IMS), the African Mountain Association and the Andean Mountain Association, besides supporting those organizations in exchange of information and experience.

There are serious problems of ecological deterioration in these watershed areas. For example, in the hillside areas of the Andean countries of South America a large portion of the farming population is now faced with a rapid deterioration of land resources. Similarly, the mountain and upland areas of the Himalayas, South-East Asia and East and Central Africa, which make vital contributions to agricultural production, are threatened by cultivation of marginal lands due to expanding population. In many areas this is accompanied by excessive livestock grazing, deforestation and loss of biomass cover. Soil erosion can have a devastating impact on the vast numbers of rural people who depend on rainfed agriculture in the mountain and hillside areas. Poverty, unemployment, poor health and bad sanitation are widespread.

Promoting integrated watershed development programmes through effective participation of local people is a key to preventing further ecological imbalance. An integrated approach is needed for conserving, upgrading and using the natural resource base of land, water, plant, animal and human resources. In addition, promoting alternative livelihood opportunities, particularly through development of employment schemes that increase the productive base, will have a significant role in improving the standard of living among the large rural population living in mountain ecosystems.

Following are the objectives of this watershed development programme area are:

— By the year 2000, to develop appropriate land-use planning and management for both arable and non-arable land in mountain-fed watershed areas to prevent soil erosion, increase biomass production and maintain the ecological balance;

— To promote income-generating activities, such as sustainable tourism, fisheries and environmentally sound mining, and to improve infrastructure and social services, in particular to protect the livelihoods of local communities and indigenous people;

— To develop technical and institutional arrangements for affected countries to mitigate the effects of natural disasters through hazard-prevention measures, risk zoning, early-warning systems, evacuation plans and emergency supplies.

Sustainable Agriculture Development

Major adjustments are needed in agricultural, environmental and macroeconomic policy, at both national and international levels, in developed as well as developing countries, to create the conditions for sustainable agriculture and rural development (SARD).

The major objective of SARD is to increase food production in a sustainable way and enhance food security. This will involve education initiatives, utilization of economic incentives and the development of appropriate and new technologies, thus ensuring stable supplies of nutritionally adequate food, access to those supplies by vulnerable groups, and production for markets; employment and income generation to alleviate poverty; and natural resource management and environmental protection.

The priority must be on maintaining and improving the capacity of the higher potential agricultural lands to support an expanding population. However, conserving and rehabilitating the natural resources on lower potential lands in order to maintain sustainable man/land ratios is also necessary. The main tools of SARD are policy and agrarian reform, participation, income diversification, land conservation and improved management of inputs. The success of SARD will depend largely on the support and participation of rural people, national Governments, the private sector and international cooperation, including technical and scientific cooperation.

All countries need to assess comprehensively the impacts of such policies on food and agriculture sector performance, food security, rural welfare and international trading relations as a means for identifying appropriate offsetting measures. The major thrust of food security in this case is to bring about a significant increase in agricultural production in a sustainable way and to achieve a substantial improvement in people's entitlement to adequate food and culturally appropriate food supplies.

United Nations agencies, such as FAO, the World Bank, IFAD and GATT, and regional organizations, bilateral donor agencies and other bodies should, within their respective mandates, assume a role in working with national Governments in the following activities:

— Implement integrated and sustainable agricultural development and food security strategies at the subregional level that use regional production and trade potentials, including organizations for regional economic integration, to promote food security;

— Encourage, in the context of achieving sustainable agricultural development and consistent with relevant internationally agreed principles on trade and environment, a more open and non-discriminatory trading system and the avoidance of unjustifiable trade barriers which together with other policies will facilitate the further integration of agricultural and environmental policies so as to make them mutually supportive;

— Strengthen and establish national, regional and international systems and networks to increase the understanding of the interaction between agriculture and the state of the environment, identify ecologically sound technologies and facilitate the exchange information on data sources, policies, and techniques and tools of analysis.

The greater the degree of community control over the resources on which it relies, the greater will be the incentive for economic and human resources development. At the same time, policy instruments to reconcile long-run and short-run requirements must be set by national Governments. The approaches focus on fostering self-reliance and cooperation, providing information and supporting user-based organizations.

Emphasis should be on management practices, building agreements for changes in resource utilization, the rights and duties associated with use of land, water and forests, the functioning of markets, prices, and the access to information, capital and inputs. This would require training and capacity-building to assume greater responsibilities in sustainable development efforts.

Agriculture needs to be intensified to meet future demands for commodities and to avoid further expansion onto marginal lands and encroachment on fragile ecosystems. Increased use of external inputs and development of specialized production and farming systems tend to increase vulnerability to environmental stresses and market fluctuations.

There is, therefore, a need to intensify agriculture by diversifying the production systems for maximum efficiency in the utilization of local resources, while minimizing environmental and economic risks. Where intensification of farming systems is not possible, other on-farm and off-farm employment opportunities should be identified and developed, such as cottage industries, wildlife utilization, aquaculture and fisheries, non-farm activities, such as light village-based manufacturing, farm commodity processing, agribusiness, recreation and tourism, etc.

International institutions, such as FAO and IFAD, international agricultural research centres, such as CGIAR, and regional centres should diagnose the world's major agro-ecosystems, their extension, ecological and socio-economic characteristics, their susceptibility to deterioration and their productive potential. This could form the basis for technology development and exchange and for regional research collaboration.

Poverty and malnutrition are already endemic in many regions. The destruction and degradation of agricultural and environmental resources is a major issue. Techniques for increasing production and conserving soil and water resources are already available but are not widely or systematically applied. A systematic approach is needed for identifying land uses and production systems that are sustainable in each land and climate zone, including the economic, social and institutional mechanisms necessary for their implementation.

Land Degradation

Land degradation is the most important environmental problem affecting extensive areas of land in both developed and developing countries. The problem of soil erosion is particularly acute in developing countries, while problems of salinization, waterlogging, soil pollution and loss of soil fertility are increasing in all countries. Land degradation is serious because the productivity of huge areas of land is declining just when populations are increasing rapidly and the demand on the land is growing to produce more food, fibre and fuel.

Efforts to control land degradation, particularly in developing countries, have had limited success to date. Well planned, long-term national and regional land conservation and rehabilitation programmes, with strong political support and adequate funding, are now needed. While land-use planning and land zoning, combined with better land management, should provide long-term solutions, it is urgent to arrest land degradation and launch conservation and rehabilitation programmes in the most critically affected and vulnerable areas.

Plant genetic resources for agriculture (PGRFA) are an essential resource to meet future needs for food. Threats to the security of these resources are growing, and efforts to conserve, develop and use genetic diversity are underfunded and understaffed. Many existing gene banks provide inadequate security and, in some instances, the loss of plant genetic diversity in gene banks is as great as it is in the field. The primary objective is to safeguard the world's genetic resources while preserving them to use sustainably. This includes the development of measures to facilitate the conservation and use of plant genetic resources, networks of in situ conservation areas and use of tools such as ex situ collections and germ plasma banks.

Special emphasis could be placed on the building of endogenous capacity for characterization, evaluation and utilization of PGRFA, particularly for the minor crops and other underutilized or non-utilized species of food and agriculture, including tree species for agro-forestry. Subsequent action could be aimed at consolidation and efficient management of networks of in situ conservation areas and use of tools such as ex situ collections and germ plasma banks. Major gaps and weaknesses exist in the capacity of existing national and international mechanisms to assess, study, monitor and use plant genetic resources to increase food production.

Existing institutional capacity, structures and programmes are generally inadequate and largely underfunded. There is genetic erosion of invaluable crop species. Existing diversity in crop species is not used to the extent possible for increased food production in a sustainable way. The objectives of this programme area are:

— To complete the first regeneration and safe duplication of existing ex situ collections on a world-wide basis as soon as possible;

— To collect and study plants useful for increasing food production through joint activities, including training, within the framework of networks of collaborating institutions;

— Not later than the year 2000, to adopt policies and strengthen or establish programmes for in situ on-farm and ex situ conservation and sustainable use of plant genetic resources for food and agriculture, integrated into strategies and programmes for sustainable agriculture;

— To take appropriate measures for the fair and equitable sharing of benefits and results of research and development in plant breeding between the sources and users of plant genetic resources.

The appropriate United Nations agencies and regional organizations should strengthen the Global System on the Conservation and Sustainable Use of PGRFA by, inter alia, accelerating the development of the Global Information and Early Warning System to facilitate the exchange of information; developing ways to promote the transfer of environmentally sound technologies, in particular to developing countries; and taking further steps to realize farmers' rights.

World food demand projections indicate an increase of 50 per cent by the year 2000 which will more than double again by 2050. Conservative estimates put preharvest and post-harvest losses caused by pests between 25 and 50 per cent. Pests affecting animal health also cause heavy losses and in many areas prevent livestock development. Chemical control of agricultural pests has dominated the scene, but its overuse has adverse effects on farm budgets, human health and the environment, as well as on international trade.

New pest problems continue to develop. Integrated pest management, which combines biological control, host plant resistance and appropriate farming practices and minimizes the use of pesticides, is the best option for the future, as it guarantees yields, reduces costs, is environmentally friendly and contributes to the sustainability of agriculture. Integrated pest management should go hand in hand with appropriate pesticide management to allow for pesticide regulation and control, including trade, and for the safe handling and disposal of pesticides, particularly those that are toxic and persistent.

Plant Nutreint Depletion

Plant nutrient depletion is a serious problem resulting in loss of soil fertility, particularly in developing countries. To maintain soil productivity, the FAO sustainable plant nutrition programmes could be helpful. In sub-Saharan Africa, nutrient output from all sources currently exceeds inputs by a factor of three or four, the net loss being estimated at some 10 million metric tons per year. As a result, more marginal lands and fragile natural ecosystems are put under agricultural use, thus creating further land degradation and other environmental problems.

The integrated plant nutrition approach aims at ensuring a sustainable supply of plant nutrients to increase future yields without harming the environment and soil productivity. In many developing countries, population growth rates exceed 3 per cent a year, and national agricultural production has fallen behind food demand. In these countries the goal should be to increase agricultural production by at least 4 per cent a year, without destroying the soil fertility. This will require increasing agricultural production in high-potential areas through efficiency in the use of inputs. Trained labour, energy supply, adapted tools and technologies, plant nutrients and soil enrichment will all be essential.

In rural areas of the developing countries, the chief sources of energy are fuelwood, crop residues and manure, together with animal and human energy. More intensive energy inputs are required for increased productivity of human labour and for income-generation. To this end, rural energy policies and technologies should promote a mix of cost-effective fossil and renewable energy sources that is itself sustainable and ensures sustainable agricultural development.

Rural areas provide energy supplies in the form of wood. The full potential of agriculture and agroforestry, as well as common property resources, as sources of renewable energy, is far from being realized. The attainment of sustainable rural development is intimately linked with energy demand and supply patterns.

Our planet's essential goods and services depend on the variety and variability of genes, species, populations and ecosystems. Biological resources feed and clothe us and provide housing, medicines and spiritual nourishment.

The natural ecosystems of forests, savannahs, pastures and rangelands, deserts, tundras, rivers, lakes and seas contain most of the Earth's biodiversity. Farmers' fields and gardens are also of great importance as repositories, while gene banks, botanical gardens, zoos and other germplasm repositories make a small but significant contribution. The current decline in biodiversity is largely the result of human activity and represents a serious threat to human development.

Biological resources constitute a capital asset with great potential for yielding sustainable benefits. Urgent and decisive action is needed to conserve and maintain genes, species and ecosystems, with a view to the sustainable management and use of biological resources. Capacities for the assessment, study and systematic observation and evaluation of biodiversity need to be reinforced at national and international levels. Effective national action and international cooperation is required for the in situ protection of ecosystems, for the ex situ conservation of biological and genetic resources and for the enhancement of ecosystem functions.

Biotechnology is the integration of the new techniques emerging from modern biotechnology with the well-established approaches of traditional biotechnology. Biotechnology, an emerging knowledge-intensive field, is a set of enabling techniques for bringing about specific man-made changes in deoxyribonucleic acid (DNA), or genetic material, in plants, animals and microbial systems, leading to useful products and technologies. By itself, biotechnology cannot resolve all the fundamental problems of environment and development, so expectations need to be tempered by realism.

Nevertheless, it promises to make a significant contribution in enabling the development of, for example, better health care, enhanced food security through sustainable agricultural practices, improved supplies of potable water, more efficient industrial development processes for transforming raw materials, support for sustainable methods of afforestation and reforestation, and detoxification of hazardous wastes.

Biotechnology also offers new opportunities for global partnerships, especially between the countries rich in biological resources but lacking the expertise and investments needed to apply such resources through biotechnology and the countries that have developed the technological expertise to transform biological resources so that they serve the needs of sustainable development. Biotechnology can assist in the conservation of those resources through, for example, ex situ techniques.

Most of the investment in modern biotechnology has been in the industrialized world. Significant new investments and human resource development will be required in biotechnology, especially in the developing world.

The improvement of human health is one of the most important objectives of development. The deterioration of environmental quality, notably air, water and soil pollution owing to toxic chemicals, hazardous wastes, radiation and other sources, is a matter of growing concern. This degradation of the environment resulting from inadequate or inappropriate development has a direct negative effect on human health.

Malnutrition, poverty, poor human settlements, lack of good-quality potable water and inadequate sanitation facilities add to the problems of communicable and non-communicable diseases. As a consequence, the health and well-being of people are exposed to increasing pressures.

Well-coordinated multidisciplinary efforts involving cooperation between scientists, financial institutions and industries will be required. At the global level, this may mean collaboration between research institutions in different countries, with funding at the intergovernmental level, possibly supported by similar collaboration at the national level.

Training and technology transfer is needed at the global level, with regions and countries having access to, and participation in exchange of, information and expertise, particularly indigenous or traditional knowledge and related biotechnology. It is essential to create or enhance endogenous capabilities in developing countries to enable them to participate actively in the processes of biotechnology production.

Environmental protection is an integral component of sustainable development. The environment is threatened in all its biotic and abiotic components: animals, plants, microbes and ecosystems comprising biological diversity; water, soil and air, which form the physical components of habitats and ecosystems; and all the interactions between the components of biodiversity and their sustaining habitats and ecosystems.

Biotechnology is one of many tools that can play an important role in supporting the rehabilitation of degraded ecosystems and landscapes. This may be done through the development of new techniques for reforestation and afforestation, germ plasm conservation, and cultivation of new plant varieties. Biotechnology can also contribute to the study of the effects exerted on the remaining organisms and on other organisms by organisms introduced into ecosystems.

Several fundamental principles could underlie many of these safety procedures, including primary consideration of the organism, building on the principle of familiarity, applied in a flexible framework, taking into account national requirements and recognizing that the logical progression is to start with a step-by-step and case-by-case approach, but also recognizing that experience has shown that in many instances a more comprehensive approach should be used, based on the experiences of the first period, leading, inter alia, to streamlining and categorizing; complementary consideration of risk assessment and risk management; and classification into contained use or release to the environment.

In developing countries, enabling factors such as training capacity, know-how, research and development facilities and funds, industrial building capacity, capital (including venture capital) protection of intellectual property rights, and expertise in areas including marketing research, technology assessment, socio-economic assessment and safety assessment are frequently inadequate.

Efforts will therefore need to be made to build up capacities in these and other areas and to match such efforts with appropriate levels of financial support. There is therefore a need to strengthen the endogenous capacities of developing countries by means of new international initiatives to support research in order to speed up the development and application of both new and conventional biotechnologies to serve the needs of sustainable development at the local, national and regional levels. National mechanisms to allow for informed comment by the public with regard to biotechnology research and application should be part of the process.

The activities are generally uncoordinated, however, involving many different organizations, priorities, constituencies, time-scales, funding sources and resource constraints. There is a need for a much more cohesive and coordinated approach to harness available resources in the most effective manner. As with most new technologies, research in biotechnology and the application of its findings could have significant positive and negative socio-economic as well as cultural impacts. These impacts should be carefully identified in the earliest phases of the development of biotechnology in order to enable appropriate management of the consequences of transferring biotechnology.

The marine environment - including the oceans and all seas and adjacent coastal areas - forms an integrated whole that is an essential component of the global life-support system and a positive asset that presents opportunities for sustainable development. The implementation by developing countries of the activities set forth below shall be commensurate with their individual technological and financial capacities and priorities in allocating resources for development needs and ultimately depends on the technology transfer and financial resources required and made available to them.

More than half the world's population lives within 60 km of the shoreline, and this could rise to three quarters by the year 2020. Many of the world's poor are crowded in coastal areas. Coastal resources are vital for many local communities and indigenous people. The exclusive economic zone (EEZ) is also an important marine area where the States manage the development and conservation of natural resources for the benefit of their people. For small island States or countries, these are the areas most available for development activities. Despite national, subregional, regional and global efforts, current approaches to the management of marine and coastal resources have not always proved capable of achieving sustainable development, and coastal resources and the coastal environment are being rapidly degraded and eroded in many parts of the world.

Coastal States, with the support of international organizations, upon request, should undertake measures to maintain biological diversity and productivity of marine species and habitats under national jurisdiction. Inter alia, these measures might include: surveys of marine biodiversity, inventories of endangered species and critical coastal and marine habitats; establishment and management of protected areas; and support of scientific research and dissemination of its results. Coastal States, where necessary, should improve their capacity to collect, analyse, assess and use information for sustainable use of resources, including environmental impacts of activities affecting the coastal and marine areas.

Coastal States should promote and facilitate the organization of education and training in integrated coastal and marine management and sustainable development for scientists, technologists, managers and users, leaders, indigenous peoples, fisherfolk, women and youth, among others.

Management and development, as well as environmental protection concerns and local planning issues, should be incorporated in educational curricula and public awareness campaigns, with due regard to traditional ecological knowledge and socio-cultural values. International organizations, whether subregional, regional or global, as appropriate, should support coastal States, upon request, in the areas indicated above, devoting special attention to developing countries.

Degradation of the marine environment can result from a wide range of sources. Land-based sources contribute 70 per cent of marine pollution, while maritime transport and dumping-at-sea activities contribute 10 per cent each. The contaminants that pose the greatest threat to the marine environment are, in variable order of importance and depending on differing national or regional situations, sewage, nutrients, synthetic organic compounds, sediments, litter and plastics, metals, radionuclides, oil/hydrocarbons and polycyclic aromatic hydrocarbons (PAHs).

Many of the polluting substances originating from land-based sources are of particular concern to the marine environment since they exhibit at the same time toxicity, persistence and bioaccumulation in the food chain. There is currently no global scheme to address marine pollution from land-based sources. Degradation of the marine environment can also result from a wide range of activities on land. Human settlements, land use, construction of coastal infrastructure, agriculture, forestry, urban development, tourism and industry can affect the marine environment.

Marine pollution is also caused by shipping and sea-based activities. Approximately 600,000 tons of oil enter the oceans each year as a result of normal shipping operations, accidents and illegal discharges. With respect to offshore oil and gas activities, currently machinery space discharges are regulated internationally and six regional conventions to control platform discharges have been under consideration. The nature and extent of environmental impacts from offshore oil exploration and production activities generally account for a very small proportion of marine pollution.

A precautionary and anticipatory rather than a reactive approach is necessary to prevent the degradation of the marine environment. This requires, inter alia, the adoption of precautionary measures, environmental impact assessments, clean production techniques, recycling, waste audits and minimization, construction and/or improvement of sewage treatment facilities, quality management criteria for the proper handling of hazardous substances, and a comprehensive approach to damaging impacts from air, land and water.

National planning and coordinating bodies should be given the capacity and authority to review all land-based activities and sources of pollution for their impacts on the marine environment and to propose appropriate control measures. An international funding mechanism should be created for the application of appropriate sewage treatment technologies and building sewage treatment facilities, including grants or concessional loans from international agencies and appropriate regional funds, replenished at least in part on a revolving basis by user fees.

The provisions of the United Nations Convention on the Law of the Sea on the marine living resources of the high seas sets forth rights and obligations of States with respect to conservation and utilization of those resources. There are problems of unregulated fishing, overcapitalization, excessive fleet size, vessel reflagging to escape controls, insufficiently selective gear, unreliable databases and lack of sufficient cooperation between States. Action by States whose nationals and vessels fish on the high seas, as well as cooperation at the bilateral, subregional, regional and global levels, is essential particularly for highly migratory species and straddling stocks. Such action and cooperation should address inadequacies in fishing practices, as well as in biological knowledge, fisheries statistics and improvement of systems for handling data.

Marine fisheries yield 80 to 90 million tons of fish and shellfish per year, 95 per cent of which is taken from waters under national jurisdiction. Yields have increased nearly fivefold over the past four decades.

The provisions of the United Nations Convention on the Law of the Sea on marine living resources of the exclusive economic zone and other areas under national jurisdiction set forth rights and obligations of States with respect to conservation and utilization of those resources. Marine living resources provide an important source of protein in many countries and their use is often of major importance to local communities and indigenous people. Such resources provide food and livelihoods to millions of people and, if sustainably utilized, offer increased potential to meet nutritional and social needs, particularly in developing countries.

To realize this potential requires improved knowledge and identification of marine living resource stocks, particularly of underutilized and unutilized stocks and species, use of new technologies, better handling and processing facilities to avoid wastage, and improved quality and training of skilled personnel to manage and conserve effectively the marine living resources of the exclusive economic zone and other areas under national jurisdiction.

Fisheries in many areas under national jurisdiction face mounting problems, including local overfishing, unauthorized incursions by foreign fleets, ecosystem degradation, overcapitalization and excessive fleet sizes, underevaluation of catch, insufficiently selective gear, unreliable databases, and increasing competition between artisanal and large-scale fishing, and between fishing and other types of activities.

Coral reefs and other marine and coastal habitats, such as mangroves and estuaries, are among the most highly diverse, integrated and productive of the Earth's ecosystems. They often serve important ecological functions, provide coastal protection, and are critical resources for food, energy, tourism and economic development. In many parts of the world, such marine and coastal systems are under stress or are threatened from a variety of sources, both human and natural.

The marine environment is vulnerable and sensitive to climate and atmospheric changes. Rational use and development of coastal areas, all seas and marine resources, as well as conservation of the marine environment, requires the ability to determine the present state of these systems and to predict future conditions. The high degree of uncertainty in present information inhibits effective management and limits the ability to make predictions and assess environmental change.

Systematic collection of data on marine environmental parameters will be needed to apply integrated management approaches and to predict effects of global climate change and of atmospheric phenomena, such as ozone depletion, on living marine resources and the marine environment.

In order to determine the role of the oceans and all seas in driving global systems and to predict natural and human-induced changes in marine and coastal environments, the mechanisms to collect, synthesize and disseminate information from research and systematic observation activities need to be restructured and reinforced considerably. There are many uncertainties about climate change and particularly about sealevel rise. Small increases in sealevel have the potential of causing significant damage to small islands and low-lying coasts. Response strategies should be based on sound data.

Increased ultraviolet radiation derived from ozone depletion has been reported in some areas of the world. An assessment of its effects in the marine environment is needed to reduce uncertainty and to provide a basis for action. States, in accordance with provisions of the United Nations Convention on the Law of the Sea on marine scientific research, commit themselves to improve the understanding of the marine environment and its role on global processes.

UN General Assembly should provide for regular consideration, within the United Nations system, at the intergovernmental level of general marine and coastal issues, including environment and development matters, and should request the Secretary-General and executive heads of United Nations agencies and organizations to:

— Strengthen coordination and develop improved arrangements among the relevant United Nations organizations with major marine and coastal responsibilities, including their subregional and regional components;

— Strengthen coordination between those organizations and other United Nations organizations, institutions and specialized agencies dealing with development, trade and other related economic issues, as appropriate;

— Improve representation of United Nations agencies dealing with the marine environment in United Nations system-wide coordination efforts;

— Promote, where necessary, greater collaboration between the United Nations agencies and subregional and regional coastal and marine programmes;

— Develop a centralized system to provide for information on legislation and advice on implementation of legal agreements on marine environmental and development issues.

Environmental measures addressing international environmental problems should, as far as possible, be based on an international consensus. Domestic measures targeted to achieve certain environmental objectives may need trade measures to render them effective. Should trade policy measures be found necessary for the enforcement of environmental policies, certain principles and rules should apply.

These could include, inter alia, the principle of non-discrimination; the principle that the trade measure chosen should be the least trade-restrictive necessary to achieve the objectives; an obligation to ensure transparency in the use of trade measures related to the environment and to provide adequate notification of national regulations; and the need to give consideration to the special conditions and development requirements of developing countries as they move towards internationally agreed environmental objectives.

Small island developing States have all the environmental problems and challenges of the coastal zone concentrated in a limited land area. They are considered extremely vulnerable to global warming and sealevel rise, with certain small low-lying islands facing the increasing threat of the loss of their entire national territories.

Most tropical islands are also now experiencing the more immediate impacts of increasing frequency of cyclones, storms and hurricanes associated with climate change. These are causing major set-backs to their socio-economic development. Because small island development options are limited, there are special challenges to planning for and implementing sustainable development. Small island developing States will be constrained in meeting these challenges without the cooperation and assistance of the international community.

Small island developing States, with the support, as appropriate, of international organizations, whether subregional, regional or global, should develop and strengthen inter-island, regional and interregional cooperation and information exchange, including periodic regional and global meetings on sustainable development of small island developing States with the first global conference on the sustainable development of small island developing States, to be held in 1993.

Since populations of small island developing States cannot maintain all necessary specializations, training for integrated coastal management and development should aim to produce cadres of managers or scientists, engineers and coastal planners able to integrate the many factors that need to be considered in integrated coastal management. Resource users should be prepared to execute both management and protection functions and to apply the polluter pays principle and support the training of their personnel. Educational systems should be modified to meet these needs and special training programmes developed in integrated island management and development. The total capacity of small island developing States will always be limited. Existing capacity must therefore be restructured to meet efficiently the immediate needs for sustainable development and integrated management.

At the same time, adequate and appropriate assistance from the international community must be directed at strengthening the full range of human resources needed on a continuous basis to implement sustainable development plans. New technologies that can increase the output and range of capability of the limited human resources should be employed to increase the capacity of very small populations to meet their needs. The development and application of traditional knowledge to improve the capacity of countries to implement sustainable development should be fostered.

Fresh Water Resources

Freshwater resources are an essential component of the Earth's hydrosphere and an indispensable part of all terrestrial ecosystems. The freshwater environment is characterized by the hydrological cycle, including floods and droughts, which in some regions have become more extreme and dramatic in their consequences. Global climate change and atmospheric pollution could also have an impact on freshwater resources and their availability and, through sea-level rise, threaten low-lying coastal areas and small island ecosystems. Water is needed in all aspects of life.

The general objective is to make certain that adequate supplies of water of good quality are maintained for the entire population of this planet, while preserving the hydrological, biological and chemical functions of ecosystems, adapting human activities within the capacity limits of nature and combating vectors of water-related diseases.

Innovative technologies, including the improvement of indigenous technologies, are needed to fully utilize limited water resources and to safeguard those resources against pollution. The widespread scarcity, gradual destruction and aggravated pollution of freshwater resources in many world regions, along with the progressive encroachment of incompatible activities, demand integrated water resources planning and management. Such integration must cover all types of interrelated freshwater bodies, including both surface water and groundwater, and duly consider water quantity and quality aspects.

The multisectoral nature of water resources development in the context of socio-economic development must be recognized, as well as the multi-interest utilization of water resources for water supply and sanitation, agriculture, industry, urban development, hydropower generation, inland fisheries, transportation, recreation, low and flat lands management and other activities.

Rational water utilization schemes for the development of surface and underground water-supply sources and other potential sources have to be supported by concurrent water conservation and wastage minimization measures. Priority, however, must be accorded to flood prevention and control measures, as well as sedimentation control, where required. Transboundary water resources and their use are of great importance to riparian States. In this connection, cooperation among those States may be desirable in conformity with existing agreements and/or other relevant arrangements, taking into account the interests of all riparian States concerned.

Water demands are increasing rapidly, with 70-80 per cent required for irrigation, less than 20 per cent for industry and a mere 6 per cent for domestic consumption. The holistic management of freshwater as a finite and vulnerable resource, and the integration of sectoral water plans and programmes within the framework of national economic and social policy, are of paramount importance for action in the 1990s and beyond. The fragmentation of responsibilities for water resources development among sectoral agencies is proving, however, to be an even greater impediment to promoting integrated water management than had been anticipated.

Integrated water resources management is based on the perception of water as an integral part of the ecosystem, a natural resource and a social and economic good, whose quantity and quality determine the nature of its utilization. To this end, water resources have to be protected, taking into account the functioning of aquatic ecosystems and the perenniality of the resource, in order to satisfy and reconcile needs for water in human activities.

In developing and using water resources, priority has to be given to the satisfaction of basic needs and the safeguarding of ecosystems. Beyond these requirements, however, water users should be charged appropriately. Integrated water resources management, including the integration of land- and water-related aspects, should be carried out at the level of the catchment basin or sub-basin.

Water resources development and management should be planned in an integrated manner, taking into account long-term planning needs as well as those with narrower horizons, that is to say, they should incorporate environmental, economic and social considerations based on the principle of sustainability; include the requirements of all users as well as those relating to the prevention and mitigation of water-related hazards; and constitute an integral part of the socio-economic development planning process.

Planning considerations should reflect benefits investment, environmental protection and operation costs, as well as the opportunity costs reflecting the most valuable alternative use of water. Actual charging need not necessarily burden all beneficiaries with the consequences of those considerations. The role of water as a social, economic and life-sustaining good should be reflected in demand management mechanisms and implemented through water conservation and reuse, resource assessment and financial instruments.

The delegation of water resources management to the lowest appropriate level necessitates educating and training water management staff at all levels and ensuring that women participate equally in the education and training programmes. Particular emphasis has to be placed on the introduction of public participatory techniques, including enhancement of the role of women, youth, indigenous people and local communities.

Skills related to various water management functions have to be developed by municipal government and water authorities, as well as in the private sector, local/national non-governmental organizations, cooperatives, corporations and other water-user groups. Education of the public regarding the importance of water and its proper management is also needed.

Although water is managed at various levels in the socio-political system, demand-driven management requires the development of water-related institutions at appropriate levels, taking into account the need for integration with land-use management. In creating the enabling environment for lowest-appropriate-level management, the role of Government includes mobilization of financial and human resources, legislation, standard-setting and other regulatory functions, monitoring and assessment of the use of water and land resources, and creating of opportunities for public participation.

International agencies and donors have an important role to play in providing support to developing countries in creating the required enabling environment for integrated water resources management. This should include, as appropriate, donor support to local levels in developing countries, including community-based institutions, non-governmental organizations and women's groups. Water resources assessment, including the identification of potential sources of freshwater supply, comprises the continuing determination of sources, extent, dependability and quality of water resources and of the human activities that affect those resources.

Major impediments are the lack of financial resources for water resources assessment, the fragmented nature of hydrologic services and the insufficient numbers of qualified staff. At the same time, the advancing technology for data capture and management is increasingly difficult to access for developing countries. Water resources assessment necessitates the strengthening of existing systems for technology transfer, adaptation and diffusion, and the development of new technology for use under field conditions, as well as the development of endogenous capacity.

Water resources assessment requires the establishment and maintenance of a body of well-trained and motivated staff sufficient in number to undertake the above activities. Education and training programmes designed to ensure an adequate supply of these trained personnel should be established or strengthened at the local, national, subregional or regional level. In addition, the provision of attractive terms of employment and career paths for professional and technical staff should be encouraged.

Human resource needs should be monitored periodically, including all levels of employment. Plans have to be established to meet those needs through education and training opportunities and international programmes of courses and conferences. Because well-trained people are particularly important to water resources assessment and hydrologic forecasting, personnel matters should receive special attention in this area. The aim should be to attract and retain personnel to work on water resources assessment who are sufficient in number and adequate in their level of education to ensure the effective implementation of the activities that are planned.

Freshwater is a unitary resource. Long-term development of global freshwater requires holistic management of resources and a recognition of the interconnectedness of the elements related to freshwater and freshwater quality. There are few regions of the world that are still exempt from problems of loss of potential sources of freshwater supply, degraded water quality and pollution of surface and groundwater sources. Major problems affecting the water quality of rivers and lakes arise, in variable order of importance according to different situations, from inadequately treated domestic sewage, inadequate controls on the discharges of industrial waste waters, loss and destruction of catchment areas, ill-considered siting of industrial plants, deforestation, uncontrolled shifting cultivation and poor agricultural practices. This gives rise to the leaching of nutrients and pesticides.

Aquatic ecosystems are disturbed and living freshwater resources are threatened. Under certain circumstances, aquatic ecosystems are also affected by agricultural water resource development projects such as dams, river diversions, water installations and irrigation schemes. Erosion, sedimentation, deforestation and desertification have led to increased land degradation, and the creation of reservoirs has, in some cases, resulted in adverse effects on ecosystems. Many of these problems have arisen from a development model that is environmentally destructive and from a lack of public awareness and education about surface and groundwater resource protection.

Ecological and human health effects are the measurable consequences, although the means to monitor them are inadequate or non-existent in many countries. There is a widespread lack of perception of the linkages between the development, management, use and treatment of water resources and aquatic ecosystems. A preventive approach, where appropriate, is crucial to the avoiding of costly subsequent measures to rehabilitate, treat and develop new water supplies.

Safe water-supplies and environmental sanitation are vital for protecting the environment, improving health and alleviating poverty. Safe water is also crucial to many traditional and cultural activities. An estimated 80 per cent of all diseases and over one third of deaths in developing countries are caused by the consumption of contaminated water, and on average as much as one tenth of each person's productive time is sacrificed to water-related diseases. Concerted efforts during the 1980s brought water and sanitation services to hundreds of millions of the world's poorest people. The most outstanding of these efforts was the launching in 1981 of the International Drinking Water Supply and Sanitation Decade, which resulted from the Mar del Plata Action Plan adopted by the United Nations Water Conference in 1977.

The implementation of water-supply and sanitation programmes is a national responsibility. To varying degrees, responsibility for the implementation of projects and the operating of systems should be delegated to all administrative levels down to the community and individual served. This also means that national authorities, together with the agencies and bodies of the United Nations system and other external support agencies providing support to national programmes, should develop mechanisms and procedures to collaborate at all levels.

This is particularly important if full advantage is to be taken of community-based approaches and self-reliance as tools for sustainability. This will entail a high degree of community participation, involving women, in the conception, planning, decision-making, implementation and evaluation connected with projects for domestic water-supply and sanitation. Overall national capacity-building at all administrative levels, involving institutional development, coordination, human resources, community participation, health and hygiene education and literacy, has to be developed according to its fundamental connection both with any efforts to improve health and socio-economic development through water-supply and sanitation and with their impact on the human environment.

Capacity-building should therefore be one of the underlying keys in implementation strategies. Institutional capacity-building should be considered to have an importance equal to that of the sector supplies and equipment component so that funds can be directed to both. This can be undertaken at the planning or programme/project formulation stage, accompanied by a clear definition of objectives and targets.

Scarcity of freshwater resources and the escalating costs of developing new resources have a considerable impact on national industrial, agricultural and human settlement development and economic growth. Better management of urban water resources, including the elimination of unsustainable consumption patterns, can make a substantial contribution to the alleviation of poverty and improvement of the health and quality of life of the urban and rural poor.

A high proportion of large urban agglomerations are located around estuaries and in coastal zones. Such an arrangement leads to pollution from municipal and industrial discharges combined with overexploitation of available water resources and threatens the marine environment and the supply of freshwater resources.

Sustainability of food production

Sustainability of food production increasingly depends on sound and efficient water use and conservation practices consisting primarily of irrigation development and management, including water management with respect to rain-fed areas, livestock water-supply, inland fisheries and agro-forestry. Achieving food security is a high priority in many countries, and agriculture must not only provide food for rising populations, but also save water for other uses. The challenge is to develop and apply water-saving technology and management methods and, through capacity-building, enable communities to introduce institutions and incentives for the rural population to adopt new approaches, for both rain-fed and irrigated agriculture.

The rural population must also have better access to a potable water-supply and to sanitation services. It is an immense task but not an impossible one, provided appropriate policies and programmes are adopted at all levels - local, national and international. While significant expansion of the area under rain-fed agriculture has been achieved during the past decade, the productivity response and sustainability of irrigation systems have been constrained by problems of waterlogging and salinization. Financial and market constraints are also a common problem.

Soil erosion, mismanagement and overexploitation of natural resources and acute competition for water have all influenced the extent of poverty, hunger and famine in the developing countries. Soil erosion caused by overgrazing of livestock is also often responsible for the siltation of lakes. Most often, the development of irrigation schemes is supported neither by environmental impact assessments identifying hydrologic consequences within watersheds of interbasin transfers, nor by the assessment of social impacts on peoples in river valleys.

The non-availability of water-supplies of suitable quality is a significant limiting factor to livestock production in many countries, and improper disposal of animal wastes can in certain circumstances result in pollution of water-supplies for both humans and animals. The drinking-water requirements of livestock vary according to species and the environment in which they are kept. It is estimated that the current global livestock drinking-water requirement is about 60 billion litres per day and based on livestock population growth estimates, this daily requirement is predicted to increase by 0.4 billion litres per annum in the foreseeable future.

Fisheries of inland waters should be so managed as to maximize the yield of aquatic food organisms in an environmentally sound manner. This requires the conservation of water-quality and quantity, as well as of the functional morphology of the aquatic environment. On the other hand, fishing and aquaculture may themselves damage the aquatic ecosystem; hence their development should conform to guidelines for impact limitation.

An International Action Programme on Water and Sustainable Agricultural Development (IAP-WASAD) has been initiated by FAO in cooperation with other international organizations.

The main objective of the Action Programme is to assist developing countries in planning, developing and managing water resources on an integrated basis to meet present and future needs for agricultural production, taking into account environmental considerations. The Action Programme has developed a framework for sustainable water use in the agricultural sector and identified priority areas for action at national, regional and global levels.

Quantitative targets for new irrigation development, improvement of existing irrigation schemes and reclamation of waterlogged and salinized lands through drainage for 130 developing countries are estimated on the basis of food requirements, agro-climatic zones and availability of water and land. FAO global projections for irrigation, drainage and small-scale water programmes by the year 2000 for 130 developing countries are as follows:

(a) 15.2 million hectares of new irrigation development;

(b) 12 million hectares of improvement/modernization of existing schemes;

(c) 7 million hectares installed with drainage and water control facilities; and

(d) 10 million hectares of small-scale water programmes and conservation.

The development of new irrigation areas at the above-mentioned level may give rise to environmental concerns in so far as it implies the destruction of wetlands, water pollution, increased sedimentation and a reduction in biodiversity. Therefore, new irrigation schemes should be accompanied by an environmental impact assessment, depending upon the scale of the scheme, in case significant negative environmental impacts are expected. When considering proposals for new irrigation schemes, consideration should also be given to a more rational exploitation, and an increase in the efficiency or productivity, of any existing schemes capable of serving the same localities.

Technologies for new irrigation schemes should be thoroughly evaluated, including their potential conflicts with other land uses. The active involvement of water-users groups is a supporting objective. It should be ensured that rural communities of all countries, according to their capacities and available resources and taking advantage of international cooperation as appropriate, will have access to safe water in sufficient quantities and adequate sanitation to meet their health needs and maintain the essential qualities of their local environments.

The Ministerial Declaration of the Second World Climate Conference states that "the potential impact of such climate change could pose an environmental threat of an up to now unknown magnitude ... and could even threaten survival in some small island States and in low-lying coastal, arid and semi-arid areas". The Conference recognized that among the most important impacts of climate change were its effects on the hydrologic cycle and on water management systems and, through these, on socio-economic systems. Increase in incidence of extremes, such as floods and droughts, would cause increased frequency and severity of disasters. The Conference therefore called for a strengthening of the necessary research and monitoring programmes and the exchange of relevant data and information, these actions to be undertaken at the national, regional and international levels.

Following objectives, consistent with the United Nations Framework Convention on Climate Change:

— To understand and quantify the threat of the impact of climate change on freshwater resources;

— To facilitate the implementation of effective national countermeasures, as and when the threatening impact is seen as sufficiently confirmed to justify such action;

— To study the potential impacts of climate change on areas prone to droughts and floods.

The Conference secretariat has estimated the average total annual cost of implementing the activities of this programme to be about $100 million, including about $40 million from the international community on grant or concessional terms. These are indicative and order-of-magnitude estimates only and have not been reviewed by Governments. Actual costs and financial terms, including any that are non-concessional, will depend upon, inter alia, the specific strategies and programmes Governments decide upon for implementation.

The development and implementation of response strategies requires innovative use of technological means and engineering solutions, including the installation of flood and drought warning systems and the construction of new water resource development projects such as dams, aqueducts, well fields, waste-water treatment plants, desalination works, levees, banks and drainage channels.

Substantial Use of Chemicals

A substantial use of chemicals is essential to meet the social and economic goals of the world community and today's best practice demonstrates that they can be used widely in a cost-effective manner and with a high degree of safety. However, a great deal remains to be done to ensure the environmentally sound management of toxic chemicals, within the principles of sustainable development and improved quality of life for humankind.

Two of the major problems, particularly in developing countries, are

(a) lack of sufficient scientific information for the assessment of risks entailed by the use of a great number of chemicals, and

(b) lack of resources for assessment of chemicals for which data are at hand.

Gross chemical contamination, with grave damage to human health, genetic structures and reproductive outcomes, and the environment, has in recent times been continuing within some of the world's most important industrial areas. Restoration will require major investment and development of new techniques. The long-range effects of pollution, extending even to the fundamental chemical and physical processes of the Earth's atmosphere and climate, are becoming understood only recently and the importance of those effects is becoming recognized only recently as well. A considerable number of international bodies are involved in work on chemical safety.

In many countries work programmes for the promotion of chemical safety are in place. Such work has international implications, as chemical risks do not respect national boundaries. However, a significant strengthening of both national and international efforts is needed to achieve an environmentally sound management of chemicals. Collaboration on chemical safety between the United Nations Environment Programme (UNEP), the International Labour Organisation (ILO) and the World Health Organization (WHO) in the International Programme on Chemical Safety (IPCS) should be the nucleus for international cooperation on environmentally sound management of toxic chemicals. All efforts should be made to strengthen this programme. Cooperation with other programmes, such as those of the Organisation for Economic Cooperation and Development (OECD) and the European Communities (EC) and other regional and governmental chemical programmes, should be promoted.

Globally harmonized hazard classification and labelling systems are not yet available to promote the safe use of chemicals, inter alia, at the workplace or in the home. Classification of chemicals can be made for different purposes and is a particularly important tool in establishing labelling systems. There is a need to develop harmonized hazard classification and labelling systems, building on ongoing work.

Establishment of pollution prevention procedures and setting standards for chemicals in each environmental medium, including food and water, and in consumer goods, constitute another example of risk reduction. In a wider context, risk reduction involves broad-based approaches to reducing the risks of toxic chemicals, taking into account the entire life cycle of the chemicals.

Such approaches could encompass both regulatory and non-regulatory measures, such as promotion of the use of cleaner products and technologies, pollution prevention procedures and programmes, emission inventories, product labelling, use limitations, economic incentives, procedures for safe handling and exposure regulations, and the phasing out or banning of chemicals that pose unreasonable and otherwise unmanageable risks to human health and the environment and of those that are toxic, persistent and bio-accumulative and whose use cannot be adequately controlled.

In the agricultural area, integrated pest management, including the use of biological control agents as alternatives to toxic pesticides, is one approach to risk reduction. The OECD Council has decided that OECD member countries should establish or strengthen national risk reduction programmes. The International Council of Chemical Associations (ICCA) has introduced initiatives regarding responsible care and product stewardship aimed at reduction of chemical risks. The Awareness and Preparedness for Emergencies at Local Level (APELL) programme of UNEP is designed to assist decision makers and technical personnel in improving community awareness of hazardous installations and in preparing response plans.

The objective of the programme area is to eliminate unacceptable or unreasonable risks and, to the extent economically feasible, to reduce risks posed by toxic chemicals, by employing a broad-based approach involving a wide range of risk reduction options and by taking precautionary measures derived from a broad-based life-cycle analysis.

Many countries lack national systems to cope with chemical risks. Most countries lack scientific means of collecting evidence of misuse and of judging the impact of toxic chemicals on the environment, because of the difficulties involved in the detection of many problematic chemicals and systematically tracking their flow. Significant new uses are among the potential hazards to human health and the environment in developing countries.

In several countries with systems in place there is an urgent need to make those systems more efficient. Basic elements for sound management of chemicals are:

(a) adequate legislation,

(b) information gathering and dissemination,

(c) capacity for risk assessment and interpretation,

(d) establishment of risk management policy,

(e) capacity for implementation and enforcement,

(f) capacity for rehabilitation of contaminated sites and poisoned persons,

(g) effective education programmes and

(h) capacity to respond to emergencies.

There is currently no global international agreement on traffic in toxic and dangerous products. However, there is international concern that illegal international traffic in these products is detrimental to public health and the environment, particularly in developing countries, as acknowledged by the General Assembly in resolutions 42/183 and 44/226. Illegal traffic refers to traffic that is carried out in contravention of a country's laws or relevant international legal instruments. The concern also relates to transboundary movements of those products that are not carried out in accordance with applicable internationally adopted guidelines and principles.

Effective control of the generation, storage, treatment, recycling and reuse, transport, recovery and disposal of hazardous wastes is of paramount importance for proper health, environmental protection and natural resource management, and sustainable development. This will require the active cooperation and participation of the international community, Governments and industry.

The prevention of illegal traffic in hazardous wastes will benefit the environment and public health in all countries, particularly developing countries. It will also help to make the Basel Convention and regional international instruments, such as the Bamako Convention and the fourth Lom Convention, more effective by promoting compliance with the controls established in those agreements. Article IX of the Basel Convention specifically addresses the issue of illegal shipments of hazardous wastes. Illegal traffic of hazardous wastes may cause serious threats to human health and the environment and impose a special and abnormal burden on the countries that receive such shipments.

Environmentally sound waste management must go beyond the mere safe disposal or recovery of wastes that are generated and seek to address the root cause of the problem by attempting to change unsustainable patterns of production and consumption. This implies the application of the integrated life cycle management concept, which presents a unique opportunity to reconcile development with environmental protection.

The exhaustion of traditional disposal sites, stricter environmental controls governing waste disposal and increasing quantities of more persistent wastes, particularly in industrialized countries, have all contributed to a rapid increase in the cost of waste disposal services. Costs could double or triple by the end of the decade.

Some current disposal practices pose a threat to the environment. As the economics of waste disposal services change, waste recycling and resource recovery are becoming increasingly cost-effective. Future waste management programmes should take maximum advantage of resource-efficient approaches to the control of wastes.

Safe waste disposal programmes are relevant to both developed and developing countries. In developed countries the focus is on improving facilities to meet higher environmental quality criteria, while in developing countries considerable investment is required to build new treatment facilities.

Radioactive Wastes

Radioactive wastes are generated in the nuclear fuel cycle as well as in nuclear applications. The radiological and safety risk from radioactive wastes varies from very low in short-lived, low-level wastes up to very large for high-level wastes. Annually about 200,000 m3 of low-level and intermediate-level waste and 10,000 m3 of high-level waste is generated world wide from nuclear power production. These volumes are increasing as more nuclear power units are taken into operation, nuclear facilities are decommissioned and the use of radionuclides increases.

The high-level waste contains about 99 per cent of the radionuclides and thus represents the largest radiological risk. The waste volumes from nuclear applications are generally much smaller, typically some tens of cubic metres or less per year and country. However, the activity concentration, especially in sealed radiation sources, might be high, thus justifying very stringent radiological protection measures.

The safe and environmentally sound management of radioactive wastes, including their minimization, transportation and disposal, is important, given their characteristics. In most countries with a substantial nuclear power programme, technical and administrative measures have been taken to implement a waste management system.

APPENDIX: PROTECTION OF THE ATMOSPHERE: REPORT OF THE UN SECRETARY-GENERAL

Introduction

1. The purpose of the present report is to provide a succinct summary of factual material relating to the protection of the atmosphere. The summary is based primarily on the in-depth review of the ninth session of the Commission on Sustainable Development, supplemented by more recent material that has come available from the work of the Intergovernmental Panel on Climate Change (IPCC) established by the

United Nations Environment Programme (UNEP) and the World Meteorological Organization (WMO). There have been several distinct tendencies in atmospheric conditions during the decade of the 1990s and since the United Nations Conference on Environment and Development held at Rio that have continued from previous decades.

I. Global atmospheric trends

2. The Earth's climate has been relatively stable since the last ice age, with global temperature changes of less than 1° Celsius over a century during the past 10,000 years. During this time, modern society has evolved and, in most cases, successfully adapted to the prevailing local climate and its natural variability. However, the Earth's climate is now changing. The Earth's surface temperature during the twentieth century was clearly warmer than during any other century for the last thousand years, that is to say, the climate of the twentieth century was clearly atypical. According to IPCC, the Earth's atmosphere near the surface warmed overall by between 0.4° and 0.8° C over the past 100 years, with air over land areas warming more than the ocean surface, and with the last two decades of the twentieth century being the hottest in that century. Recent research by WMO shows that the 10 warmest years have all occurred since 1983, with of these having occurred since 1990. As a new century begins, the global mean temperature is 0.6° C above the estimate for the start of the twentieth century. The year 2000 continued the run of warm years in spite of the persistent cooling influence of the tropical Pacific La Niña event and

was the twenty-second consecutive year with the global mean surface air temperature above the 1961-1990 normal.

3. In addition to the direct evidence from temperature records of global-scale warming of the atmosphere near the Earth's surface, there is substantiation from increasing sea level (owing partly at least to thermal expansion), the retreat of many of the world's glaciers, and the thinning of Arctic sea ice.

4. Increases in temperature will change the distribution of vectors for malaria and other tropical diseases, and adversely influence agricultural patterns in already vulnerable parts of the world. Rises in sea level will place low-lying countries at risk for severe flooding, cholera and other waterborne diseases. In addition, extreme weather events are expected to increase in frequency and/or severity, and have important health impacts, with the burden falling disproportionately on the poor.

A. Global and regional precipitation

5. There is evidence that precipitation patterns are changing in systematic ways with large areas of the world's continents experiencing extended upward and downward trends. Precipitation increased by 0.5-1 per cent per decade in the twentieth century over most mid and high latitudes of the northern hemisphere continents and also over much of Australia and South America, except for the west coast of both continents. Rainfall decreased during the twentieth century over much of the tropical and subtropical land areas north of the equator, including

Africa, East Asia and the Americas, although it has recovered in some areas during recent years. In Western Europe, Southern Africa and parts of Central Asia, there appear to be no distinct trends.

B. Global-scale greenhouse gas concentrations

6. The atmospheric concentrations of greenhouse gases have increased because of human activities, primarily owing to the combustion of fossil fuels (coal, oil and gas), deforestation and agricultural practices.

7. The concentration of atmospheric carbon dioxide (CO2) has now risen to over 360 parts per million from a pre-industrial level of about 270 parts per million.

Changes in the ratio of carbon isotopes in atmospheric CO2 confirm that the increase is a consequence of human activities. CO2 has an effective lifetime in the atmosphere of about 100 years, so that its global mean concentration responds only very slowly to changes in emissions. This means that about one third of the CO2 resulting from human activities in the recent past will still be present in 100 years' time. Anthropogenic CO2, then, is making the largest direct additional contribution to radiative forcing at present and is likely to do so for some time into the future. Stabilization of CO2 emissions at current values could slow the consequent projected climate change but still leave atmospheric concentrations rising. Emission reductions of about 60-70 per cent would be needed to prevent CO2 concentrations from rising further.

8. In addition to the higher concentration of CO2 in the atmosphere (about 30 per cent), the concentration of

methane has more than doubled, while that of nitrous oxide (N2O) has increased by about 15 per cent. Methane and N2O also act as greenhouse gases. The burning of fossil fuels has, in addition, caused the atmospheric concentrations of sulphate aerosols to increase in some regions, primarily in the northern hemisphere. However, while greenhouse gases tend to warm the atmosphere near the Earth's surface, aerosols can result in cooling.

C. Global stratospheric ozone concentrations

9. The combined abundance of ozone-depleting chlorine compounds in the stratosphere has apparently peaked and is now slowly declining. Chlorine is no longer increasing because the total consumption of chlorofluorocarbons (CFCs) worldwide had decreased dramatically from about 1.1 million tons in 1986 to 156,000 tons by 1998. The parties to the Vienna Convention for the Protection of the Ozone Layer have phased out 85 per cent of the production of those chemicals that destroy the ozone layer. The remaining 15 per cent is mainly produced and consumed in developing countries which have until 2010 to phase out most of the major ozone depleting substances. By July 2000, 176 countries had ratified the Vienna Convention and 175 countries the Montreal Protocol on Substances that Deplete the Ozone Layer.

10. Although total chlorine is declining, total bromine is increasing according to the Scientific Assessment Panel of the Montreal Protocol. Bromine is much more effective than chlorine at destroying ozone.

11. One measure of the success of the Montreal Protocol and its subsequent Amendments and Adjustments is that without the Montreal Protocol, by the year 2050, the amount of ozone depleting chemicals in the atmosphere would have been five times greater. Ozone depletion would have risen to 50 per cent in the northern hemisphere mid latitudes and 70 per cent in southern hemisphere mid latitudes, about 10 times worse than current levels. The result would have been a doubling of ultraviolet radiation of relative short wavelengths (UVB) reaching the Earth in northern hemisphere mid latitudes and a quadrupling in the southern hemisphere. The implications for human health would have been very serious: 19 million additional cases of non-melanoma skin cancer, 1.5 million more cases of melanoma and 129 million more cases of eye cataracts.

12. The severe destruction of stratospheric ozone over the Antarctic continent (the "ozone hole") was first detected in the mid-1980s using ground-based measurements from stations operating under the WMO Global Atmosphere Watch network. The stratosphere contains 90 per cent of total atmospheric ozone. The seasonal occurrence of the Antarctic ozone hole (during southern hemisphere springtime) has continued up to the present time. Its formation requires stratospheric temperatures below -78° C, which allow the formation of polar stratospheric clouds, levels of chlorine above about 2 parts per billion by volume and sunlight to activate the ozone destroying chemistry of chlorine. The chlorine loading (currently at 4 parts per billion by volume) is a direct result of the use of CFCs as refrigerants, insulators, cleaning agents and propellants in spray cans.

13. At its maximum each year, the ozone hole can cover an area greater than 20 million square kilometres with almost total destruction of the stratospheric ozone at times in some locations within the hole. The Vienna Convention came into force in 1985, and together with its Montreal Protocol (1987) and the subsequent Amendments thereto, has effectively curtailed the release of CFCs into the atmosphere. Because CFCs have such long lifetimes however, the chlorine associated with them is not expected to decline below the critical 2 parts per billion by volume in the stratosphere until mid-century. It is expected, therefore, that the low springtime Antarctic ozone levels will occur for some time.

14. Fortunately for most of humanity, this extreme loss of atmospheric ozone, with its attendant increase in harmful ultraviolet radiation reaching the Earth's surface, occurs over largely uninhabited areas. Its effect on marine ecosystems is unknown at this point, but studies are under way in various countries to determine any impacts.

15. Ozone depleting substances, which include CFCs, are being replaced by hydrofluorocarbons (HFCs) and, to a lesser extent, by perfluorocarbons (PFCs); and consequently, concentrations of the latter substances in the atmosphere are increasing. HFCs and PFCs have significant global warming potential and the Kyoto Protocol to the United Nations Framework Convention on Climate Change has included HFCs and PFCs in a basket of six gases whose emissions are to be reduced by industrialized countries. The global warming potentials of substitutes for ozone depleting substances have been evaluated by the Scientific Assessment Panel of the Montreal Protocol

and IPCC. Options for reducing global warming contributions by substitutes for ozone depleting substances have been evaluated by the Technology and Economic Assessment Panel of the Montreal Protocol and IPCC. Both Assessment Panels of the Montreal Protocol are working closely with IPCC to address the problem of HFCs and PFCs in the context of the two Protocols.

II. Regional air pollution

16. Large-scale regional air pollution is found principally in eastern North America and Europe and increasingly in East Asia. Although naturally occurring episodes of regional "pollution" can be caused by lightning-initiated forest and grassland fires, the chronic regional pollution that is so much a matter of concern is often the consequence of human activities.

17. In the three regions mentioned, a combination of intense industrialization, large population numbers and density, and the ubiquitous automobile results in high pollution levels over large areas. Sulphur, nitrogen oxides, heavy metals and organic compounds are among the principal pollutants. Sulphur and nitrogen, carried aloft by air currents, can lead to the formation of acid rain which may fall to Earth hundreds and thousands of kilometres from their source regions. Acid rain is thought to have contributed to the disappearance of fish from thousands of lakes in both Europe and North America and to extensive damage to forests.

18. Substantial progress in reducing regional air pollution has been achieved in North America and

Europe where a number of international agreements are now in place limiting emissions of sulphur, nitrogen oxides, volatile organic compounds, heavy metals and persistent organic pollutants. These have resulted in significant reductions with, for example, in Europe, sulphur emissions having fallen from more than 40 million tons to 22 million tons per year between 1990 and 1998.

19. More recently, regional pollution has become an important issue in many developing countries. In a number of regions, agreements have been adopted to address the problem. They include East and South-East Asia, southern South America and Southern Africa. Nevertheless, because of rapid industrialization and urbanization, the situation is most acute in East Asia and particularly so in South-East Asia, which is also affected by extensive, episodic biomass burning events.

20. Each ecosystem reacts differently to the same input of acid rain and other pollutants. Sensitivity maps showing the most susceptible ecosystems indicate that, in 1990, there were few areas at risk in East and South-East Asia. However, deposition scenarios for 2025 indicate that large areas will be at risk by that date.

III. Urban air pollution

21. The urban environment is where an increasing share of the world's population lives. According to the United Nations, 4.9 billion inhabitants out of 8.1 billion are predicted to live in cities by 2030. This compares with 2.9 billion out of 6.1 billion at the

present time. With increased urbanization comes increased urban air pollution associated with the transportation, energy and industrial sectors. In some of the world's major cities, for example, Los Angeles, Mexico City and Beijing, local topography and climate exacerbate levels of urban pollution. Urban pollution characteristics vary enormously spatially, temporally and between individual cities.

22. Common pollutants in urban areas are non-methane hydrocarbons (NMHCs), nitrogen oxides, sulphur dioxide and various types of particulate matter. Urban smog, common in many cities, is a result of the action of sunlight on NMHCs and oxides of nitrogen, and the same process also produces harmful levels of ozone. Pollution is harmful to human health and the built environment. For instance, many world heritage sites located in cities are subject to pollution damage, and increased incidence of diseases and deaths may result from exposure to increased levels of air pollution (for example, small particulates less than 2.5 microns in diameter). The fact that outdoor air pollution levels also interact with indoor air pollution levels is a particular problem where biomass and coal are used for domestic cooking and heating.

23. Many developed-country cities and some developing-country cities now have monitoring systems that provide air quality information. In some cities, the authorities can enact control measures such as restricting traffic or ordering certain industries to reduce operations to lower pollution levels. To assist city authorities, the World Health Organization (WHO) has produced air quality guidelines based on health studies and WMO is working with national

meteorological services to improve urban air pollution forecasting.

IV. *Issues for further consideration*

24. In view of the recent findings of IPCC in its Third Assessment Report that there is evidence of substantial vulnerabilities to the projected climatic changes, particularly for the poor populations and populations in coastal areas, there is a need to draw greater attention to the adaptive capacity and vulnerabilities of populations, natural systems and regions, and to the links between climate change and sustainable development and equity.

25. Overarching issues such as capacity-building, education and training, and raising public awareness, need to be taken into careful consideration, as well as the increased need for assessments of climate and environmental change and quantitative methods for comparative assessment and decision support analyses.

4

Conserving Water Resources

Water is needed in all aspects of life. The general objective is to make certain that adequate supplies of water of good quality are maintained for the entire population of this planet, while preserving the hydrological, biological and chemical functions of ecosystems, adapting human activities within the capacity limits of nature and combating vectors of water-related diseases.

Over the past several decades, many businesses have improved the efficiency of water use ana reduced the discharge of pollutants to surfacewaters and aquifers. In fact, in some areas, despite increases in population and economic activity, freshwater consumption has dropped since 1980 in response to water conservation, reuse, recycling efforts, and changing priorities for water use. The business case for strategically addressing water challenges is getting stronger. While each organization must assess the business case arising from its own relationship to water risks and opportunities, companies are increasingly encountering four strategic water signals that the business case to address water issues is building in multiple industry sectors.

Businesses are experiencing increases in water-related costs, not only those reflected in direct prices. In fact, water prices in many locations fail to accurately represent shifting supply and demand for water. Other direct and indirect water-related costs have emerged or risen in both industrialized and developing countries.

Wastewater treatment and pollution mitigation costs to meet more stringent pollutant discharge and runoff standards as regulatory approaches shift from technology-based requirements to watershed health-based limits and levels necessary to support endangered species protection and restoration efforts. Supply expansion costs associated with dam construction, water diversion, well drilling, and securing new water allocations Indirect costs from suppliers with water-intensive processes or significant water impacts.

Many companies now realize that even greater risks lie in the potential for water-related constraints 3 on business activity. Current "allocations" of water rights for use and for discharge of pollutants are not assured into the future. In many regions of the world, pressures are growing to give higher priority to ecosystem and basic human needs for water.

Changing local water supply and quality levels, combined with increasing competition for clean, freshwater resources, make past allocations vulnerable to disruption and revision. Businesses lacking contingency plans and failing to take proactive steps to address facility and local water challenges may find it difficult to avoid or respond quickly to surprises. Potential water-related business risks include:

— Water supply disruptions due to temporary or chronic water shortages, infrastructure deterioration, surface and groundwater contamination, or terrorist activity

— Pressures to change water allocations to address other industrial, agricultural, residential, and ecosystem needs, particularly in times of tight supply

— Supplier disruptions from water shortages in other regions, particularly those affecting energy and agricultural inputs

— Opposition to proposed facility siting or expansion stemming from existing or anticipated company or community water uses or impacts

— Public opposition to or government prohibitions against certain wastewater discharge techniques or certain types of water quality impacts

Many publicly traded companies are experiencing shareholder initiatives aimed at corporate environmental performance or decision-making. Such initiatives and associated shareholder expectations can create pressure for a company to alter its water-related practices or strategic plans. At the same time, some companies are finding ways to enhance revenues by applying core competencies to address water-related needs experienced by others, such as products that use less water or services that reduce customers' water dependency.

Critical customers are no longer just shareholders and those who buy a company's products and services. They include those individuals and groups-financial markets, suppliers, neighbours, non-governmental organizations, and regulators-whose behaviour or responsiveness a business depends on to maintain its "license to operate" and to deliver consistently increasing shareholder value.

Business has a strategic opportunity to get out in front of water sustainability challenges before they impose constraints on business activity. Localized environmental issues of water availability and quality-that could often be "solved" through technical, policy, or behavioural approaches-are transforming, in many communities, into sustainability challenges that demand ongoing balancing efforts to satisfy competing needs.

Individual companies face the challenge of understanding what all of these evolving water signals mean for them and what steps they should take. Each company has a different relationship to water throughout its value chain-from production inputs, raw materials, and suppliers to ultimate service or product use and disposition. Each company must assess its own business case for action. By understanding some of these signals early, companies may find paths that prevent future crises.

While water challenges persist at the local level, businesses are finding advantages in taking a more coordinated and strategic approach to addressing water challenges. Coordinated corporate attention to water challenges can support, promote, and transfer successes across facilities and sites, while engaging multiple business functions in reducing water-related risks and pursuing value-adding opportunities.

Historically, at many companies, water-related responsibilities have been divided among separate functions, such as facilities management, engineering, and environmental affairs, with ownership of overall strategic water considerations falling through the cracks.

Leadership, however, can come from many places-and plant managers will undoubtedly have a growing responsibility to navigate facility operations through local water challenges.

The Global Environmental Management Initiative (GEMI) has developed this analytical process-the Water Sustainability Tool-to assist individual companies and other organizations to better understand what emerging water issues might mean for them, given their operations, needs, and circumstances. The tool is designed to help individual companies build a business water strategy. The tool encourages businesses to:

— Conduct a systematic assessment of their relationship to water

— Identify specific opportunities and risks associated with this relationship

— Assess the business case for action

— Tailor a water strategy that addresses specific needs and circumstances of the organization

Water opportunities and risks are emerging throughout companies' value chains. For example, certain suppliers may be vulnerable to water supply availability risks that could impact a business' costs or availability of key production inputs, from raw materials to energy.

At the other end of the value chain, the use or final disposition of a company's products or services could affect water resources in beneficial or detrimental ways. In order to help businesses consider upstream and downstream opportunities and risks related to water, this tool utilizes a five-stage value chain. The value chain approach is designed to help companies identify and assess water uses and impacts in places where they might not be immediately obvious.

For example, water-related risks and opportunities may appear in raw material or production stages, linked with key process inputs and suppliers, or in later stages, associated with product use or final disposition. Companies may find that they rely upon or impact water in unexpected ways. Understanding how a product, facility, or company is connected to water-through direct and indirect water use and through impacts to water from business activities and products-is the critical first step in determining how an organization should respond to water risks and opportunities in a sustainable manner.

Each stage in a company's value chain, tool users are encouraged to think broadly about water use. Tool users should begin developing an understanding of key water uses at the company, from raw material or production stages, through customer use and final disposition. There are several areas of water use and reliance shared by many companies, such as facility landscaping, process heating/ cooling, cleaning of parts during production, and transportation of materials.

There are also areas of water use that are common to specific industry sectors. In addition, companies are often connected to water in very indirect, yet critical ways. These connections may be associated with the way your suppliers, employees, and customers use water. Each stage of the value chain also has unique water uses that are common to many companies. Exploring these water uses from a variety of approaches will help the user complete a comprehensive picture of a company's key connections to water. Tool users need to collect sufficient information about key water uses to identify associated opportunities and risks.

Water impacts may be associated with water discharges. Examples of water discharges include water released from a facility wastewater treatment plant, stormwater runoff from company property, and cooling water returned to a nearby waterway. Water impacts can result from business activities that do not directly relate to water use, but involve other materials potentially impacting the quality of water sources. For example, air deposition can affect the quality of surfacewaters. Leaching of materials and chemicals can impact the quality of groundwater aquifers. Spills or leaking tanks can impact surface and groundwater quality. In certain stages of the value chain, such as "process/production," direct water impacts will often be easy to identify because they involve activities that are likely to be regulated by government agencies. At each end of the value chain, however, direct and indirect impacts may be less obvious. Using several different approaches will help to identify hidden water impacts. For water discharges, be sure to consider all the ways that water quality can be changed by an activity.

In looking for possible impacts arising from contact with raw materials, production intermediates or finished product, consider all of the materials used in your company's supply chain as potential sources. Then, consider the value chain. Use it as a lens to focus a systematic search for water-related impacts. For example, customers may require water to use, clean, or maintain a company's products or services. Tool users should consider potential impacts, and not just those that may occur routinely. Companies should explore the vulnerabilities associated with sources that the company directly and indirectly relies upon and/or impacts. Tool users should consider information such as the general description of the source, the size of source, the source's rate of replenishment, the source's quality, other industrial, agricultural, domestic, commercial, and ecosystem demands on the source, as well as climatic conditions or weather patterns, such as drought. In many cases, it will be sufficient for the tool user to perform a brief assessment of primary water sources on which the facility or company relies or impacts.

The Procter and Gamble Company (P&G) markets approximately 250 brands of consumer products to nearly five billion consumers in more than 130 countries. The products include laundry detergents, toothpastes, shampoos, feminine hygiene products, pharmaceuticals, snacks, diapers, cosmetics and cold remedies. As P&G looked at their water use and impacts along the value chain, the company identified a number of areas for improving water management. Over the past few years, it has significantly reduced water usage and pollution at its manufacturing plants.

However, one of the company's biggest challenges is to address consumer use of water. Water is essential for the use and disposal of virtually all of P&G's products. Nearly 85% of sales are associated in some way with household water use. P&G is pursuing cleaning and laundry products that use less water, cold water, non-potable water and even salt water. They are developing shampoo and personal cleaning products that use less water or no water at all. To help consumers improve the quality of their water use, P&G is also developing filtration and treatment systems that treat and recycle water in the home.

In US, using a "Water Balance" to Identify and Characterize Water Uses Texas Instruments Incorporated

Texas Instruments (TI) has found that developing "water balance" diagrams that map water inflows, outflows and intermediate reuse between production and support areas in a manufacturing plant provide valuable information for improving water management and reducing costs.

A water balance is very beneficial during the design of manufacturing plants as well as during efforts to optimize subsequent plant operations, particularly where appropriate flow meters are installed. Identifying the amount and quality of water needed in all water use areas allows the development of a better-integrated water use program during process design that may reduce demand for freshwater. A water management system can also match water use requirements with other water streams in the facility of appropriate quality, enabling reuse without additional treatment.

TI's semiconductor fabrication plant in Miho, Japan has been in operation since the early 1980s as a zero industrial wastewater effluent plant. The plant was built this way at the request of the local neighbours and government. At the time, the area lacked the infrastructure to support a more conventional plant design, which typically uses over a million gallons of water per day.

The production area at the Miho plant reuses process water over and over again, enabling the plant to consume a much smaller amount of water than comparable semiconductor plants. Some generated production "by-products" are segregated from process water and collected for reuse as raw materials at other companies or disposed of as concentrated waste solutions. The Miho plant has found water balances to be useful tools for improving process designs and communicating about water use. Understanding the business sensitivity to water-related changes, as well as the relative likelihood of these changes occurring, provides important information regarding potential business risks. Such information enables business managers to assess and articulate the business case for developing a strategy to mitigate potential water-related constraints to business activity. Most businesses employ well-established procedures for identifying and evaluating potential business risks.

Tool users are encouraged to seek opportunities for incorporating the risk information and evaluation criteria into such core business risk evaluation processes, including due diligence assessments for site acquisition, issue identification systems, environmental management system risk assessment processes, and other risk assessment activities.

A business would be highly sensitive to a change if it, or the company's response options, would result in significant business constraints. External changes can result in steep increases in water costs, production delays, limits on production, or strong community opposition to company activities. For each water use, consider how sensitive the business is to a change in:

1) water price,
2) water availability,
3) water quality, or
4) the loss of a specific source.

For example, an aquifer that is being rapidly depleted or contaminated would likely be vulnerable to changes or response actions such as public policy changes or price increases that can affect the business. However, changes in water prices and allocations are often not directly related to the vulnerability of local water sources, but may instead stem from broader changes in public opinion and policy related to the needs of other water users.

A business would be highly sensitive to a change if the change, or the company's response options, would result in significant business constraints. For example, stricter effluent standards can result in significantly higher treatment costs to remove contaminants. Community concerns about a company's water impacts can affect your "license to operate." Certain spills have potential for high liability and impact on company reputation. In some industries, product use has been linked to water quality problems.

Water uses and impacts that fall in the high and medium risk quadrants are likely to demand further consideration and assessment. The Coca-Cola Company oversees the operation of more than a thousand beverage manufacturing plants in nearly 200 countries around the world. Water is an essential ingredient to their products. To assure a continuous supply of high quality freshwater, all facilities are expected to evaluate the reliability of water sources on which they depend.

The Coca-Cola Company has recently undertaken source protection planning, a cost-effective program to improve the safety of their water treatment systems, without increasing treatment costs. Source protection plans must include a comprehensive assessment of potential sources of contamination, strategies to protect wellheads and aquifer recharge zones, and active participation in local watershed management efforts. Each of the 25 plants located in areas of water scarcity received increased technical and financial support from the regional offices, sometimes using consulting services to assess in-depth water supply reliability.

Watershed management initiatives may reduce treatment costs by improving the quality of the water inputs at the source. Reduced microbial load and lower concentration of nutrients, which will generate less algae, limit the need for expensive treatment steps. For example, since 1995, a Coca-Cola bottling plant in Brazil has invested more than $2 million in partnership with the municipality and other businesses to protect the Jundiaí River watershed, the primary source of water for that community.

Ross Products, a division of Abbott Laboratories and a leading manufacturer of adult and pediatric nutritionals, including infant formula, has reduced costs and risk at several facilities by eliminating "non-value-added water use" and pursuing water reuse and recycling opportunities. At its Michigan plant, the installation of a new cooling tower enabled Ross Products to shut down three groundwater wells, reducing water use by over a million gallons per day. At other facilities, before discharge, boiler blowdown water is circulated through a heat recovery exchanger system to preheat water. Heat recovery projects save each facility over $30,000 per year. Water from process cooling is used for irrigation and cooling tower make-up water. Recovered water systems save some Ross Products facilities over $100,000 per year.

Ross Products' Arizona and Michigan facilities have taken creative steps to minimize potential wastewater discharge impacts to local surfacewaters from its nutritional operations. Wastewater with high biological oxygen demand (BOD) concentrations is applied to local fields used to produce straw grass for livestock feed. The recycled wastewater serves as a fertilizer while also reducing agricultural watering needs.

In New Jersey, Bristol-Myers Squibb Company (BMS) developed a comprehensive Watershed Management Program to demonstrate corporate commitment to sustainable development principles. The Program is an integrative approach to managing water resources on-campus and downstream. The centerpiece of the Program is a water reuse initiative that will replace up to 500 gallons per day of groundwater and surfacewater with treated effluent from the on-site wastewater treatment plant. This treated water will be reused for non-potable uses, including heating, ventilation and air conditioning (HVAC) make-up water, fire protection water, and toilet flushing water.

Currently, water from on-site groundwater extraction wells and diversion of surfacewater from an on-site stormwater detention pond serves these uses. Using a structured method for gathering information, BMS conducted a rigorous study to assess water uses in the existing facility and proposed future development. They found that internal metering at multiple points is the most helpful assessment tool to determine water use. After evaluating opportunities for wastewater reuse, they developed a conceptual design and began construction in early 2002. Using existing infrastructure in the design controlled capital costs. When the system is operational, the watershed management project will support continued expansion of the Hopewell Campus by addressing community concerns, and providing increased ecosystem benefits to the local stream, wetlands, forest and agricultural habitats.

United Agri Products, a ConAgra Foods company, has pioneered an innovative service through its mPOWER3 subsidiary that helps to improve agricultural productivity while reducing water use and improving water quality. The Greeley, Colorado company developed applications in its suite of software and web-based tools that assist growers to enhance the efficiency and effectiveness of agricultural and irrigation resources.

Farmers synchronize mPOWER3's software on their personal computers with the company's web-based systems to share and process data. This software and information management service uses databases, historical algorithms, and geographic information systems (GIS) to process data on weather, soil, hydrology, and other factors that influence crop yields. The resulting information and maps enable growers to release water to plants when they need it, and not according to predetermined schedules.

mPOWER3's systems also generate information that allows growers to better target and time pesticide and fertilizer use and application. The result: less pesticide and fertilizer use, less runoff of pesticides and fertilizer to surface waters, and healthier crops. mPOWER3 is discovering that the market for these services extends beyond growers. Irrigation authorities, local governments, and other organizations are finding

mPOWER3's information management and aerial imagery services to be powerful tools for managing water in a more sustainable manner. In US, Kodak company wanted to demonstrate that an innovative regulatory option to reduce silver discharges from photoprocessing facilities could achieve environmental goals more effectively and efficiently than traditional regulatory approaches, delivering cost savings and simplifying municipal pretreatment program administration. Kodak worked with The Silver Council, the Association of Metropolitan Sewerage Agencies, the U.S. EPA, and others to develop a best management practices approach to maximizing the recovery of silver and minimizing its release to the environment by recommending specific technologies, equipment, and management practices for controlling silver discharges.

In 1995, the results of this collaboration produced the Code of Management Practice (CMP) for Silver Dischargers. Pollution prevention recommendations for facilities to minimize wastes and conserve water were also a key part of the CMP. Both customers and regulatory authorities have experienced the benefits of the CMP. Municipalities can now implement the CMP as a legally authorized and fully enforceable element of their industrial wastewater pretreatment program, or as a voluntary program. Either approach provides a cost-effective alternative to traditional numerical discharge limits for silver and results in consistent and significantly improved silver recovery. The photographic industry's customers now have cost-saving tools for recycling a non-renewable natural resource, conserving water, and ensuring environmental protection.

Johnson Company Controls is a leading manufacturer of automotive parts and a global leader in integrated facility management services and building controls systems. One of the company's goals is to provide energy efficient building systems and operations, designed explicitly to help customers conserve energy and protect the environment. As part of their efforts to provide integrated, energy efficient systems in large commercial buildings, Johnson Controls develops Water

Management Programs to reduce facility water use and provide cost savings. By adding water management as a new facility service, Johnson Controls has been able to create new markets, build top-line value, and offer a full scope of facility solutions.

Johnson Controls has found that the cost savings from proposed water conservation measures often provide the additional funds needed to achieve paybacks from energy efficiency upgrades in a reasonable period. The company is also expanding markets by promoting the construction of "green buildings" that include efficient water systems. They have participated in the U.S. Green Building Council's program, "Leadership in Environmental Energy and Design (LEED)," a building rating system that evaluates environmental performance from a "whole building" perspective, including impacts on local water resources.

In US, Southern Company is one of the largest electricity producers, with more than 34,000 megawatts of electric generating capacity across the Southeast. The region's population has exploded by 63% since 1970, and is projected to almost double by 2015. This growth has placed significant pressures on the availability and quality of regional water resources. Southern Company subsidiaries rely on water in the production of power in its hydroelectric projects. Coal, gas, oil, and nuclear plants also require large quantities of water for cooling and other purposes. In light of the increasing pressures, Southern Company recognized the importance of working cooperatively in the region to balance and meet competing demands for freshwater resources. Southern Company is in the process of applying to the Federal Energy Regulatory Commission (FERC) for new operating licenses for its hydroelectric projects on the

Chattahoochee River. The river supports a wide diversity of uses, including other industries, recreation, municipal water treatment, and ecosystem functions.

Some companies have developed or adapted "total cost assessment" or probabilistic risk assessment tools to support their efforts to determine costs and benefits. Nonetheless, business managers are accustomed to making decisions that involve weighing difficult-to-quantify costs and benefits. Yet the common toolbox of valuation and decision-making tools, such as net present value (NPV), can lead companies to underestimate the value of decisions and investments that create options for future action.

New tools, however, are emerging to assist business managers in making investment decisions amidst significant uncertainty about the future. The concept of "real options" adapts financial options tools to the evaluation of a business' opportunities. Incorporating the value of future "options"-such as secured access to sufficient quantities of clean freshwater at an affordable price-into corporate decision-making can significantly improve the financial attractiveness of strategic investments.

For example, a company's investment in watershed protection could contribute to a valuable future "option" for its facility to expand production capacity in the future by alleviating local water quality pressures. Even when the benefits of pursuing an action outweigh the costs, the activity may not compete effectively for limited organizational investment resources and attention.

Some water sustainability projects may be too small to easily attract management interest, or they may have a lower return on investment than other projects under consideration. To the extent that investments in water sustainability initiatives can reduce costs, increase competitiveness, safeguard the business' "license to operate," and remove potential constraints to future growth, these benefits are likely to resonate with company leadership.

Most companies have three explicit or implicit core goals related to water: comply with all applicable regulatory requirements; assure continued access to sufficient supplies of clean freshwater at an affordable price to meet the company's needs; and maintain "license to operate" through attentiveness to community needs and concerns.

Tool users should seek to understand the organization's explicit and implicit goals related to water and sustainability. Through their environmental management systems, many companies have developed vision statements, policies, and goals stating their commitment to environmental performance and, sometimes, sustainability. These may include specific goals addressing water security, water use, and water impacts. If not, they may provide insight into implicit water goals. For example, "working with communities in which the company operates to address their environmental concerns" may be a commitment that implies certain goals or focus areas related to water. For businesses that pursue a coordinated water strategy, there may be value in engaging multiple levels of the business-facility, business unit, corporate-as well as critical customers and interested members of the community, in establishing clear water-related goals and targets.

For some companies, particularly those with a weak or narrowly focused business case, a water strategy may concentrate on specific opportunities or risks. Such a strategy might not engage many functions in the organization and not establish many water-focused activities, such as creation of a water task force. For other companies, the business case may be sufficient to engage the organization in a broad-based effort to pursue a coordinated water strategy. Such an approach would ideally involve multiple business functions to ensure that the water strategy and goals are effectively integrated into existing business processes.

Most tool users are probably well aware of their business' organizational culture and strategy, planning, and decision-making processes. From this understanding, one can identify who within the organization needs to be aware of the business case for pursuing a water strategy. There may be other personnel or functions within the business that may be affected by a key water opportunity or risk. For example, opportunities to develop partnerships with community-based water organizations may be of significant interest to senior business managers and external affairs staff. In many organizations, business personnel are accustomed to thinking about water resources as a "limitless frontier," without constraints or significant direct or indirect costs associated with water use. Georgia-Pacific (G-P) is one of the world's leading manufacturers and distributors of pulp and paper and building products. Paper mills use a significant amount of water in their operations and their wastewater discharges can impact water quality. Manufacturing packaging materials and thermosetting resins had the potential to save money by recycling or reusing wastewater.

In 1994, in order to support G-P management's recognition that strong environmental and safety performance is vital to strong financial performance, the company established clear environmental performance goals in all the environmental media. By setting environmental performance as a top and measurable priority, the CEO led the company on a path toward environmental leadership. G-P's 1994 Environmental and Safety Report established nearly 60 goals, with associated performance measures, to track environmental progress in each of the categories. The five water pollution prevention goals included:

— Beneficially reuse process wastewater or become closed loop at all G-P chemical plants by 1998.

— Beneficially reuse process wastewater or become closed loop at all G-P packaging plants by 2000.

— Reduce, through waste treatment plant upgrades, total suspended solids (TSS) per ton of product 25% by 1998 and biochemical oxygen demand (BOD) per ton of product 15% from pulp and paper mills by 1998, using 1993 as a base year.

— Measure the impact of color discharges from each major pulp and paper mill to the receiving water body using a delta system, with 1995 as a baseline. Apply Best Management Practices (BMPs) to develop site-by-site cumulative color delta reduction targets to be achieved by 1998.

— Complete underground storage tank upgrades or removals by 1998. In 2000, after making significant progress toward meeting these goals, G-P developed, with input from employees, new performance measures to track continuous improvement of corporate-wide and individual business unit performance. The measures are designed to help employees, shareholders, communities, and others better understand and evaluate environmental performance.

For example, water use is now measured in terms that are more directly integrated into the business bottom line, such as gallons per ton of product produced. These measurements provide incentives for individual business units to reduce costs associated with water use and discharge. In addition to the measurable improvements to performance since 1994, G-P has found that the principles and goals have helped build a new culture among G-P employees. Using the goals and the performance measures established in 1994, environmental protection and safety awareness have moved beyond being special programs and have become a way of life throughout the company.

Gerber Products Company, a producer of baby foods, discovered that employee education and involvement related to water management at its Fremont, Michigan plant can yield significant returns. Gerber is a business unit of Novartis Consumer Health, Inc. In January 2000, the plant's Water Team kicked off a yearlong effort to cut water consumption. By year's end, they had saved 67.5 million gallons of water compared to 1999. The Water Team worked with all areas of the plant to survey water use, collect water conservation suggestions from employees, and identify specific opportunities.

The Water Team produced a video to increase employees' awareness of water issues and plant water use. Among other topics, the video encourages employees to routinely check for leaks and drips to reduce wasted water. Employee involvement with Water Team activities, combined with the video and other awareness raising efforts, has helped to change employees' water management behaviours while enlisting them in company efforts to continually improve the plant's water-related performance.

Many of the companies profiled in the case studies have found signifi cant benefit in engaging multiple business functions in developing and implementing the organization's water strategy. Cross-functional involvement broadens ownership for tracking and managing water opportunities and risks. It also promotes incorporation of water awareness into established business processes and activities.

High quality water is an essential ingredient throughout Anheuser-Busch's (A-B) value chain, from irrigation water for grain crops to brewing water for beer. To ensure that sufficient organizational attention focuses on water conservation and other water issues, A-B is engaging multiple parts of the organization in developing and implementing the company's water strategy. A-B facilities use this information to develop a "roadmap" of water uses and flow rates, using a "materials balance" approach. For example, in 2000, a multi-disciplinary Utilities Task Force at A-B's Williamsburg, Virginia brewery identified opportunities to save over 175 million gallons per year. A review of the facility's automated cleaning processes revealed an opportunity to reduce rinse water by 36 million gallons per year. In addition, at an employee's suggestion, bottle and can rinsing equipment in the packaging area was recalibrated, saving 24 million gallons of water annually.

A-B brewmasters play an essential role in assuring the long-term reliability of local water supplies. Brewmasters are responsible for building relationships with local water utilities and suppliers to help ensure that local water sources are managed in a sustainable manner.

A-B has developed a "water reliability survey of long-term fundamentals" to assist plant staff in working and planning with local water supply managers to maintain the health and reliability of local and regional water sources. A-B established a Corporate Water Council to support and coordinate efforts across the company to address water opportunities and risks.

DuPont began to explore potential water metrics in the mid-1990s as part of the company's growing focus on sustainability. The effort met initial internal resistance at the facility level due to "metrics fatigue" and concerns that certain metrics definitions related to water "consumption" would unfairly penalize some facilities when compared to others.

Over time, EHS staff built awareness at the facility level, used examples illustrating the benefits of metrics, and made a sufficient business case for proceeding. DuPont formed a team of corporate and facility personnel, supplemented by water resource and engineering experts, to determine how to best approach water performance measurement.

Issues of Water Scarcity

About one-fifth of the world's population lacks access to safe drinking water, and about half lacks adequate sanitation. About 40 percent of the world's population lives in countries with moderate to high water stress. By 2025, this figure could rise to 50 percent. Yet, with the help of policy and legal reform, international cooperation, community and private sector participation, and technical innovation-there are encouraging signs that the crisis could be averted. The international community is beginning to develop a common understanding of the complexity of managing marine ecosystems. In high-risk areas such as the Black Sea and the Nile River, nations are working together to devise strategies that will reduce pollution, restore fisheries, and manage resources, while at the same time taking into consideration the interests of both upstream and downstream users. South Africa, Brazil, and Mexico have enacted pioneering water laws emphasizing a national approach to water issues. Many communities are working cooperatively to manage their water resources. New innovative technologies promise significant improvements in water-use efficiency. International forums continue to emphasize the importance of management and policy reforms, particularly reducing water subsidies, taking a more integrated approach to water resources management, and using catchments and basin areas as natural management units.

While encouraging, these efforts are still insufficient. Much more needs to be done in five key areas: full-cost water pricing and improved incentives to encourage private sector participation; increased investments for water, sanitation, and health for the poor; greater multinational cooperation on transboundary water issues; stronger efforts to prevent and remedy pollution in coastal waters; and greater emphasis on cross-sectoral approaches and decentralized decision-making on water basin management. In the Millennium Declaration, the international community acknowledged the importance of global action to increase and protect water resources. This declaration cogently describes the links between poverty, hunger, and water security and emphasizes the critical role of improved water resources management in sustainable development. Increasing the income levels of the poor will require more water use and the intensive development of marine ecosystems. Growing and harvesting additional food will require more irrigation and greater exploitation of inland and ocean fisheries. Providing more people with safe drinking water will require not only more water, but also enormous investments in sewage collection and treatment systems to reduce disease. Achieving these goals depends on access to water resources—not just access to water.

Water supplies are scarce in some regions and relatively abundant in others. And though water quality has improved in many developed countries, it is still a significant problem in most developing countries. The effects of long-term climate change are also likely to vary significantly across regions. Over the past century, world population tripled, but the aggregate use of water rose sixfold. Just 35 years ago, people were using about one-fourth of readily available freshwater. Today they are using roughly half. Most freshwater is used for agriculture. It is estimated that about 41 percent of the world's population currently lives in areas characterized by water stress or water scarcity. Assuming the U.N.'s low-range population projection of 7.27 billion people, some 48 percent of the population could be living in such areas by 2025.

The World Commission on Water expects that by 2025 water stress will increase significantly in more than 60 percent of the world, including large areas of Africa,

Asia, and Latin America. In the Asia and Pacific region, arid countries such as Afghanistan and the Islamic Republic of Iran already have chronic water shortages. Most other developing countries in the region are faced with growing water scarcity. In many parts of the region, misuse and overexploitation of water resources have resulted in the depletion of aquifers, falling water tables, shrinking inland lakes, and diminished streamflows. In West Asia, water is a particularly limited resource. In the region as a whole and the Arabian Peninsula in particular, groundwater resources are being withdrawn at rates that far exceed natural recharge rates. In the Syrian Arab Republic, suggest that overall demand for groundwater will outstrip the supply by 2005. In the northeastern part of the country, some springs have dried up and the flow of permanent rivers such as the Khabur have been seriously reduced because of groundwater overexploitation. In Africa, water resources are distributed very unevenly. For example, the Congo River watershed accounts for about 30 percent of the continent's annual runoff but contains only 10 percent of Africa's population. By contrast, the more populous Northern and Southern regions receive just 9 and 12 percent, respectively, of the continent's rainfall. By 2025, it is estimated that nearly half of Africa's population will be living in countries facing either water scarcity or water stress.

Water scarcity carries the potential to increase tensions among nations that share water basins. About 43 percent of the world lives in multicountry basins, which cover almost half of the planet's land surface and contain over 80 percent of the freshwater river flow. There are 261 major basins and countless aquifers that cross political boundaries. Most of the river basins in South

Asia, South America, and Africa fall into this category. About 50 African rivers-including the Nile, Niger, Volta, and Zambezi-run through two or more countries. As a result of manmade diversions and extractions, many major rivers no longer reach the sea during the dry season, including the Colorado, Huang He (Yellow), Ganges, Nile, Syr Darya, and Amu Darya. The Amu Darya and Syr Darya rivers once contributed 55 billion cubic meters of water annually to the Aral Sea, but diversions for irrigation have reduced this volume to 7 billion cubic meters, with devastating consequences for the Aral Sea.

About 20 percent of the world's population lacks access to safe drinking water, and about 50 percent lacks adequate sanitation. Since the 1970s, levels of suspended solids in Asia's rivers have risen by a factor of four: they typically contain 4 times the world average and 20 times OECD levels. The fecal coliform count in Asia's rivers is 50 times higher than recommended by the World Health Organization (WHO) guidelines. In Latin America, only about 10 percent of sewage receives any treatment; sewage pollution of groundwater is also common in many developing countries. Polluted water is estimated to affect the health of about 1.2 billion people every year. It contributes annually to the death of 15 million children under the age of five, and is responsible for 1.5 billion cases of intestinal parasites, 1 billion cases of diarrheal diseases, and 400 million cases of malaria. The WHO reports that about 3.5 million people die from these diseases each year-2.2 million from diarrheal diseases alone. During the month of March 2002, 100,000 new cases of dengue fever were reported in Rio de Janeiro during a wet season, after decades of control. In Africa alone, the annual costs of malaria are estimated at $2 billion; globally, lost productivity from preventable water-related diseases exceeds $100 billion each year.

Quality issues

Sewage pollution is the largest water quality problem, but not the only one. In addition Overuse of pesticides has degraded water quality in many areas. Industrial wastes have led to significant water pollution, contaminating water with heavy metals (lead, mercury, arsenic, and cadmium) and persistent organic compounds. Over-abstraction of groundwater has led to sea-water intrusion along shorelines, causing salinization of coastal agricultural lands. In many areas, including Lake Victoria and the Black Sea, non-native invasive species have had devastating impacts. The accidental introduction of a jellyfish—like creature into the Black Sea in 1982 soon dominated the aquatic food web, where it directly competed with native fish for food. This, combined with overfishing and other factors, collapsed the Black Sea fish catch to one-third of its former volume by 1992. In Lake Victoria, the introduction of the Nile perch and Nile tilapia had major consequences on the lake's native fish stocks. Invasive plants such as water hyacinths also have proven to be a major problem in many rivers and lakes. Strategic partnerships have helped reverse these trends.

Roughly 75 per cent of global pollution of marine waters is from land-based sources. Pollutants include toxic chemicals (organic chemicals, heavy metals, and radioactive waste), nutrients (agricultural fertilizers and sewage), sediments, and solid waste. Nutrient pollution, especially from nitrates and phosphates, is rising dramatically, largely as a result of the excessive use of fertilizers, growth in the quantities of domestic and industrial sewage, and increased aquaculture, which releases considerable amounts of waste directly into the water.

Regional seas such as the Baltic and Black Seas receive massive amounts of pollutants from watersheds that cover a wide geographic area. Pollution in the Baltic Sea has been a serious problem for over 50 years. Contributing factors include a high population (about 77 million people in the basin), inadequate wastewater treatment facilities, and emissions from industrial enterprises. Eutrophication and concentrations of toxic organic compounds are growing. The Danube, Dnieper, Dniester, and Don rivers carry nutrients, oil, heavy metals, pesticides, and other pollutants into the Black Sea. At risk are the 170 million people who live in the catchment area. In addition, eutrophication and overfishing have decimated the fishery.

Today the capacity of the global fishing fleet is about 40 percent greater than global fisheries can support. Aided by high-technology fishing gear and other technical advances, the global fishing fleet caught nearly 105 million tons of fish in 1997, more than double the 50 million tons caught in 1975. The marine catch has followed a predictable pattern: as fishing pressure in one region leaves major fish stocks depleted or in decline, the global fleet increases its activities in other fishing regions around the world. According to the Food and Agriculture Organization of the United Nations (FAO), more than one-quarter of all fish stocks are already depleted, and almost half of all fish stocks are being fished at their biological limit and are vulnerable to depletion.

Dramatic increase in extreme weather events, including both floods and droughts, may be linked to climate change. Between 1986 and 1995, economic losses from natural disasters were estimated to be eight times higher than in the 1960s. The Munich Reinsurance Company recorded 700 major disasters in 1998, compared with between 530 and 600 during previous years. Floods account for about one-third of natural catastrophes, cause more than half of the fatalities, and are responsible for about one-third of the economic losses. In addition, surface warming of the oceans could reduce phytoplankton productivity, which forms the basis of the entire marine food chain.

The links between water, health, and poverty are numerous and complex. Issues include lack of access to safe water and adequate sanitation, the amount of time spent by rural women to obtain water, the higher risk of waterborne disease in poor communities, and the fact that the urban poor often must buy water from vendors that costs 10-20 times more than piped water. Access to saltwater resources is another key element for poverty reduction. Many coastal communities depend on harvesting living marine resources for income and for food. About 40 percent of the world's people live in coastal and riverine floodplain areas and are critically dependent on fish and other marine products. In the Pacific Ocean region alone, coastal settlements account for about 60 percent of the population. In many cases, water development and other programmes have in the past compromised the security of poor communities by reducing or eliminating their access to water or by increasing their vulnerability to flooding. Redressing the denial of traditional formal or informal property rights has been neglected or ignored in some nations. But many countries now realize that the security of poor communities often depends on access to water ecosystems such as functioning wetlands and floodplains. Three important dimensions of poverty reduction include:

— Protecting and expanding the asset base for the poor
— Improving land tenure regimes and securing water rights
— Expanding social protection and community participation, especially by women.

Countries are increasingly recognizing the advantages of working together to manage transboundary basins and marine ecosystems. Solutions have already been developed to reduce ship-related pollution, expand general policies on wetlands, and control movement and disposal of hazardous wastes. A growing number of countries now support international conventions that recommend norms, targets, and compliance measures. The goal of the U.N. Convention on the Law of the Sea (UNCLOS) and the U.N. Convention on the Law of Non-Navigational Uses of International Watercourses is to implement global solutions through region-specific partnerships among nations experiencing problems. UNCLOS, which entered into force in 1994, sets out the rights and duties of states with respect to the use and conservation of the oceans and their resources. This document includes fundamental global norms for conservation of marine resources and for preservation and protection of the marine environment. These global norms are translated into more specific goals and commitments through specialized agreements. For land-based sources of pollution, for example, the UNCLOS framework calls on governments to establish detailed rules and guidelines and to harmonize policies at the regional level. Several regional seas agreements have specific language on land-based pollution. The UN Watercourses Convention adopted in 1997 has yet to enter into force. It represents a global framework agreement designed to ensure the safe use, development, conservation, management, and protection of international watercourses. Nonbinding 'soft' law complements binding legal arrangements, helping countries overcome barriers to action.

The Global Programme of Action (GPA) for the Protection of the Marine Environment from Land-Based Activities is an example of such soft law. Adopted in late 1995, GPA recognizes that more than 75 percent of coastal and marine water pollution originates from land-based sources. In addition to pollution loading, GPA addresses the modification of physical habitat, such as wetlands conversion, in establishing priority action areas and defining strategies and programs to take advantage of numerous instruments that currently exist. Other prominent international action programs have been adopted in accordance with the FAO Code of Conduct for Responsible Fisheries. In recent years, numerous international forums have sought to galvanize the plan of action originally outlined in Agenda 21, the global action plan for sustainable development adopted at the 1992 Rio Earth Summit. In the freshwater area, these include the deliberations of the World Commission on Water for the 21st Century, the second World Water Forum in the Hague in 2000, and the International Conference on Freshwater in Bonn in 2001.

In the marine area, an Intergovernmental Review Meeting was held in Montreal in November 2001 to assess progress under the GPA, and two important conferences reviewed progress on addressing marine fisheries and coastal management. These important global policy discussions, and the new tools that have emerged from a decade of experience, have led to consensus on an action agenda that addresses poverty reduction as well as water-related human health and governance issues. In cases involving shared river basins and regional seas, cooperation among affected nations is the only way to successfully attack pollution and water resource management problems. Two pioneering examples involve the Black Sea and Danube River, and the Nile River.

Following the signing of the Danube and the Black Sea regional conventions, the 17 participating countries carried by GEF to build capacity, help identify needed policy, legal, and institutional reforms, and establish priorities for investments in the agricultural, municipal, and industrial sectors. To accelerate implementation of these reforms and investments, the GEF Council approved the first $29 million of a $95-million Strategic Partnership for the Danube and Black Sea Basin. The partnership harnesses the comparative advantages of each of the three GEF implementing agencies the UN Development Programme (UNDP), the UN Environment Programme (UNEP), and the World Bank-to help the countries address top priorities that complement actions funded through the European Union.

The partnership is leveraging three times the GEF contribution through cofinancing to assist the countries in this region. Wetlands were also considered a priority for accelerating restoration of the river and sea. In Romania, for example, wetlands between the villages of Chilia Veche and Periprava were drained in the early 1980s to increase agricultural production, which in turn destroyed fishery habitat and valuable reeds traditionally harvested by local people. After a GEF-supported programmes breached the dike in four places, 20 species of fish returned to the wetlands in just two years, and the reed bed regained its former health.

Following six years of preparation, the 10 Nile Basin countries launched the International Consortium for Cooperation on the Nile in June 2001. The consortium received pledges from the donor community for an initial $140 million for the Shared Vision Program of the Nile Basin Initiative, with an additional $3 billion anticipated in investments for sustainable development. GEF played a significant role by providing preparation funds for the formulation of a GEF international waters project that would underpin the initiative. The consortium produced a transboundary environmental analysis to build confidence and set priorities. This analysis was produced through a participatory process and included in country consultations, national, and in country interministerial coordination. The Transboundary Environmental Analysis was approved by the Nile Council of Ministers in March 2001, marking the first time such a substantive document received approval of all Nile riparian countries. This catalytic process proved to be a turning point for expanding the dialogue among the water ministries to include other ministries in each of the 10 countries as well as NGOs.

Like the Black Sea and Nile River cases, partnerships are being used to enhance the management of large marine ecosystems. For example, the Benguela Current Large Marine Ecosystem (BCLME), which is shared by Angola, Namibia, and South Africa, provides annual benefits worth hundreds of millions of dollars. This globally important fishery has been stressed by overfishing, oil and gas extraction, and diamond mining. But it is also threatened by extreme weather events. In the 1980s, scientists found changes in the Benguela that were related to increased temperatures and currents. The fisheries and the region's sensitive biodiversity, including penguins and seals, were adversely affected. The three BCLME countries received GEF assistance in 1998 to prepare a Strategic Action Programme of reforms and actions to sustainably manage the large marine ecosystem and its biological diversity. The countries will enact policy, legal, and institutional reforms to jointly manage the large marine ecosystem and to address mineral and energy extraction issues. This international waters program was formed in partnership with BENEFIT, a science-based capacity building program funded by European nations.

Several nations-including South Africa, Brazil, and Mexico-have recently enacted national water laws that take a new approach to water resources management. South Africa. South Africa's 1998 National Water Act is a pioneering effort to incorporate sustain-ability and international cooperation into a national water law. The law reflects the growing consensus among South Africans that further expansion of water supplies is unrealistic. South Africa is already using nearly 60 percent of its available water, compared with just 5-10 percent in countries such as Namibia and Botswana. Furthermore, South Africa's water resources are greatly influenced by climate and topography. Only one-fourth of the nation has perennial rivers, another fourth has rivers that only flow periodically, and half of the nation has rivers that only flow after infrequent storms. Under the new law, water is specifically reserved for two priority uses: to meet basic human needs and to maintain ecological functions. Provisionally, the law allocates 25 liters a person a day to each individual for drinking, food preparation, and personal hygiene. The law also seeks to balance human use with the long-term sustainability of aquatic and associated ecosystems throughout South Africa. Remaining water must be allocated so that all people have equitable access for productive purposes and for benefits that flow from water use, such as jobs.

The new law greatly broadens local participation in water management decisions. Within an individual watershed, the responsibility for allocating water to users rests with local catchment management agencies, which are expected to operate with broad participation from all interested parties. The Department of Water Affairs and Forestry is authorized to develop water pricing strategies, such as charges to cover the full financial costs of providing access to water, including infrastructure; a watershed management charge, which can cover the use of rivers and water bodies for both water consumption and waste disposal; and a resource conservation charge, which can be applied when a particular water use significantly affects others in the watershed. Finally, the law recognizes the need to manage transboundary water resources cooperatively. Brazil enacted a new water law in 1997 and a national system of water resource management in 1998.

Under the new law, Brazil adopted the river basin as the basic territorial management unit. Rivers that lie wholly within a state are now the responsibility of that state, while the federal government is responsible for rivers that cross more than one state. Basin committees for state and federal rivers are the focal point for the development of a water resources management system. Federal government approval is not required, so basin committees decide how much and when to charge for the use of rivers. They establish charging mechanisms, suggest values to be charged, and determine the criteria for the distribution of costs linked to multiple uses or that are of common or collective interest. The pricing provisions of the law are intended to promote recognition that water is a real asset, make consumers aware of its economic value, motivate the rational use of water resources, and obtain funding for programs and activities that are required in water resource plans. In Mexico, the 1992 National Water Law is based on an integrated ecosystem-based approach to the modernization of water resources management. The law authorizes the establishment of river basin councils to coordinate activities and produce agreements among the National Water Commission, other federal, state, and municipal agencies, and water user representatives. The National Water Commission also has reorganized its regional structure, with boundaries based on river basins.

There are many opportunities to reduce poverty through sustainable, community-based fisheries management. In southern India, the Gulf of Mannar Biosphere Reserve includes 21 islands with 44 villages and a total population exceeding 100,000. A GEF programme implemented by the UNDP set up 20 village marine conservation councils (VMCCs) to ensure stakeholder consultations. About half of these council members are women. Working with existing village panchayat councils, the VMCCs established user-rights agreements between the government and fishing cooperatives, including trawlers. In addition, contracted with a local NGO to manage a microcredit scheme to support mariculture and sustainable fisheries. The Lake Victoria export fishery is now recovering, with the return on investment estimated at $600 million over two years.

In India, the Centre for Science and Environment (CSE) is sponsoring a national campaign to promote the use of rainwater harvesting. CSE's National Water Harvester's Network, which promotes community water management programs based on water harvesting, has members and affiliates throughout India. With groundwater levels declining in many parts of India, rainwater harvesting is gaining political support. An elaborate plan for water harvesting is being implemented on the estate.

There are encouraging examples of the private sector working with urban and rural communities to provide affordable water supply services and sewage treatment collection systems. Some companies work with community groups to plan the services, and community labor helps to reduce the costs. Following the adoption of South Africa's water law, for example, a number of pilot partnerships were launched to test low-cost techniques for delivering water to both rural communities and those on the outskirts of cites such as Durban. Although these public-private partnerships were established for an affordable fee, the water still remains under the regulatory control of the government as a public good. In rural areas of South Africa—the Eastern Cape, Northern Province, KwaZulu/Natal, and Mpumalanga-over 2 million people have been served since 1997 in a BOTT (Build-Operate-Train-Transfer) Partnership. Standpipes that use electronic pre-payment cards and those financed through community revenue collection provide water from wells and from an extensive scheme of 50 reservoirs. The transfer of these services to local companies resulted in sustainable operations and fee collections even in rural areas. In poor sections of Durban, community groups' participation in urban planning created a demand for affordable sewage collection systems. In 1999, a partnership was initiated to use labor from the communities to reduce the cost of shallow, small-bore sewer systems similar to ones popularized in Brazil. The resulting 50-percent savings in capital costs made extending sewerage systems affordable. These private-sector partnerships overcame years of inaction and inequities experienced by poor communities in South Africa.

Trends in Freshwater Supply

Today, freshwater is not uniformly distributed. A number of regions are experiencing chronic freshwater shortages. Less than one percent of the world's freshwater is readily accessible and located in the lakes, rivers and streams that cross our continents. Although freshwater is a finite resource, the world's water cycle is constantly renewing itself. Rain and snow supply enough new water every year to inundate all of Europe under almost seven feet of water. But freshwater resources are not uniformly distributed, and many regions are suffering from shortages. The Middle East, North Africa and the Southwestern U.S., among other regions, have long been familiar with water shortages. Increasingly, shortages are occurring even in places that have access to relatively large amounts of water.

China is facing severe surface and groundwater supply problems as it irrigates croplands to feed its enormous population. The Ganges River in India and the Chao Phraya River in Thailand, both of which are in monsoon regions, now experience times in the year when little or no water reaches the ocean. The Pacifi c Northwest of the U.S., well known for its wet weather, and states from Maine to Georgia have recently experienced several summers of drought. The severity of water shortages varies greatly from place to place.

Some areas face issues such as hydroelectric power shortages, decreased crop yields, and loss of species habitat, while some less developed nations confront the true crisis of insufficient water for basic human needs. Despite this range of differences, an important commonality is emerging in all global water resource issues. Shortages and conflicts are less the result of insufficient technological or infrastructure capacity for accessing new sources and more a result of water demands surpassing the availability of local freshwater resources.

Increasing human demands for water and unsustainable rates of water withdrawal are likely to worsen water shortages. Other factors also have the potential to affect long-term water availability. 40% of the world will live in water-scarce regions by 2025. Factors likely to contribute to these predicted water shortages include population growth and unsustainable rates of water withdrawal.

The United Nations currently estimates global annual population growth at 1.2%, which translates to an increase of 77 million people per year. Current data indicates that 10% of the global agricultural harvest-180 million tons of grain-is produced by depleting groundwater supplies. Extensive surfacewater withdrawals for irrigation have also contributed to the dramatic shrinking of some of the world's great freshwater bodies including the Aral Sea and Lake Chad. Given that agricultural irrigation is the world's largest use of freshwater, accounting for twice as much as the industrial and domestic sectors combined, these unsustainable rates of withdrawal have already caused water shortages and will likely cause more.

Pollution of existing freshwater supplies exacerbates water constraints and shortages. At the same time, water management advances are providing water quality and availability improvements. Surfacewater and groundwater pollution effectively decreases the quantity of usable freshwater. Many of the world's lakes, large rivers, and most of its estuaries have been contaminated with industrial, municipal, and agricultural runoff and effluent discharges.

Contamination of surfacewater has led many regions of the world to turn to groundwater. While most of the planet's groundwater remains pure, contaminants such as pesticides, nitrogen, petrochemicals, radioactive waste, and a variety of heavy metals increasingly threaten these supplies. The pollution of groundwater aquifers is not just signifi cant for localized groundwater users but also for surfacewater users since the base flow for major rivers such as the Mississippi, Niger, and Yangtze comes from groundwater sources. Signifi cant progress has been made in developing technologies and best practices for conserving, purifying, recycling, and desalinating water, all actions that effectively increase freshwater availability.

In the developed world, basic efficiency measures are now widely practiced in the industrial and commercial sectors and include the use of low-volume plumbing fixtures, reduction of irrigation schedules, and efficiency improvements for water-cooling technologies and equipment. Industrial dischargers generally employ best available pollution control technologies. Basic drinking water and sewage treatment are in place throughout the developed world and some developing nations. More efficient and effective technologies are gradually emerging. While desalination is not yet cheap enough to be broadly applicable, the technology has advanced significantly, most notably in the technique of reverse osmosis (RO), which uses pressure and semipermeable membranes to filter salt or other contaminants from water.

In Singapore, recycled and reclaimed water is emerging as an essential alternative to water from the mainland. By 2010, the island country aims to meet 20% of its water needs through reclaimed water. A new water treatment facility will have the capacity to produce "Newater", reclaimed water with an even higher purity than the standard potable supply. In arid Namibia, wastewater-recycling technology has helped meet water needs in the capitol city of Windhoek at less than half the cost of developing new sources of supply. Expansion of freshwater supplies is increasingly costly and controversial.

In the past, as demand for water has increased, society's focus has been on addressing this demand through increases in supply. However, this solution is becoming increasingly difficult and costly and may soon be infeasible in many areas. No longer does the drilling of additional wells sufficiently address agricultural supply issues. The area of irrigated land using water from the Ogallala Aquifer in the Western U.S. has decreased since the 1970s because of falling water tables and rising pumping costs.

Dimensions of Water Issues Inadequate supplies of clean freshwater contribute to a broad range of public health issues, especially in the non-industrial nations and some developing nations. Human health can be affected by freshwater problems ranging from contamination of municipal water supply sources to pollution of water bodies used for fishing or recreation. Pathogens that cause acute illness and disease, or chemicals that can be carcinogens in high concentrations, can affect drinking water supplies. Non-industrial and developing nations face the most serious threats to human health from inadequate freshwater supplies. Various sources estimate that 1 to 1.5 billion people lack access to safe drinking water, 2 to 3 billion people lack access to proper sanitation, and 14,000 to 30,000 people die each day from water-borne illnesses. These astonishing numbers represent a signifi cant challenge for individuals, governments, and businesses in coming decades.

Freshwater shortages, and attempts to address them through diversion and storage projects, have displaced large numbers of people. As lakes and rivers dry, people dependent on these resources are forced to move. Experts estimate that dams displaced 40 million people in the 20th century. Water scarcity is increasingly leading to conflict, especially in arid areas. Violent conflict over water resources has occurred in many regions of the world, most notably in the Middle East where scarce water resources exacerbate existing religious and political tensions.

Ecosystem needs for freshwater are broadly affected by human activities. Due to the finite nature of water resources, there is a constant trade-off between meeting human and environmental freshwater needs. Water taken from a watershed for municipal drinking water supplies, for example, can affect the habitat and health of local species. Indirect impacts of human activities on ecosystem freshwater needs are common. Habitat degradation, urbanization, pollution, and introduction of foreign species can all adversely impact the ability for ecosystems to receive an adequate quantity and quality of freshwater. As society recognizes the value of ecosystem services and natural capital, environmental needs for freshwater are receiving higher priority. Often, and especially in times of severe shortage, human needs are given immediate priority over those of the environment. However, there is increasing recognition for the social and economic value provided by the environment and various ecosystem services.

Irrigation Management

Changes in water management systems are also important. For example, irrigation systems could be improved through better timing of water releases. Farmers could adopt water-conservation technology and use better information and communication technologies to reduce non-beneficial irrigation, apply water uniformly to crops, and reduce stress. Farmers could also plant more drought-resistant crop varieties or varieties that use water more efficiently. In addition, they could adapt better soil management and other conservation practices. Options to improve the productivity of irrigation include land leveling and efficient sprinklers to apply water more uniformly; surge irrigation to improve water distribution; low-energy precision application sprinklers to cut evaporation and wind drift losses; furrow diking to promote soil infiltration and reduce runoff; and drip irrigation to cut evaporation and other water losses and to increase crop yields.

Sufficient water must be set aside to maintain ecosystem health and services. Upstream, the management of forests and land is essential for moderating hydrological variability, reducing silt, and con-serving biodiversity. Downstream, water is vital for the conservation and management of wetlands and floodplains and to support fisheries and crop pro-duction systems. Many water utilities and hydropower companies are developing partnerships with upstream commu-nities for maintenance of catchment quality. In 1998, the leaders established a fund for the protection of the catchment. Water consumption fees will be negotiated with the various users and invested in catchment protection. The Nature Conservancy, the Ecuadorian Forest and Natural Areas Institute, Quito's Municipal Sewage and Water Agency, and other companies and local groups in the Quito area. In downstream areas, new practices include incorporating ecological flows in the design of new infrastructure and recalibrating the operating rules in river basins. Streamflow regulation is another important component of watershed management.

Developed countries have historically relied on massive infrastructure to control streamflow and manage floods. More recently, nonstructural solutions, such as watershed management and land use planning, have proved to be effective complements to traditional infrastructure. Many developing countries also are investing heavily in nonstructural solutions. Ecosystem-based irrigation management is built on the needs of the ecosystem and the watershed's inhabitants. For example, in Western Africa, a dam constructed in 1978 for rice irrigation in Cameroon severely restricted the downstream floodplain along the Logone River, causing ecosystem degradation and the disruption of traditional livelihoods. In 1988, The World Conservation Union (IUCN) initiated a programme to rehabilitate the Logone floodplain. The restored floodplain is providing important new economic benefits for traditional users.

There is a new recognition that fluctuating climatic conditions can pose long-term threats to the benefits these water-related ecosystems provide for both national economies and local communities. An action agenda to address these new realities must ensure access to freshwater and marine ecosystems for the poor; recognize water-related human health issues by enacting reforms and incentives for improved service delivery; reduce subsidies and phase in full-cost water pricing to generate revenue and attract private sector participation; and establish transboundary and large marine ecosystem-specific partnerships to undertake reforms and foster investments that can reverse existing trends in pollution and depletion.

5

Sustainable Development: Role of Economy

Financial support for the environment continues to lag, undermining the ecosystems and natural resources that billions of people-especially the poor-depend on for survival.In late 2001, an international consulting firm polled 30,000 people in 30 countries, including OECD countries; developing countries in Africa, Asia, and Latin America; and eastern European and central Asian economies in transition. In the Philippines and Mexico, for example, more than 80 percent of the respondents affirmed that their own health was affected "a great deal" by environmental problems.

Governments have the ultimate responsibility and should make the budget and policy reforms needed to promote sustainable development. For example, substantial resources could be freed, and economic efficiency improved, through the reduction or elimination of subsidies that encourage the excessive use of natural resources. A recent study of six developing countries and Russia found that fossil fuel subsidies alone amounted to some $50 billion a year. Governments can also promote sustainable development by levying environmental taxes and through initiatives that sell environmental services like the "ecomarkets" program in Costa Rica.

Historically, official development assistance (ODA) has supported economic growth and financial stability in developing countries. It is increasingly important for governments to foster private investment through regulatory, tax, and other reforms.Although it accounts for a dwindling proportion of the resources flowing to developing countries, ODA continues to be essential. A greater share of ODA funds could be used to support capacity building and institutional and policy reforms at the country level. International financial institutions, in particular, could promote greater use of innovative financial instruments such as partial risk and credit guarantees and payments for environmental services. This would leverage increasingly scarce ODA by attracting private financing for sustainable development, especially in the areas of water and energy use. The private sector is the largest potential source of financing for sustainable development in developing countries.

Attracting substantial private funding for environmentally oriented investments will, however, continue to be a major challenge because of high perceived risk. With the help of donors and international financial institutions, developing country governments can take steps to improve the general investment climate and help overcome the reluctance of private investors. Progressive business organizations such as the World Business Council for Sustainable Development can also assist by highlighting the compatibility between sustainable development and profitability. During the 1990s, the Global Environment Facility (GEF) was the major source of grant financing for environmental initiatives in its four main areas of concern: conserving biodiversity, reducing risks of climate change, preventing the degradation of international waters, and protecting the ozone layer. In its first decade, GEF's financial commitments for the environment totaled $4.2 billion, and leveraged an additional $12.4 billion in co-financing.

Although more modest in size and scope, other important funding sources for global environmental initiatives include the Multilateral Fund for the Implementation of the Montreal Protocol, which has provided resources to help countries phase out the use of ozone-depleting substances, and the G7 Pilot Program to Conserve the Brazilian Rain Forest. At the same time, developing countries should both continue to seek additional resources for local and national environmental problems and strengthen their own environmental laws and policy frameworks.

Many OECD and some developing countries have instituted national taxes with environmental objectives in recent years. Revenues from environmental taxes presently account for about 2 percent of GDP in OECD countries, or about 6 percent of their total tax revenues. Denmark, at more than 4 percent, has the highest ratio of environmental taxes to GDP. The United States, at less than 1 percent, has one of the lowest ratios.

New environmental taxes have usually been accompanied by a commensurate reduction in the burden of other taxes with nonenvironmental objectives. The transportation sector, a major contributor to greenhouse gas emissions and urban air pollution, accounts for over 90 percent of the revenue from environmental taxes. Denmark, Finland, Italy, the Netherlands, Norway, and Sweden have each instituted some form of carbon tax. Although these taxes vary according to the carbon content of fuels, they are generally not considered pure carbon taxes because of exemptions and rebates based on nonenvironmental considerations such as sector competitiveness or income distribution.

Sweden, for example, refunds 65 percent of the carbon tax on fuels used in manufacturing, agriculture, and forestry. An international carbon tax based on the consumption and carbon content of fossil fuels could provide a new source of funding for global environmental initiatives.

A carbon tax is clearly defined, since it is already in force in six countries. The revenue-generating potential is large even at relatively low rates of taxation. While revenue estimates vary greatly depending upon the assumptions used regarding tax rates and coverage, a recent U.N. technical note concluded that a carbon tax on gasoline applied universally-equal to 4.8 cents per U.S. gallon-has the potential to raise $125 billion a year. A U.N. High-Level Panel on Financing for Development concluded that the "international community should recognize the carbon tax as a promising possibility."

The Intergovernmental Panel on Climate Change (IPCC) estimates that CO_2 emissions from aircraft accounted for 2.4 percent of total emissions from fossil fuels in 1992. The IPCC also estimates that aviation's share of greenhouse gas emissions could grow to between 3.5 and 15 percent by the year 2050. Despite its substantial impact on climate change, international aviation is not included in international agreements on quantitative reductions of greenhouse gas emissions. Levying taxes and fees on international travel could provide incentives to reduce emissions and also help finance investments in environmental protection.

Taxes or fees on international travel, which would adhere in a general way to the polluter-pays-principle, could be assessed in a variety of ways. One simple approach would be a surcharge on all passenger tickets and air freight. The revenue-generating potential of such a tax could be substantial. It is estimated that a 1-percent tax on passenger tickets and air freight would yield approximately $2.2 billion per year-$800 million on passenger tickets alone. Similar revenues could be raised through the collection of the equivalent of $3.50 from each traveller; worldwide, tourist arrivals reached about 618 million in 1998. Such fees could be collected as a flat rate or as a percentage of a travel package.

Another potential revenue source is aviation fuel. Currently, aviation fuel used on domestic flights is seldom taxed-and fuel used on international flights is exempt from taxation. This latter exemption, based on the 1944 Chicago Convention on Civil Aviation, was originally designed to stimulate commercial aviation and to ensure fair international competition. In order to tax aviation fuel used for international flights, an international agreement would be needed, including decisions on the appropriate taxing authority.

An important issue would be to mitigate the possible effects of such a tax on the economies of developing countries that rely on tourism for a significant share of their foreign exchange earnings. An emissions-based user charge determined by the aircraft type, engine type, air route, distance, and weight is another possible approach.

The International Civil Aviation Organization could play an important role in collecting an emissions-based levy, which could be used to improve energy-efficient technologies or to intensify the use of renewable energy sources. In many developed and developing countries, government subsidies lower the prices of resources such as energy and water, and encourage excessive use. If large enough, subsidies can also contribute to public budget deficits and macroeconomic instability, and discourage investment by the private sector. For example, subsidies associated with the production and sale of electricity were estimated at $112 billion per year in 1996 in developing and transitional economies. These huge subsidies encourage waste and contribute not only to local air pollution, but to global climate change as well. Phasing out electricity subsidies could have a "win-win" effect. A reduction of 10 percent would generate annual revenues of $11 billion, reduce greenhouse gas emissions, and-as part of internationally agreed-upon emissions trading mechanisms-enable the sale of these emission reductions in the international market. Water used for drinking, irrigation, and sanitation is also heavily subsidized in many developed and developing countries-annual water subsidies were estimated at $56 billion in 1996. These subsidies directly contribute to the overuse of water resources and are creating critical water scarcity conditions in some regions.

The World Commission on Water estimates that $100 billion more than is currently being spent on infrastructure is required each year just to meet the basic needs of people in developing countries. Since official development assistance to this sector is small, most of this financing will have to come from private sources. However, it is unlikely that the private sector will make investments of this magnitude unless national policies are changed to permit full-cost pricing of water resources. In OECD countries, agricultural subsidies amount to about $360 billion each year.

There are two key concerns are how to increase capital flows to low-income countries, particularly those that have been largely ignored by investors, and how to maximize the use of foreign investment to help solve developing countries' social and environmental problems. Some studies suggest that improved environmental performance and an improved bottom line for private corporations can be compatible. Several factors are strengthening linkages between profitability and environmental progress. First, partly as a result of increased pressure from shareholders and consumers in OECD countries, multinational corporations that operate in developing countries have a strong incentive to engage in environmentally sound practices.

For example, an "Eco-OK" certification program for bananas was established in Costa Rica in 1993 in response to the environmental concerns of foreign consumers. Improved productivity, or "eco-efficiency," is a second factor that leads to beneficial environmental outcomes. The privatization of Mexico's steel concern, AHMSA, for example, has led to reduced emissions into the air, the elimination of acidic wastewater discharges, and increased rates of recycling.

Commercial banks, governments, multilateral agencies, and company managers are sensitive to environmental impacts when making financial decisions. Commercial banks, for example, now often require that private sector investments in major projects follow World Bank environmental guidelines or the equivalent. However, many environmentally friendly projects in developing countries have difficulty attracting long-term capital. This is due to a host of factors, including the modest size of most businesses in these countries; traditional lenders' lack of familiarity with activities such as organic agriculture, sustainable forestry, and eco-tourism; and the relatively higher risk involved.

Water and wastewater treatment, renewable energy, and natural foods are now of interest to some venture capitalists. For example, the Environmental Enterprises Assistance Fund, a $10 million nonprofit fund that focuses on Central America, has over the past few years made more than 25 investments in renewable energy, organic agriculture, environmental technologies, and forestry.

The GEF/IFC Terra Capital Fund provides financing for biodiversity-related private investments in Latin America; other investors include the Swiss government and private sources. And the IFC and GEF are collaborating to provide financing for small and medium enterprises that work to conserve biodiversity and mitigate climate change. If these initiatives can demonstrate the long-term financial viability of small- and medium-size environmental projects, it will encourage traditional commercial sources to support similar enterprises.

Another important development is the growing public support for socially responsible investments, which enable investors to direct their savings into firms that engage in ethical and sustainable production and marketing. This investment approach originated in North America and Europe in the 1970s and expanded rapidly after firms adhering to sustainable development values proved, on the whole, to be more profitable than those that did not.

At present, global funds that endorse socially responsible investments are managing $1.4 trillion in assets. Most of these funds are invested in developed countries, and the direct impact on developing countries has been limited. But this may change in the future. For example, when a transnational corporation is being considered as an investment opportunity, fund managers now look at the social and environmental practices of the corporation's subsidiaries in developing countries-creating an incentive for firms to improve their environmental and social performance.

Many governments and private companies have adopted voluntary payment systems to finance environmental initiatives. Utility companies, for example, use "green pricing" to encourage greater use of renewable energy sources.

In addition, some U.S. state governments allow taxpayers to contribute to various environmental causes by checking boxes on their tax forms. BP Amoco's Global Choice program is linked to the introduction of a new type of gasoline that is being marketed as a highly refined, low-emissions product in Australia. When a motorist fills a gasoline tank with this new brand of fuel, BP Australia agrees to invest a percentage of the purchase price in environmental projects-for example, renewable energy, new forests, innovative technology-designed to offset greenhouse gas emissions. All such activities are certified by the government and are independently verified.

Since automobiles are major contributors to greenhouse gas emissions and urban air pollution, it would be environmentally beneficial to link green payments to new car sales or annual registrations. Available estimates suggest that over the 100,000-mile useful lifetime of an automobile, total carbon emissions are around 10 tons for a 35-mile per gallon car and 20 tons for a 20-mile per gallon car. If the costs of remedial action to offset these emissions are assumed to be a conservative $10 per ton of carbon, each new owner of a 20-mile per gallon vehicle could be asked to contribute a maximum of $200 for the environment.

A survey on green pricing carried out in Germany, for example, found that many customers thought mandatory premiums were more equitable than voluntary contributions. Potential contributors would also have to be convinced that revenues generated through voluntary contributions were being applied efficiently and effectively in worthy environmental projects. Such programs would require a simple and highly transparent administrative structure. The support of major automobile manufacturers and retailers is, of course, essential to the success of any program of voluntary contributions based on new-car sales.

Subsidies for Sustainable Development

A subsidy play a crucial role in helping development around the globe become more sustainable. Many of today's subsidies encourage practices that are economically perverse or trade-distorting or ecologically destructive or socially inequitable. Prices are the most efficient information system; they largely determine decisions by producers and consumers. When prices do not reflect the full costs and benefits of production and consumption, the true facts about resource scarcity and environmental values aren't made known. Nor are the true costs of producing or consuming goods and services. A market failure results when the price of goods does not reflect either the full costs or the full benefits. Other examples are the failure of markets to reflect the real value of wetlands or the well-known "tragedy of the commons" which can lead to the exhaustion of shared natural resources, like high-seas fisheries.

A market failure, on the other hand, implies a lack of government action, but does not imply that the markets cannot work. On the contrary, governments could often play an active role in helping the markets to function properly. If governments want to promote sustainable development, they have to make sure that prices and incentives are right. That job requires identifying subsidies, measuring them and assessing their impact. In theory, the best benchmark for helping identify a subsidy would be something economists call marginal private costs.

For some goods and services, world prices are a quick and easy substitute for prices based on opportunity costs. And a sure benchmark to define a subsidy. Any domestic price below the world price level indicates a subsidy somewhere, since domestic producers could get more selling on the world market. But some goods and services aren't traded on the world market and therefore have no world market price. For these, the preferred benchmark would be long-run marginal costs.

In the short run, these marginal costs might be high, if you had to pay overtime or find new capital to expand; in the long run, however, the extra equipment would be depreciated and the labour force optimized. So any price below the long-run marginal cost would point to a subsidy. For most things that aren't traded on world markets, a benchmark almost as good as long-run marginal cost is the average cost of producing one item. If the selling price is below that average unit cost of production, there's a subsidy.

There are several indicators have been developed by economists to reveal how much the various forms of government support, including subsidies, depart from a level playing field. Such indicators include two elements: the relative price impact and the associated transfer of income. The former looks at the effect of price changes that arise from government intervention; what's important here isn't the absolute size of the change but how the price for one resource is changed relative to the price for another.

So increasing the minimum wage or cutting the prime lending rate will each have an impact on the relative prices for labour or capital. And the combination of labour and capital chosen to increase production - a process called the "allocation of resources" -depends on this relative price impact. The associated transfer of income has a more indirect effect. Getting a government subsidy means a producer can afford to pay a little more than a competitor for labour, capital or raw materials.

For instance, economic impact can be gauged by effects on income or by growth in a country's economy measured in terms of the Gross Domestic Product (GDP). Reduction of emissions or depletion of natural resources will help assess the environmental implications. Loss in purchasing power or the distribution of benefits between rich and poor may be considered to determine the social impact. Merely tracking down subsidies and measuring their impact is a gruelling enough task, as our safari through the economics jungle showed. Actually trying to reform them is, for politicians, like swimming across a river teeming with hungry crocodiles.

The political and international impacts of subsidies must be evaluated as well. It is almost always easier to introduce a subsidy than to remove one. Eliminating subsidies raises heavy opposition from vested interests and groups that benefit from the subsidy. Opposition is equally vocal on behalf of producer and consumer subsidies, even though they originally were created for different reasons. Producer subsidies are usually initially motivated by concerns for employment and removing them is believed to threaten jobs.

Subsidies to consumers are often aimed at supporting the poor, and reducing them will likewise cause wide protest. Considering the usually heavy opposition, enormous political will and courage are required to reduce subsidies. But there is also the chance of a large political payoff. Since most subsidies are financed through either taxes or deficits, reducing them frees up funds. These can be used for deficit reduction, returned to the private sector through tax cuts or directed towards financing sustainable development. This revenue-creating capacity is politically very attractive, particularly where countries are running a deficit, because this "found" money can help smooth the transition and mobilize public support for subsidy reform.

Funds generated from subsidy removal can also be used to develop alternative policies that target the original objectives of subsidies more cost-effectively, for instance by switching to direct income support. Another major impact of subsidy reform is in the area of international competitiveness. Years of addiction to subsidies have convinced many policy-makers that removing them would fatally damage the relative competitiveness of their country or irreversibly harm the competitive position of the supported industry.

Interventions that use the market, rather than trying to replace it, can play a vital role in sustainable development because they help reconcile environmental concerns and development needs. In particular, economic incentives are ideal for shifting behaviour as well as production and consumption patterns towards sustainability; cost-effective and flexible, these policies can also correct markets and adapt easily to changing circumstances.

To promote sustainable development, it is essential that government policy establish the right incentive structure. To start, governments should identify the existing policy distortions - interventions that warp the economy and subsidize waste and environmental degradation. With this information, governments can begin to reduce subsidies that have adverse effects on the environment and on the overall efficiency of the economy.

Water is the most essential substance for life on Earth, yet it is among the least valued by governments and market forces. Without water, plants cannot use the sun to convert carbon dioxide into carbohydrates - the basis of our food chain; without safe water, a person perishes in days; without sufficient water, mighty civilizations quickly shrivel and vanish. From the very beginning, humanity has appreciated the vital importance of water in principle but has been reckless about its use in practice. While the Earth from space appears awash with blue, less than one per cent of all the water on our planet is both fresh and available.

The hydrological cycle delivers roughly 40,000 cubic kilometres of fresh water as an annual renewable supply. But almost two-thirds of this precipitation is taken up by trees and plants and returned directly to the atmosphere; another 2,000 cubic kilometres is too remote geographically to be of much help. Still, what's left for our use as a stable, renewable, easily accessible supply seems a lot - 12,500 cubic kilometres a year, enough fresh water to flood all Europe to a depth of slightly more than a metre. More than half of that is already being used, often wastefully, and global demand has been doubling every 20 years.

Water withdrawal can exceed 100 per cent because excess water might be taken from a lake or river shared with another country or from an aquifer that doesn't replenish each year, known as fossil water. It's like running up an overdraft at the bank - in this case a continuing overdraft. Some striking annual water-withdrawal percentages: Libya (404 per cent), Qatar (174 per cent) and Saudi Arabia (106 per cent). Other countries like Egypt, Israel and Jordan are soon expected to be using all their renewable water resources.

These percentages and per capita figures camouflage a crucial fact: More than two-thirds of the water taken from the world's rivers, lakes and aquifers is currently used for agriculture. To produce one tonne of grain requires 1,000 tonnes of water.

Countries like Bangladesh, the Philippines and Thailand experience water losses of 50 per cent. In Middle East countries like Jordan, Yemen and others with rising water scarcity, more than 40 per cent of the available water cannot be traced.

According to the World Bank, nearly two-thirds of all water losses in these countries could be avoided, equal to increasing their actual water supplies by one-quarter.

In 1980, an alarming two-billion-plus people did not have enough safe water. The 1980s were proclaimed as the International Drinking Water Supply and Sanitation Decade, and 1.6 billion people were provided with adequate water, particularly in rural areas, where access to safe water doubled from 30 to 63 per cent. Despite this progress, only a few developing countries reached the objective of supplying water for all citizens.

Table 1: How many people don't have safe water

Countries	(in millions)
China	367
India	186
Indonesia	93
Sudan	14
Philippines	11
Egypt	6
Nigeria	65
Brazil	20
Bangladesh	18
Mali	6
Colombia	5

The World Bank estimates that safe and adequate water and sanitation supplies would avoid two million deaths of children from diarrhea each year and hundreds of millions of infections from roundworm, schistosomiasis and other water-borne diseases. Water pollution from industrial waste also harms aquatic life in rivers and lakes with severe economic consequences for fisheries. Less visible but no less serious is the contamination of groundwater, both by improper use of chemicals and hazardous wastes and by poorly managed irrigation.

Each time irrigation water passes through the soil, it picks up mineral salts; these become more concentrated through evaporation in reservoirs. If not enough water is applied to flush these salts, then fatal chemical concentrations quickly build up at the plant roots. Ten per cent of the irrigated land in Mexico and India is damaged by excess salinity, 21 per cent in Pakistan, and roughly a quarter of irrigated land in China and the United States.

Pakistan today spends more on pumping out salt-laden water than on irrigation. And there's a historical cost as well - perhaps a fifth of the arable land in present-day Iraq, site of the ancient Sumerian civilization, has been permanently destroyed by high salinity. Excess pumping of groundwater amounts to depleting your resource capital, as opposed to pumping only what the hydrological cycle will naturally replenish, which is like living off the interest. Not only does this abuse permanently reduce the available water supply, it can also lead to land subsidence and waterlogged soil, increasing erosion. And it's a global phenomenon: Aquifer depletion in North African currently amounts to 10 cubic kilometres a year, and water tables in India and China have also fallen sharply. But the world's biggest natural underground reservoir - the Ogallala-High Plains Aquifer System in the USA has also witnessed the biggest modern environmental vandalism.

Since the early 1960s, farmers have been pumping out 20 to 40 times more water than nature has been putting back in; the result has been enormous wealth for a favoured few in the states of Texas, Colorado, New Mexico, Kansas and Oklahoma, and enormous insecurity for future generations. Insecurity can also develop when water is shared by two or more countries, with the concern rising as levels drop for the downstream states. Studies have found that user charges are usually high enough in Western industrialized countries to cover the annual operating and maintenance costs of public water supplies. Yet subsidization of capital costs through grants is common, usually amounting to a minimum of one-fifth of the total financing bill and often rising to two-fifths. For irrigation projects, however, subsidization of capital costs can reach four-fifths.

In the U.S., one study found, such subsidies conferred supernormal profits - which economists carefully call "economic rents" - of as much as $500 per irrigated hectare. In Australia, water charges are largely nominal in the major agricultural region, the Murray-Darling river basin. In the United States, the federal government actually incorporated a two-stage subsidy in the way it set prices for irrigation water. First, the contractual water prices were based on an irrigator's ability to pay rather than on the actual cost of supplying the water. Second, no interest was charged on the loans to fund construction costs.

The World Bank estimates that governments recover about a third of the cost of providing drinking water services in developing countries, sticking themselves with an annual underpricing bill of some $13 billion. This bill is sure to grow, since cities are burgeoning and the unit costs of new water supplies will soon double and even triple, without including environmental costs.

Farmers in perpetually parched Tunisia pay no more than a seventh of the cost of the irrigation water they receive. Based on a cost recovery rate of 20-25 per cent and total costs of about $25 billion, subsidies to irrigation in developing countries can be tentatively calculated between $20 billion and $25 billion annually. In total, subsidies for drinking water and irrigation in developing countries amount to $45 billion per year.

One theoretical study, however, predicted that there might be an economic cost to drastically overhauling the subsidies in Morocco's agricultural sector. While water use would be slashed by about a third, both real GDP and real income could fall by as much as one per cent. Since 92 per cent of all Morocco's water is already used in agriculture, with only 10 per cent cost recovery, and since a water deficit is projected soon for the country, that one-per-cent drop might be thought bearable in the circumstances.

Studies have shown that water supply projects achieve only half the average rate of return of World Bank projects generally. In strict economic terms, then, the Bank could get a lot more development bang for its bucks by investing in other areas. Other studies point to an environmental payoff when prices for irrigation water are tied to the volume actually used or applied in incremental tiers. This is to be expected since research had already found large price elasticities for agricultural water; a 10 per cent hike in price could be expected to trigger a drop in demand of 15 to 20 per cent.

The environmental payoff comes in a push for greater efficiency throughout the entire system. For example, cost-conscious farmers are less liable to overuse water, thus reducing the risk of soil salinization and waterlogging. There is a double misconception in the widespread belief that water subsidise are necessary to support the poor. First, it is fallacious to assume that the poor need low water prices because they would not be able to pay high prices.

In a multicountry study of rural water demand, the World Bank found that the willingness of most people, and in particular the poor, to pay for water services is often very high, if the service is reliable. In fact, poor people are already paying more. The price of privately sold water, on which poor people rely, is typically between $2 and $3 per cubic metre, 12 times higher on average than the price of piped city water. The latter is subsidized, the former isn't. Second, it is fallacious to assume that water subsidies mostly benefit the poor.

In the village of Bhadresar in Gujurat, India, upper castes owned 120 of the 128 electric pumps in 1988. The evidence reveals a vicious circle. When water services are heavily subsidized, their quality is low and service expansion relatively slow because of lack of resources and their inefficient use. The consequences are that the rich benefit while the poor still have relatively high water expenses. At the same time, the health of the poor suffers most from low quality water services.

Later, when water had become a symbol of ritual purity, it was felt it should not be tainted by grubby mechanisms of the market. Even today, some cultures ban the buying and selling of water. That redefining has to start with introducing demand-management policies for water to compliment the traditional supply-oriented thinking. This new unified policy approach should help in the most difficult question: the equitable reallocation of water between different users, and different uses.

First, recognize that water has an economic value in all its competing uses, whether those devised by nature or by humanity. It follows that a greater use of economic instruments in water policies is desirable; sound water pricing in general, and subsidy removal in particular, will achieve more sustainable patterns of water use. Water prices should at least cover operating, maintenance and capital costs of systems, earning an appropriate rate of return. Moving toward sound water pricing also will generate the new resources necessary to expand water services, giving access to the poor and other marginal groups.

Eventually, social and environmental costs should be incorporated as well. Treating water as an economic good also necessitates the reform of irrigation policies. Begin by removing subsidies and then adjust pricing to encourage sustainable practices. Similarly, a demand-oriented approach means the water use must not only be effectively metered but competently policed as well; this is one of the surest ways to reduce water losses. And demand can be reduced through improved technology, such as low-flow devices in showers and toilets and better surveillance and control in agriculture.

The domestication of wild grains - wheat, rye, barley, oats, millet and spelt - gave birth to agriculture 15 millennia ago on the shores of the eastern Mediterranean. And also independently in other regions, historians speculate. This emergence of agriculture in places as far apart as the valleys of the Tigris and Euphrates, the Indus, the Yellow River and the Nile is not as odd as it first sounds.

Agriculture, after all, stems from making use of the immediate environment: land, wood and water. Little wonder that cultivation, herding and harvesting have so permeated the world's religions, cultures and history: Agriculture was the first engine of economic development. With the Industrial Revolution began a decline in the relative economic importance of agriculture which has accelerated during the past 25 years.

While the world's economy grew by 3.7 per cent annually from 1965 to 1990, agriculture grew at a annual rate of merely 2.1 per cent. More telling is the race between two other statistics: population growth and food production. Throughout the fifties, sixties and seventies, the news was largely good, with the Green Revolution - improved seeds, intensive cropping and extensive use of fertilizers, pesticides and irrigation - bringing leaps in agricultural productivity.

Changes in population, income and food production help determine the flow in agricultural trade. On average, food imports have increased by 1.5 per cent annually between 1980 and 1993, even more in Africa and North America where per capita food production has declined. Exports of food have dropped dramatically in the former Soviet Union, but risen in Asia and, to a lesser extent, Europe. In Africa, the drop in both the volume of food exports and in their prices has cut export earnings of many countries and worsened their external debt. While the Green Revolution seemed to rout the prophets of mass famine, the victory may have been only temporary. As we have seen, recent trends in agriculture are not encouraging.

The FAO optimistically forecasts that increased yields will generate two-thirds of the projected growth in agricultural production in most developing countries until the year 2010, with expansion of arable land and more intense cultivation accounting for the rest. Land expansion for agricultural purposes, however, usually comes at an ecological cost: It often involves cutting down forests, and land without trees often cannot sustain agriculture for long. The FAO's rosy scenario is for the global picture only. Somewhat less clear is the availability of food for specific regions and countries. There are three kinds of potential barriers: physical, economic (too poor to buy enough food) and political.

Equally important is the challenge of increasing global agriculture production without continuing the unsustainable demands made on the environment in recent decades - practices often spurred and propped up by subsidization. There's not much point in feeding the nearly eight billion passengers expected on Spaceship Earth by the year 2020 if the spaceship is damaged beyond repair in the process. Some damage is already close to irreparable, such as the declining fertility, widespread contamination and mass erosion of soil. This gloomy assessment is possible only because the United Nations co-ordinated scores of researchers to produce the first account of global soil degradation in 1990.

Overuse of land or cultivation of marginal lands usually involves extensive irrigation and overuse of fertilizers and pesticides, all aggravating soil degradation. Another environmental legacy of such exploitation can be desertification, if the loss of vegetation or deforestation is severe enough. Yet the complex relationship between agriculture and environment is surely not only negative.

Agriculture might produce environmental benefits as well, such as conserving the rural landscape, biodiversity and ecosystems. Consider, for instance, two possible effects of taking land out of cultivation. On the one hand, there may be environmental benefits, while on the other, this preservation could equally lead to overexploitation of the land remaining in cultivation. Governments have never made any apologies for intervening heavily in the agricultural sector, ostensibly for the best of reasons - safeguarding an adequate and reliable food supply at reasonable prices to consumers and maintaining farm income. Agricultural support measures in the Western industrialized countries are many and varied. About 60 per cent of total assistance is dedicated to supporting market prices, although this proportion is slowly dropping as governments shift towards straightforward budgetary payments. Examples of market support include export subsidies, import taxes and intervention prices; non-price support measures include subsidies for inputs such as fertilizers and pesticides, as well as for inspection services, research and training.

In earthier terms, OECD agricultural support policies were the equivalent of transferring $16,000 to each full-time farmer, or an additional $1,500 on the annual food bill for a family of four. Over all, agricultural subsidies to producers amounted to $182 billion in 1995. Livestock products receive 60 cents of every dollar of producer subsidies, with milk getting the largest share; the remaining 40 cents was spent subsidizing crops, with half devoted to rice, for which subsidies can amount to 90 per cent of the value of production.

In relative terms, agricultural support is highest in Switzerland, Norway, Finland and Japan; these countries provide the most support per capita, per full-time farmer, per hectare of agricultural land and as a percentage of production. In absolute terms, the biggest subsidizers are the European Union, the USA and Japan. Both New Zealand and Australia have modest support levels, measured either relatively or absolutely. This continued high level of support, measured in almost every way, emphasizes the addictive hold of subsidies, despite the noble founding principles of bodies like the European Union. While there is a wide variation among countries, total agricultural transfers in the OECD have increased from the mid-1980s to the mid-1990s in absolute terms, per capita, per full-time farmer and per hectare.

A 1992 World Bank study concluded that agricultural producers in 18 developing countries effectively paid an average 30 per cent tax between 1960 and 1984 because of direct and indirect government policies. Many developing countries, like the 18 under study, have overvalued their currencies because of large budget deficits and their desire to protect domestic manufacturers. These rates hurt agriculture by raising domestic prices relative to world prices and by reducing the purchasing power of farm households. Such indirect interventions accounted for three-quarters of the tax on agriculture in the World Bank study; direct interventions such as export taxes and food crop quotas were less important. As a result of this discrimination, income transfers out of agriculture have been enormous, averaging 46 per cent of agricultural GDP annually.

The rationale behind these policies was to use the revenue from taxing agriculture to force the pace of manufacturing, since many economists believed agriculture was unresponsive to price changes. In fact, the World Bank study found that growth rates - over all and for agriculture - were highest in those countries that least discriminated against agriculture. There is no hard evidence to show whether agriculture is still so heavily taxed today, but many of the underlying policies persist. To compensate farmers, governments in developing countries have generally turned to subsidizing credit and agricultural inputs such as irrigation, fertilizers and pesticides.

In some cases consumers have also been supported by policies that keep food prices low. These food subsidies have been a major drain on public budgets in food-importing countries. Together these producer and consumer subsidies accounted for almost five per cent of annual government spending over 25 years, implying subsidies of roughly several billions of dollars each year. And that's not all. Pesticides benefit from both price and non-price subsidies in developing countries, including preferential tax treatment for pesticide research. An early and comprehensive study calculated average subsidy rates of nearly 50 per cent for pesticide use. Another researcher estimated that developing countries spent $4 billion on pesticides in 1990. Some quick arithmetic produces a tentative estimate of $2 billion annually for pesticide subsidies.

Governments in developing countries also heavily subsidize the use of fertilizer, at rates ranging from 50 to 90 per cent. In India, the bill for fertilizer subsidies soared from $1-billion-plus in the early 1980s to $2.5 billion in 1992. Despite all these examples, there are no recent, comprehensive statistics on total agricultural subsidies in developing countries. The gains in agricultural production over the past decades have been impressive. Even more impressive - and unacceptable - has been the cost: the degradation of soil, the deliberate impoverishment of some farmers and just as deliberate enrichment of others, the pesticide poisoning of water, air and soil.

OECD subsidy policies focus on price support to farmers, measures that are particularly distorting because they raise domestic produce prices for farmers, spurring increased production. Moreover, such support also encourages farmers to use more agricultural inputs, just as does directly lowering the costs of inputs.

Numerous empirical studies have concluded that consumers and taxpayers in Western industrialized nations stand to gain substantially more from subsidy removal than farmers would lose. Indeed, if subsidy reform is well conceived and managed, farmers need not lose at all. For proof, look no further than the poor efficiency of OECD agricultural transfers in actually achieving the original objective of maintaining farm income.

The transfer efficiency ratio -defined as the ratio of income gained by the farm household to the costs borne by consumers and taxpayers - is very low, because higher output prices encourage farmers to spend more on inputs. Furthermore, there are opportunity costs when resources are diverted to the production of subsidized commodities. Finally, terms of trade are likely to worsen as a result of agricultural protectionism, making imports cost more. Even with a generous interpretation, the transfer efficiency ratio in the OCED is no better than about 0.2, meaning that for every $5 of support from either taxpayers or consumers, only $1 ends up as additional farm income. Of the $4 remaining, 25 cents reflects the extra costs to consumers and taxpayers from income losses and export subsidies, $1 covers the opportunity cost of diverted household resources and $2.75 is spent by farmers to purchase additional inputs.

In other words, consumers and taxpayers in Western industrialized countries divert $335 billion each year to transfer $66 billion to farmers. There is a better way. An OECD study analyzed the transfer efficiency of competing policy options and concluded that direct income support was tops in seven out of 10 categories. More specifically, direct support deters trade the least, has the least impact on resource allocation and puts more money into the hands of the intended recipients. Input subsidies, the preferred choice of many governments, have been judged the most distorting. An added benefit of OECD subsidy reform would see developing countries grow more of their own food.

Farmers will choose to invest their time, money, land and other resources based on real prices, without distorting subsidies. Decoupling has an even greater chance of success if the biggest agricultural subsidizers - the European Union, Japan and the USA embark on the reform together. Linking any remaining producer support to a sound conservation approach on the farm would further enhance environmental gains. There is also plenty of scope for improving agricultural performance in developing countries.

Although the subsidization of agricultural inputs may partly compensate financially for the taxation of output, both approaches create distortions and inefficiencies in agricultural production. Artificially lowering the costs of such essentials as pesticides and fertilizers through subsidies mostly encourages farmers to use more than they need. Some analyses indicate that such input subsidies are the most distorting, with the largest economic costs and much of the payment leaking away before reaching the target; their removal would benefit both agricultural production and the public budget.

The environmental benefits from breaking the link between subsidies and agricultural production are undeniable, even if their precise nature and size can't be calculated in advance. Too much depends on how individual farmers react to new, higher prices that will vary with specific crops and products. Yet the direction is clear. Instead of subsidizing farmers to maximize the exploitation of their lands, the incentive structure should support and encourage them to conserve. The result:

more efficient production and less exploitation of land. Reducing subsidies for inputs is also likely to be environmentally positive; the evidence indicates that excessive use of pesticides, fertilizers and other agricultural inputs generally damages the environment and, ultimately, reduces agricultural productivity.

A classic example of such unintended consequences occurred in Indonesia when overuse of pesticides routed the natural enemies of the brown rice planthopper, until then a minor pest. In what the Worldwatch Institute calls "a two-year feeding frenzy", the bug ruined some $1.5 billion worth of rice, prompting the government in 1986 to cancel pesticide subsidies. The good news is that pesticide applications each season then plunged to half previous levels and the treasury pocketed the $100 million in former annual pesticide subsidy payments.

A common political justification for agricultural support policies is to "protect the family farm" by maintaining farm income. In fact, most subsidies do nothing of the sort, since they are based on how much is grown, not on the size of the farm. And even then they are inefficient. For every $5 of support from either taxpayers or consumers in Western industrialized countries, only $1 ends up as additional farm income. Furthermore, the largest subsidy benefits go to large agricultural producers who are commonly the richest farmers.

In the United States, more than a third of government payments in 1991 went to the wealthiest five per cent of farms, with annual gross cash income of $250,000 or more. Small farms with a cash income below $40,000 got only 17 per cent. In developing countries, input subsidies, particularly for irrigation and pesticides, also tend to benefit large farms. And wherever equipment or credit subsidies favour large mechanized farms, their removal would not particularly hurt small farmers. Nor can the current multi-billion-dollar levels of agricultural support in Western industrialized countries be justified on equity grounds. Once off-farm earnings are included, OECD farmers collectively have a higher net worth than the average household.

OECD countries not only need to reduce their level of agricultural support, as they have committed to do, but they must quickly find the political will to decouple subsidies from agricultural production. This could imply replacing production-linked programs with direct payments to needy farmers or linking support to sound conservation practices. Similarly for developing countries: Instead of subsidizing agricultural inputs, move towards assisting farmers directly.

Over the past 50 years, global energy use has quadrupled, driven primarily by the seemingly insatiable appetite of the wealthy industrialized world for oil. Yet demand for oil is more price-sensitive than once thought. After the first oil shock in 1973-74, a blue-ribbon panel of economists forecast that demand in the industrialized West would drop no more than two per cent for every 10-per-cent rise in the price. In fact, the price/demand ratio was more than twice that from the mid-seventies through the mid-eighties. Still, global energy demand is expected not only to continue growing but to accelerate as commercial energy consumption in low- and middle-income countries closes the gap with the richer nations.

Industrialization in developing countries meant during the same mid-seventies to mid-eighties period that a 10-per-cent rise in income produced as much as a

20-per-cent increase in electricity use or 15-per-cent greater consumption of natural gas. These demand-favouring relationships for both price and income have led some economists to predict that the world will be consuming six times as much total energy after the next 50 years have passed. But others favour lower growth forecasts, pointing out that how people and corporations spend their income in the future may be altered by factors not reflected in these current ratios, such as materials substitution and saturation.

There are two main environmental issues for energy: specific pollution problems from energy use and the depletion of non-renewable resources. In general, the non-renewable forms of energy - coal, oil and natural gas - are more polluting than the renewable forms - solar, wind and water. Specific problems from energy production and use include:

— global warming resulting from the build-up of greenhouse gases such as carbon dioxide and methane;

— damage to property, forests, lakes and biodiversity caused by acid rain or dust, soot and ash;

— biodiversity loss from resource extraction;

— declining water quality, resulting from mine drainage and runoff, oil spills, acid deposition, fallout and sludge;

— health problems from inhaling air pollutants such as sulphur dioxide, nitrogen oxides and particulates;

— fatal respiratory infections for millions annually who inhale smoke from indoor cooking;

— specific diseases like the black lung of coal miners;

— safety risks primarily associated with nuclear energy and waste;

— land-use conflicts from coal mining and hydro energy;

— dust and soot problems from coal transport.

Some contend petroleum production will peak sometime around the year 2000 and that global reserves cannot support any substantial production much beyond 2040. Another group argues that improved technologies for exploration and exploitation will add another 10 to 20 years of potential reserves. Whoever is correct about the precise timing, the real problem remains. Current subsidies encourage overconsumption, accelerating the inevitable exhaustion of petroleum reserves. By distorting the market processes, subsidies tilt the playing field in favour of more polluting energy sources, penalizing efficiency measures and renewable energy sources.

Judging by their public pronouncements, governments around the world realize they should be following policies that encourage a transition to greater energy efficiency and lower energy use. Yet many official policies instead encourage energy profligacy and waste. Worse still, they usually favour the dirtier energy sources. Germany, for instance, for years imposed an 8.5-per-cent surcharge on power bills to subsidize the price of costly Ruhr Valley coal, thus encouraging use of a fuel that makes the greatest contribution to the green-house effect. Governments also tend to look after their own.

Policies in OECD countries mainly support energy production while developing countries subsidize energy consumption. And many and varied are the means of subsidizing energy, for both producers and consumers. For most OECD countries, the statistics on energy subsidies are very fragmentary. Information is more comprehensive about energy subsidies in the USA, where roughly two-thirds of producer subsidies are directed towards fossil fuels. The largest share for any single energy source goes to nuclear energy, with only tiny subsidies for renewable forms of energy.

In Canada, a 1995 study by the Library of Parliament concluded that the oil and gas industry received highly favourable tax breaks with a gross value of almost $6 billion. Consumer energy subsidies alone are huge in developing countries, although once again the best estimates are still rather rough and ready.

Market reforms in Russia have increased real prices of all energy sources for the industrial sector between 30 and 90 per cent between 1990 and 1994. For house-holds, however, energy prices are still a long way from real market levels. As the list opposite shows, real prices for heating and natural gas in Russian households would have to be increased by 50 to 75 times their 1994 levels to remove consumer subsidies - amounting to politically explosive 30-per-cent annual price hikes until 2010. Yet over all, fossil fuel subsidies in Russia have been roughly halved, bringing a $100 billion drop in total subsidies.

China is another example where energy policies have changed recently. To tackle the poor efficiency of the coal sector, the Chinese government is phasing out coal subsidies; domestic coal prices are already nearing world market prices. These developments, plus others in countries like the Philippines, mean that annual energy subsidies in developing countries are now probably no more than $200 billion and might be as low as $150 billion. There's something unbelievable about the world spending hundreds of billions of dollars annually to subsidize its own destruction. It seems more the stuff of myths, like the North American Indian tales of the trickster coyote snatching fire from right under the noses of fierce guardians.

The resulting global warming from excess carbon dioxide is being blamed for recent weather catastrophes that have even the insurance companies worried. So right now seems a good time to consider the impact of phasing out or reforming most energy subsidies. Studies by both the World Bank and the OECD indicate that getting rid of energy subsidies would raise real incomes globally by three-quarters of one per cent, although the gains would be unevenly distributed.

Most developing countries would be better off; in particular, the former Soviet Union and Eastern European countries would benefit, with an expected increase in income of 20 per cent. The major exception would be China, where the deterioration in terms of trade might result in an average real income loss of just below one per cent per year. According to the Bank and the OECD, the other losers would be energy-exporting countries, with an estimated decrease in real income of five per cent annually.

While reforming energy subsidies is merely beneficial to economic development, it's essential to global environmental health. Without scrapping many energy subsidies there is no way the world's 37 industrial countries have a hope of meeting the Earth Summit goal of holding emissions of greenhouse gases at or below the 1990 level in the year 2000. Even with drastic reforms, the target may well be missed.

Removing subsidies to consumers would also reduce emissions by lowering energy demand. Compared to a baseline scenario in which carbon emissions in OECD countries are assumed constant, one report concludes that phasing out consumer subsidies in non-OECD countries would reduce CO_2 emissions by seven per cent below projected levels in 2010.

Subsidy removal would allow most non-OECD countries, including so-called "transition" economies like Russia, to stabilize carbon emissions at 1990 levels, but not others like China where carbon emissions would still be more than double the 1990 level. Another group of researchers used the OECD's GREEN model to project the effects of eliminating all energy price distortions over the period until 2050. Compared with a business-as-usual scenario, carbon emissions would be reduced by 3.4 billion tonnes, or 18 per cent of world emissions. Removing energy subsidies would also significantly reduce other greenhouse gases and emissions of sulphur dioxide and nitrogen oxides. Forecasting the social impact of energy price reform is not for the faint of heart. On the macro scale, theory cautions there might be an economic rebound, with the energy price rise triggering inflation, thus reducing purchasing power.

One study in Colombia, Ghana, Indonesia, Malaysia, Turkey and Zimbabwe, referred to earlier, found the opposite in practice, with overall inflation lower in the two years after the reform. On the micro level, the effects depend on several unknown variables: the size of the price increase, the relative share of energy costs in the household budget and whether people will pay more for the same amount of energy or cut their consumption, and by how much.

Over the past 100 years, the car has liberated individuals just as surely as it has enslaved societies. Every day, vast reaches of prime agricultural land are paved and offered up as sacrifices. Every month, the population equivalents of entire towns perish from road accidents and automotive pollution. Every year, tens of millions of cars are produced - and almost all sold. Yet the car's hold on us grows still. The world's fleet of passenger cars doubled in just 17 years, from 1970 to 1987 - a period that included two global oil shocks.

Most of the people who travel in cars don't think of these billions of dollars as subsidies for them, of course; they see free parking, police patrols and even roads and bridges as simply part of the natural order, an integral part. Indeed, most economists would agree that transportation is an integral part of economic development. Efficient transportation leads to savings in time and costs, stimulating economic growth directly. Indirectly, transportation helps allocate capital efficiently across a region and between regions. The relationship, however, works in both directions; growing prosperity also increases the demand for transportation.

Developing countries face severe transportation difficulties in both urban and rural areas. In large cities, problems arising from the relatively low quality of the transport system - and often poor safety as well - are made far worse by the uncontrolled growth of private cars.

For example, nearly 500 new vehicles enter Bangkok's notoriously congested streets every day, slowing traffic in peak periods to an average of two miles per hour. There is a booming business selling plastic urine bags to drivers and passengers who spend an average of 44 days a year stuck in Bangkok's traffic jams. Outside the cities in developing countries, the low quality of highways is a potential roadblock to economic development; the World Bank estimates that at least half these paved roads are in poor condition.

More than 50 million people in OECD Europe and 36 million people in Japan are exposed to road traffic noise high enough to cause hearing loss over prolonged exposure. Transportation is also a major contributor to air pollution. It causes up to 75 per cent of carbon monoxide emissions in OECD countries and half the nitrogen oxide emissions.

In the OECD, the transportation sector also contributes a fifth of carbon dioxide emissions, one of the causes of the greenhouse effect that is warming the Earth. Air pollution in cities can be severe enough to cause health problems and even deaths. In Los Angeles, the air is officially "unhealthful" three days a week; a recent study of hospital records in Sydney, Australia, estimates that 400 people die each year as a result of local air pollution. These numbers are likely to worsen in the future if transportation growth continues or even accelerates; in developing countries in particular, uncontrolled traffic growth might trigger an outburst of environmental and health problems.

For the United States, Japan and Germany, the question isn't whether road transportation is subsidized, or whether the subsidies are huge, but how huge. Unfortunately for those who value precision in such matters, two immensely detailed U.S. studies come up with final annual subsidy estimates of $174 billion and $55 billion - a gap about the size of Norway's economy. A big part, $66 billion in fact, of the gap between the high estimate of the World Resources Institute and the low figure from an OECD-commissioned study arises from the treatment of free employee parking.

The OECD study assumes that a large portion of this supposed parking subsidy is borne by drivers indirectly, either through lower wages or higher prices for goods. This disagreement between economists, however esoteric it seems, explains much of the reason for the wide range of 20 to 50 per cent for the USA. So, American motorists either pay a fifth of the actual costs of their travel or they pay half. Or somewhere in between. Whatever the precise figure, the public subsidy is still huge. It's the same in Japan, where an OECD study estimated net subsidies of $16 billion to road users. Again, however, the researchers omitted subsidies for parking and selected some very low costs for road-related services, such as police.

In Europe, higher prices at the gas pump - including higher state levies and taxes - mean that subsidies to road users are much lower and sometimes even turn into net taxation. This is the case in the Netherlands and in France, where road users pay at least 10 per cent above their proportional share.

Road transportation subsidies are likely huge in developing countries as well, but we have only fragmentary statistics. The World Bank has estimated that developing countries spend $15 billion annually on road rehabilitation because of deterioration that could have been avoided with more efficient maintenance.

In the case of Africa, one study estimated nearly a third of the $150 billion invested in roads has been lost because of poor management and bad maintenance. Such poor roads may well hamper economic development, particularly in remote and economically backward regions. To prevent further deterioration and to restore merely those roads that are economically viable would require $1.5 billion annually over the next 10 years.

The American case study shows that removing subsidies there would reduce carbon-dioxide emissions by 11 to 14 per cent over 20 years. Yet economic growth projections would be barely affected. The Japanese case study examines a rise in fuel taxes which would cut carbon-dioxide emissions by 11 per cent compared to leaving taxes unchanged. Although car users in France pay enough in taxes and other levies to finance road expenditures and support services, they don't cover what economists call external costs - the price of their vehicle pollution, congestion and accidents. To pay that total bill would require a general fuel-tax increase, on top of targeted user fees to eliminate cross subsidies. The policies in the French scenario would also reduce carbon-dioxide emissions by 11 per cent.

In Singapore, a policy of area licensing begun in 1975 has decreased traffic entering the central zone during peak periods by 75 per cent and kept it well below predicted levels. The Singapore scheme is currently being modernized to use overhead cameras that will automatically deduct the entry fees for vehicles from "smart cards" mounted on their dashboards. Studies and experiments in Milan, London and Bergen all show that other forms of road pricing also can reduce traffic volume. A 1992 study looked at demand management policies for Mexico City, one of the most polluted megacities of the developing world. In Athens, motorists banned from entering the urban centre instead drove around it to reach their destination, increasing both driving and pollution, the opposite of the intended effect.

Subsidizing the provision of infrastructure is sometimes defended on the grounds that it redistributes resources from high-income households to the poor. However, the World Bank concluded in a 1994 report that price subsidies for all types of infrastructure in developing countries almost always benefit the better-off more than the poor. Also in the specific case of road transport in developing countries, subsidies patently benefit the better-off -car owners. In Algeria for instance, they receive almost four times more subsidized transport services than the poor. There are, however, legitimate equity concerns about some of the road-pricing measures under consideration as subsidy reforms.

Raising the cost of travel in peak periods might simply help the wealthy to speed along on less-congested roads. And city-core-bans are usually even more inequitable, since the poor can't afford one car, let alone a second to circumvent licence-plate-restrictions. A more equitable approach is to provide good public transit as an alternative while raising the costs of driving a car for everyone. Most experts agree that economic and financial instruments can help achieve sustainable forms of transportation, but they can't do the whole job. Transportation issues are so complex and so intertwined with other issues, such as land use and demographic and cultural trends, that only a coherent set of policy measures will work.

Transportation policy strategies should consist of economic, institutional, technological, information and land-use measures. A balanced strategy should set standards, use incentives to achieve full-cost recovery, inform consumers, provide alternatives for them, collaborate with the transportation sector and integrate social and urban planning.

The fundamental role for governments is to help markets work more efficiently. For that reason, subsidies are often not the right policies: They give the wrong market signals and lead to unsustainable behaviour. Subsidies tend to waste resources, they do not produce the intended results and they wind up in the pockets of the wrong people. The costs and incentives should be put back where they belong - on users instead of on taxpayers or other groups. Industrialized countries are in the strongest position to take the global lead in moving towards desubsidization.

Water subsidies in developing countries seem to have been inspired predominantly by social objectives. Subsidies for drinking water were intended to ensure that the poor had access to water, because it was assumed that poor people cannot pay high prices. Yet the reality has been the opposite; water subsidies have tended to benefit the haves instead of the have-nots.

In addition, the poor often paid (and still pay) high water prices in practice, because they must buy expensive water from private vendors. Water subsidise turn out to be a barrier to improving the conditions of the poor because governments, having spent unwisely on ineffective subsidies, then lack the money to improve the public water system. In both developed and developing countries, subsidized water remains so cheap today that it invites overuse, misuse and waste. Irrigation is extensively subsidized, causing farmers to pump water at will, with little thought for costs or cost-effectiveness.

In both developed and developing countries, agricultural subsidies were originally intended to support farm incomes. There may also have been hopes of encouraging agricultural production, particularly in food-importing countries. Agricultural subsidies are today very costly, and often ineffective, ways of tackling these objectives. For example, only 20 per cent of $335 billion in annual OECD agricultural transfers actually ends up as additional farm income. And when it does, most of it goes to the larger and richer farmers. Switching to direct income support could yield a triple dividend, benefiting farmers, consumers and taxpayers.

After the oil crises in the 1970s, many countries introduced energy subsidies to stimulate exploration and production because they wanted to be more self-sufficient in oil, and less susceptible to external shocks. But now the world is afloat in oil and increasing economic globalization has diminished the dominance of any single producer or group of producers. Energy subsidies have instead become very expensive protection for sectoral interests and employment.

The promotion of economic development seems to have been the driving force behind subsidies for private road transport in both developed and developing countries. Greater mobility may very well promote and enhance economic development. However, subsidizing road transport has not primarily achieved this objective; instead, the subsidies have all too often encouraged overuse, increasing pollution and congestion. The proof can be seen daily in grid-locked cities and bumper-to-bumper highways. In addition, road transport subsidies put a heavy burden on the public budget and, in developing countries, mostly benefit the better-off, i.e. car owners. To be fair, governments may sometimes feel that no better policy is available than a subsidy. This cramped outlook can sometimes be traced, in part, to the powerful forces which defend subsidies and oppose their reform.

Many taxpayers are won over by such tactics for the simple reason that few fully grasp any specific subsidy issues. All too often the existence of individual subsidies is hidden at the same time as their costs are spread across a broad public. That's what some governments prefer. Those getting the subsidies may also prefer implicit forms of support or support geared to production, out of fear that subsidies that are too high-profile will be cut first in times of fiscal stress. Closely related are fears about how subsidy reform will play out: who is going to be harmed and by how much.

Uncertainty about the outcome of subsidy reform may create a political bias for the status quo. When the result of reform is unclear, even those who could benefit may prefer the certainty of the present to the uncertainty of the future. Uncertainty about the benefits may also cause some countries to await international action before implementing reform at home. It's equally possible, however, for international considerations themselves to be an impediment.

Countries may be reluctant to act unilaterally and risk losing relative competitiveness internationally. A country may also fear that gains through domestic reform will leak away through an increase in imports. For developing countries and economies in transition like those of Eastern Europe and Russia, the lack of foreign assistance can be a big problem. These countries may need short-term foreign funds to bridge the first stages of the process.

Management and organizations that administer the subsidies may feel understandably threatened and be skeptical about the need for reform. Generally it takes strong political action to slice through the inertia and push administrative changes. In addition, many countries may lack the level and range of analytical and technical skills to assess and develop reform policies, or to implement them effectively. Numerous and varied are the barriers, but numerous and varied also are the potential strategies for overcoming them and instituting subsidy reform. International bodies such as OECD and the United Nations could play a pivotal role by nurturing the dialogue with facts and analysis. The World Trade Organization could adopt the model of international trade discussions and hold a series of "Green Rounds" to agree upon subsidy reform and provide mutual assistance. Non-governmental organizations may well be crucial, exposing and publicizing subsidies as well as building support for reform among their constituencies.

Index

Atmospheric emissions, 152
Awareness and Preparedness for Emergencies at Local Level (APELL), 208

Biophysical relationships, 13

Community-based approaches, 200
Compact Fluorescent Lamps (CFLs), 41
Convention on Biological Diversity (CBD), 2
Cost-effective policies, 153

Deoxyribonucleic Acid (DNA), 179

Ecosystem functions, 1
Environmental benefits, 291
Environmental costs, 289
Environmental groups, 5
Environmental protection, 157
Exclusive Economic Zone (EEZ), 184

Forest management, 7
Fragile ecosystems, 164

Global Climate Observing System, 150
Global Environment Facility (GEF), 40, 270
Gross Domestic Product (GDP), 35, 280

Hydrological cycle delivers, 282

Intergovernmental Panel on Climate Change (IPCC), 34, 272
International Action Programme on Water and Sustainable Agricultural Development (IAP-WASAD), 203
International Crops Research Institute for the Semi-Arid Tropics (ICRISAT), 25
International Institute of Tropical Agriculture (IITA), 47
International Labour Organisation (ILO), 207
International Mountain Society (IMS), 169
International Programme on Chemical Safety (IPCS), 207
International Water Management Institute (IWMI), 25

Landscape ecological planning (LANDEP), 158
Life-support systems, 156
Liquefied Petroleum Gas (LPG), 32

Mountain ecosystems, 167
Multi-dimensional endeavour, 150
Murray-Darling Basin (MDB), 28

Non-governmental organizations, 151

Office National de Electricité (ONE), 37
Official Development Assistance (ODA), 270
Organisation for Economic Cooperation and Development (OECD), 207
Ozone-depleting substances, 154

Parts Per Million by Volume (ppmv), 35
Plant Genetic Resources For Agriculture (PGRFA), 175
Polycyclic Aromatic Hydrocarbons (PAHs), 185
Primary Environmental Care (PEC), 158

Regeneration programmes, 162
Rehabilitation programmes, 174
Resource management, integration of, 9

Sustainable Agriculture and Rural Development (SARD), 170

Technical assistance programmes, 11
Terrestrial ecosystems, 14
Transparency mechanisms, 4
Transparent administrative structure, 278
Transport systems, 152
Transportation policy strategies, 308
Tropical hard-woods, 12

U.N. Convention to Combat Desertification (UNCCD), 17
UN Environment Programme's World Conservation Monitoring Centre (UNEP-WCMC), 20
UN Framework Convention on Climate Change (UNFCCC), 17
United Nations Environment Programme (UNEP), 166
United Nations University (UNU), 169
Unsustainable activities, 10

Woodland Mountain Institutes (WMI), 169
World Health Organization (WHO), 207